THE LEMKO REGION
IN THE SECOND POLISH REPUBLIC

JAGIELLONIAN STUDIES IN HISTORY

Editor in chief
Jan Jacek Bruski

Vol. 2

Jarosław Moklak

THE LEMKO REGION
IN THE SECOND POLISH REPUBLIC

Political and Interdenominational Issues
1918–1939

Jagiellonian University Press

The publication of this volume was financed by the Jagiellonian University in Krakow – Faculty of History

REVIEWER
Paul J. Best, Ph.D. Professor Emeritus, President and CEO Carpathian Research Institute

SERIES COVER LAYOUT
Jan Jacek Bruski

COVER DESIGN
Agnieszka Winciorek

Cover photography: The celebration of the Feast of Jordan, Sanok, 1935. At the head of the procession, the Lemko apostolic administrator, Fr. Vasyl Mastsiukh [Courtesy of the National Digital Archives (Narodowe Archiwum Cyfrowe) in Warsaw]

Translated from the Polish by Timothy Williams

ISBN 978-83-233-3438-5 (PRINT)
ISBN 978-83-233-7513-5 (PDF)

ISSN 2299–758X

WYDAWNICTWO
UNIWERSYTETU
JAGIELLOŃSKIEGO

www.wuj.pl

Jagiellonian University Press
Editorial Offi ces: Michałowskiego St. 9/2, 31-126 Krakow
Phone: +48 12 631 18 81, +48 12 631 18 82, Fax: +48 12 631 18 83
Distribution: Phone: +48 12 631 01 97, Fax: +48 12 631 01 98
Cell Phone: + 48 506006 674, e-mail: sprzedaz@wuj.pl
Bank: PEKAO SA, IBAN PL80 1240 4722 1111 0000 4856 3325

Contents

List of important abbreviations

AAL – Apostolic Administration of the Lemko Region
AAN – Central Archives of Modern Records in Warsaw
ABGK – Archives of the Greek Catholic Bishopric in Przemyśl
AKL – Archives of Father Lukashklavich
AP K – State Archives in Kraków
AP P – State Archives in Przemyśl
AP R – State Archives in Rzeszów
BBWR – Non-partisan Bloc for Cooperation with the Government
BJ – Jagiellonian Library
BP-U – Polish-Ukrainian Bulletin (Biuletyn Polsko-Ukraiński)
CDIAL – Central State Archives in Lviv
DALO – State Archives of Lviv Province
HRNO – Halych-Russian National Organization
KGPP – Chief Government Police Headquarters
KOS K – District School Board of Kraków
MSW – Ministry of the Interior
MSZ – Foreign Ministry
MWRiOP – Ministry of Religious Affairs and Public Education
n.d.p. – no date of publication
n.p.p. – no place of publication
OOL – Organization for the Defense of Lemkivshchyna
OOLZU – Organization for the Defense of Lemko Western Ukraine
PKPP – County Government Police Headquarters
p.n.n. – pages not numbered
PPP – Government Police Post(s)
RP – Polish Republic
PRM – Presidium of the Council of Ministers
RAO – Rus Agrarian Organization
RAP – Rus Agrarian Party
RNO – Russian National Organization
RSO – Russian Peasant Organization
RSRK – Auditing Union of Rusyn Cooperatives
RSUK – Auditing Union of Ukrainian Cooperatives
RZN – Russian National Union

Sejm RP – Sejm of the Polish Republic. Stenographic transcripts
Senat RP – Senate of the Polish Republic. Stenographic transcripts
SN – Nationality Affairs (*Sprawy Narodowościowe*)
SP G – County District Office in Grybów
SP NS – County District Office in Nowy Sącz
TSL – Popular School Association
ULM – Ukrainian Lemko Museum
UNDO – Ukrainian National Democratic Alliance
URP – Ukrainian Parliamentary Representation
UWKr – Kraków Province Office
ZUNR – Western Ukrainian National Republic

Introduction

As a result of the displacements of 1944–1946, and in particular Operation Vistula in 1947, the demographic structure of the previously existing Lemko Region was destroyed, and the repressed population found itself in a difficult social and moral situation. Stalinist propaganda disseminated in socialist Poland took away the Ukrainian sense of dignity, conferring an inferior status on them. This culminated in their feeling ashamed of their origins and avoiding national self-definition. The power of family traditions was not always able to overcome this barrier. For a part of the population this gave rise to certain forms of behavior which included a preference for a particular ethnographic designation. In other words, it was easier to be a Lemko than a Ukrainian. On the other hand, there were political traditions from before the war which also ruled against the use of the name "Ukrainian"; for some, there was no need to avoid the term, since they had never used it.

Political changes which took place in Poland during the "Solidarity" era awakened the political engagement of national minorities, long hidden from the realms of culture and education. Gradually this led to the rebuilding in the Lemko community of the two ideologically opposed camps which had put roots down in the Lemko region in the 19th and first half of the 20th century: the Union of Lemkos with headquarters in Gorlice, one of the Ukrainian minority organizations, and the Association of Lemkos, headquartered in Legnica, which declared the Lemkos' affinity with the modern Rusyn nation (neo-Rusyn/Carpatho-Rusyn). This polarization in attitudes bears witness to the complicated process by which the political consciousness of the Lemko population in Poland was formed.

The question of the national identity of Lemkos has given rise to much controversy. The fundamental reason for the divergence of views is the lack of thorough studies of the political history of the Lemko region. This allows many myths, legends and stereotypes to freely function, which the historian has a duty to demystify. The lack of scholarly literature means not only a gap in historiography and an open field for action toward filling it, but also ensuing difficulties in the research of the related disciplines, political science and sociology, which are attempting to grasp the various aspects of the present state of affairs, unfortunately often in isolation from the past from which it has issued. This book is an attempt to put in order the facts of the political and religious life of the region in question. Through an analysis of the pro-Russian, Old Rus and National-Ukrainian political currents and the emerging nationality policy of the Second Republic toward the Lemko region, this book should simplify the process of understanding the intertwined political and interdenominational relationships in the years 1918–1939, and also help understand the social and political attitudes of contemporary Lemkos.

The current English-language edition is a slightly condensed and revised version of the book published in 1997 in Polish. The decision to publish an English version was guided by the fact that there is a large number of English-language readers interested in the problems of the Lemko region, and furthermore in recent years research in this area has not made significant leaps forward so that the book remains up-to-date. The spelling of names of persons complies with the guidelines applied in English publications, while place names generally are assigned according to official records from the Second Polish Republic, although some modern Ukrainian names are also used.

Chapter I: Galicia and Lemkos. The formation of regional politics in the years 1849–1919

The nineteenth century was characterized by the development of modern national and political movements in Europe, which grew out of the tradition of the French Revolution. In the first half of the 19th century the national idea was echoed in Central and Eastern Europe. These processes were initiated by socioeconomic changes. The crisis of the feudal economy led to the development of the production of goods, the growth of exchange and the emergence of new money markets. Peasants freed from serfdom settled in cities, and the vernacular increasingly heard in Germanized urban centers deepened the process of urban nationalization. In Austria, a country with multiple nationalities, this caused national conflicts, accelerating the formation of modern consciousness among its Slavic peoples.

In the course of these sociopolitical changes, the ideologies of the Enlightenment and Romanticism played important roles. The Enlightenment, proclaiming the equality of all before the law, spread the concept of the nation to different social classes. Romanticism exposed elements of folk culture and brought to light evidence of a marvelous past belonging to nation-states and also stateless nations. The attempt undertaken in the late 18th and early 19th centuries to take a new look at Slavic cultural heritage found support in the philosophy of the German thinker Johann G. Herder, who showed the historic role that Slavs were to play in the future. These currents brought a rise in Slavic self-esteem and led to the activation of the intelligentsia in individual nations which in the first half of the 19th century set about gathering relics and mementos of folk culture with great enthusiasm. On eastern Galician soil this was the share of the Rusyn (Ukrainian) intelligentsia.

In 1816 through the efforts of canon Ivan Mohylnytsky an association of intelligentsia took shape in Przemyśl under the name Clerical Association, with a publishing operation intended to diffuse education in Rusyn society. The second center of Rusyn intellectual life was Vienna, to be precise, the clerical and secular intelligentsia concentrated in the orbit of the Church of St. Barbara, which kept in contact with Przemyśl. Historiography even refers to a Vienna–Przemyśl circle of Rusyn scholars. A real breakthrough came only with the activities of the Ruthenian Triad, a group of enthusiasts of Rusyn (Ukrainian) folk culture, led by Markian Shashkevych, Yakiv Holovatsky, and Ivan Vahylevych. The group's greatest achievement was publishing the *Rusalka Dnistrova* (Mermaid of the Dniester) in Pest in 1837, edited in an innovative form in the vernacular transcribed phonetically. The *Rusalka Dnistrova* raised the vernacular to the rank of literary language and became the basis for later national activities among Galician Ukrainians.

The revolutions of 1848–1849 in turn set off a period of political involvement among Rusyns. Cultural autonomy was marked the natural boundaries between Polish and Rusyn (Ukrainian) settlements in Galicia. The geographic division overlapped substantially with the nationality divide and was conducive to efforts to gain separate administrative units. The plan for dividing Galicia into two provinces was released by the Austrian authorities in 1847, but a year later became a political demand of the Supreme Rusyn Council, who strove to have the area divided into Polish and Rusyn sections. In fact the plan was never fulfilled, but was many times released anew up until the fall of the Habsburg monarchy.[1]

The Revolutions of 1848, also called the Spring of Nations, opened a new era of rivalry with the Poles, who possessed a longer national and state tradition and from whom the Rusyn peasant population differed in social status, religious denomination and language. The failure of the Ukrainian Revolution of 1848 not only left the relationship unchanged but further led to a long period of internal rivalry in the Rusyn community of Galicia, which impelled some activists of the Supreme Rusyn Council to look for political support from Russia. Pro-Russian sympathies first appeared among the political elite in the eastern part of the country. Due to its geographic placement, the Lemko region at that time was at the margins of Galician politics and until the late 19th century lay beyond the reach of the influences of rival orientations: national-Ukrainian and Old Rusyn–pro-Russian. These currents became fully formed in the 1860s and 1870s, but during the following two decades their representatives took almost no interest in the population residing in the areas west of the San River.

1. The origins of pro-Russian sympathies

Starting in the mid-19th century the Rusyn question in Galicia took on an international dimension and became an element in the rivalry between powers. For Austria the issue fulfilled the additional function of acting as a control in its internal political balance. Nonetheless Austria was relatively late in precisely defining its broader Rusyn program. Only toward the end of the 1880s did Austria consider securing the Rusyns against Russia.

Russia for its part since the time of Catherine the Great had a definite agenda for Galicia. In 1828 Nicholas I ordered that the political mood in Galicia be vigilantly

---

[1] See J. Kozik, *Między reakcją a rewolucją. Studia z dziejów ukraińskiego ruchu narodowego w Galicji w latach 1848–1849* [Between reaction and revolution. Studies in the history of the Ukrainian national movement in the years 1848–1849], Kraków 1975.

observed, reckoning with the possibility of a war with Austria. The 1830s and 1840s brought intensified penetration into Russian circles, which went through several channels. The first channel comprised the activities of the Pan-Slavists – a group of scholars grouped around Mikhail Pogodin, a historian, journalist, and professor at Moscow University, who travelled throughout the Slavic world and since 1835 had visited Galicia several times. Pogodin conducted talks with an anti-Polish attitude, mainly with Uniate priests, which in that time of proliferating Rusyn (Ukrainian) national consciousness, emerging through struggles with Polish identity, fell on fertile soil. The second direction taken by Tsarist penetration in Austria was the Russian embassy's activity in Vienna; its chaplain, Mikhail Raievski, was conducting agitation with the use of the slogan "One Tsar, One Church, One Faith." The ideological activity was given financial support to prepare the ground for the future partition of Galicia. Wilhelm Feldman in one of his works wrote that

> Many [...] roubles flowed into Galicia from the coffers of the Petersburg Benevolent Association and from the government; from those of ideological fanatics and from the gendarmerie, they flowed into the editorial offices of magazines and into financial institutions, corrupting consciences and creating parasitical forms of existence [...].[2]

After Austria's defeat at Sadová in its war with the Prussians on 3 July 1866 the Habsburg monarchy was forced to make far-reaching internal reforms and in order to keep its strong position in Galicia entrusted the government to the Poles. This had important consequences for the formation of Rusyn (Ukrainian) political attitudes. The loss of faith in help from Vienna weakened the Austrophile movement among Rusyns and made the growth of the pro-Russian orientation easier.

In forming pro-Russian sympathies, a sense of threat from the Polish nation-state, the hostility toward which was multidimensional and rooted in social, cultural and political differences, played a prominent role. Social differences led to conflict between the Polish administration and Rusyn peasantry. Cultural differences resulted from absolute identification with two different traditions: the Western world – Latin, and the Eastern – Greek and Byzantine. The anti-Polish attitude of the Rusyn intelligentsia was not, however, an agenda rooted in anti-Polish phobias, but aimed at a conscious and effective emphasis on national autonomy.

Disappointment with Austria, Russia's active propaganda, and the anti-Polish attitude of Rusyns were the key factors in the first phase of the development of Moscophilism.[3] Antipathy toward the Polish nation was quick to take root. One of

2   W. Feldman, *Stronnictwa i programy polityczne w Galicji 1846–1906* [Factions and political programs in Galicia 1846–1906], vol. 2, Kraków 1907, p. 329. See K. Ustianovych, *Raievskii i rosiiskyi panslavizm. Spomyny z prezhytoho i peredumanoho*, Lviv 1884, p. 7; C. Studziński, *Zza kulisów schizmatyckiej propagandy* [Behind the scenes of schismatic propaganda], Kraków 1899, pp. 38–40.

3   Rusyn [I. Dzieduszycki], *Ruś galicyjska, jej separatyzm, przyczyny tegoż, działania i skutki* [Galician Ruthenia, its separatism, reasons thereof, actions and effects], Gródek 1888, pp. 57–114; F. Podleski, *Rusofilizm a ukrainizm* [Russophilism and Ukrainianism], Lwów 1931, p. 22.

the main reasons was the propagation by some Polish activists of the belief that Rusyns constituted a Polish tribe who differed only in social position and religious custom. Rusyn language was seen as a dialect of Polish, and Rusyn culture a regional variant of Polish culture. The assimilation of Rusyns was considered a natural phenomenon and generally self-explanatory, although signs of nation-building processes contradicted such a conviction. The events of 1848, in particular the Polish address to the Emperor passing in silence over the Rusyn question in Galicia, caused the estrangement of many Rusyns from Polish independence movements, which finally led to the rejection of the name "Rusyn" and the adoption of the name "Ukrainian."

Prior to that development, however, the pro-Russian orientation predominated among Rusyns, and in the 1850s and 1860s a Rusyn negative attitude toward Poles was clearly delineated. Rusyns made demands: a pure Eastern liturgy, equality for Rusyn language in government offices and schools, and proportional and fair representation by deputies in the Diet of Galicia and the Austrian parliament. The heightened Polish-Ukrainian conflict gave rise to the expression of a Moscophile program. On 8 August 1866 the press organ *Slovo* (Word), published in Lviv, contained an article entitled "Pohlad v buduchnost (A look to the Future)," authored by Fr. Ivan Naumovych. This well-known politician, an undoubted Rusyn patriot, wrote: "We cannot build a Great Wall of China to separate ourselves from our brothers and withdraw from linguistic, literary, church and national unions with the entire Russian world. We are no longer the Ruthenians of 1848, we are true Russians."[4] Another leading Rusyn politician, Kost Levytsky, who represented the Ukrainian orientation, defined Naumovych's intervention as a form of defense from the Polish threat, an indictment of the Viennese government and a manifestation of insecurity, or lack of faith in the community's own powers.

Fears of Polonization in many cases led into the arms of Russia, which was nonetheles not a known quantity. Less well-informed supporters of leaning on the Eastern power did not know its social structure, nor the Tsarist government's attitude toward Dnieper Ukrainians, nor did they know about the persecution which their compatriots beyond the cordon had faced. Ignorance of the realities of Russian life was widespread, particularly in the countryside. Proponents of political Moscophilism used arguments of shared Orthodox faith, the greatness of Russian culture and the strength of Tsarist power. In the minds of Rusyn peasants, not well-versed in the larger European political situation, the argument for Russia's protective stance usually found acceptance. Pro-Russian activism in the countryside was made easier by the natural awareness of the oppression of Ukrainian peasant masses by Poles, an awareness inherent in the social situation, which bred hope for a better future in the Russian state-nation.

---

[4]   Quoted from K. Levytsky, *Istoria politychnoi dumky halytskyh Ukraintsiv 1848–1914*, vol. 1, Lviv 1926, p. 90. See O.A. Monchalovski, *Zhyttie i dieiatielnost Ivana Naumovicha*, Lvov 1899, p. 61.

We find pro-Russian sympathies among the peasant population in the Lemko region relatively early. One revealing fact is the Lemkos' sending a delegation to Tsar Nicholas I in December 1849 with a request "for protection." The delegation was led by Mykhailo Hrynda of Szlachtowa, one of the villages furthest west among Rusyn settlements.[5]

The failure to realistically assess the political strivings of Russia was often found among the intelligentsia as well. The Greek Catholic clergy especially, threatened with Latinization of the Eastern rite, became involved with pro-Russian circles with relative ease.

Moscophilism among the clergy had a twofold nature. A definite majority consisted of so-called "hard Rusyns," also known as Old Rusyns. Some of them, overburdened with a lack of self-esteem and ignorance of their own history and literature, often for reasons beyond their control, broke through the identity barrier and identified with Russian cultural values. Mykhailo Hrushevsky, an outstanding Ukrainian historian, stressing the weak self-esteem among some Rusyns of the period, wrote: "from a psychology of despairing of the possibility of independently lifting themselves up, the Russophile movement among Rusyns was spawned."[6] Ivan Franko defined the phenomenon thusly:

> [...] seeing the fruitlessness, the ignominy and the vanity of efforts of a small handful of individuals, seeing how nonetheless at every step rivals compete with us from both sides, how we fall behind in the most cardinal matters, even the hottest Rusyn patriot thinks to himself whether it might not be better to abandon this hopeless struggle for national independence and join his stronger, richer, better-organized neighbors?[7]

The lack of self-esteem Franko found to be the "psychological foundation" for not only Moscophilism, but Polonophilism as well.

This was the drama of those Rusyns who sought an escape from the cultural *cul-de-sac* of their own people. The trap was illusory and not justified by history, since the achievements of Rusyn (Ukrainian) culture existed and could provide the needed basis for a sense of worth and merit. Not widely disseminated, it did not encourage the development of the national idea. Furthermore, activists in the national movement were trying to maintain a facade of attitudinal unanimity among Rusyns. They expected Moscophilism to disappear as the Ukrainian sense of national identity became more widespread. The pro-Russian demonstration in 1866 crushed those hopes and forced the national activists to take decisive initiatives. At the end of the 1860s and beginning of the 1870s the two chief Ukrainian education institutions took form:

---

[5] See *Karpatorusskii Kalendar Lemko-Soiuza za hod 1960*, Yonkers, NY, pp. 87–92.

[6] Quoted from J. Kozik, *Moskalofilstwo w Galicji w latach 1849–1866, na tle odrodzenia narodowego Rusinów* [Moscophilism in Galicia in the years 1849–1866 in the context of the Rusyn national revival], MA thesis (typescript), Jagiellonian University, Kraków 1958, p. 64.

[7] I. Franko, *Nieco o stosunkach polsko-ruskich* [A few words on Polish-Rusyn relations], Lwów 1895, p. 6.

the Prosvita Society in 1868 and the Shevchenko Scientific Society in 1873. Those in turn led to the Moscophile creation of the Kachkovsky Society in 1874.[8] Those institutions developed wide networks of popular reading rooms throughout Eastern Galicia, and beginning in the late 19th century the networks extended into Western Galicia (the Lemko region). They started up their own publishing houses and press organs. Their emergence set in motion the era of internal rivalry between Ukrainians and Moscophiles, which later Polish ruling circles would join.

In 1890 this culminated in a Polish-Rusyn agreement to break up Russian influences in the St. George's consistory in Lviv, the main center of Galician Moscophilism, a move which initiated the process of the movement's decline in Eastern Galicia and had momentous consequences for the Lemko region. From that time on as a result of limited opportunities for action in eastern Galician areas, Moscophiles began penetration of politically virgin territories, transferring the agendas of their education and political societies there. In the Lemko region their task was easier since the national activists were then applying their energies to the eastern region of the country. A sign of the weakening of the pro-Russian current was the text of the manifesto published in December 1899, in which Moscophiles declared the equality of the "Lesser Ruthenian" language with Russian. This reflected a compromise between the pro-Russian and Old Rusyn ideas and heralded the emergence of the Moscophile–Old Rusyn bloc, which would last until the parliamentary elections of 1907.[9]

The weakening of Moscophilism in the late 19th and early 20th centuries was also caused by a change in the position of Russia, which at that time was reversing the direction of its Far East foreign policy. This was negatively perceived not only among Galician Moscophiles, but also in pro-Russian movements among other Slavs of the Habsburg Empire. The historical moment was taken advantage of by national activists who achieved a dominant position in the central areas of Galicia. The pro-Russian orientation in Austria-Hungary experienced a renaissance after Russia's defeat in its war with Japan in 1904–1905. As part of their doctrine of Neo-Slavism Russian circles cultivated active penetration among Slavs in the Habsburg territories and in the Balkans. In Galicia they looked to the so-called "young men" – the extreme pro-Russian wing led by Volodymyr Dudykevych, a lawyer in Kolomyia, thereby contributing to the revival and intensification of the Ukrainian-Moscophile rivalry in the period preceding the outbreak of the First World War.

---

[8]   J. Moklak, *Relacje między ukraińskim ruchem narodowym a moskalofilstwem w Galicji Wschodniej w latach 1866–1890* [Relations between the Ukrainian national movement and Moscophilism in Eastern Galicia in the years 1866–1890], MA thesis (typescript), Jagiellonian University, Kraków 1985, p. 80; by the same author "Mychajło Kaczkowśkyj i czytelnie jego imienia na Łemkowszczyźnie" [Mykhailo Kachkowsky and the eponymous reading rooms in the Lemko region], *Magury '87* (Warszawa) 1987, pp. 53–64.

[9]   W. Kołpaczkiewicz, "Na granicy wieków (Jeden etap ewolucji myśli politycznej starorusinów)" [At the centuries' frontier (One stage in the evolution of Old Rusyn political thought)], *BP-U* 1938, no. 5, p. 50.

2. Old Rusyns, Moscophiles, and national movement activists, 1907–1914

In early 1907 in Austria-Hungary a new electoral law took effect which hastened the disintegration of existing political configurations. The conservative position, which had theretofore dominated, was destabilized. After the elections to the Imperial Council, Polish representation in the Viennese parliament was taken over by the ND (National Democrats). This change in the configuration of power brought many changes with regard to Rusyns (Ukrainians). They resulted from the ND's political program, which – aiming to rebuild the Polish nation-state – represented a pro-Russian idea, which dictated combating the monarchist Ukrainian movement and supporting Moscophilism. The ND's support for Moscophiles increased their political importance in Galicia.

In the period preceding the 1907 elections in both Moscophile–Old Rusyn and national movement circles, the plan for an agreement on elections was discussed. The former demanded a base number of seats reserved for voting by Rusyns, i.e. 14, and in one district forced the candidacy of V. Dudykevych, a declared Russian. Furthermore, they expected support from the future deputies for the Russian declaration which they intended to submit to the Imperial Council. For those in the national movement, these conditions were unacceptable, so no agreement was reached. Only in some districts were tactical agreements concluded and shared support proffered to candidates. In the Sanok area the election campaign displayed a strong rivalry between the national movement and Moscophiles, including some events of a brawling nature.[10] The Lemko region composed districts 48 (Nowy Sącz), 49 (Jasło), 50 (Krosno) and 51 (Sanok). The Lemko population constituted a small percentage in these districts and Moscophile candidates in the first three were not elected. Only in Sanok County did judicial counsellor Volodymyr Kurylovych win. The national movement put forth a candidate only in Sanok (Roman Zalozetsky, professor at the Lviv Polytechnic), a fact which reveals the weakness of the Ukrainian movement in the Lemko region in the first decade of the 20th century.

The national movement camp focused its attention mainly on Eastern Galicia. The electoral campaign was directed by the National Committee in Lviv, led by Kost Levytsky. In the electoral program it was stipulated that there would be agrarian reform, repeal of taxes (except for the progressive income tax), reduced taxes on the army and increased taxes on education, a rise in the number of Ukrainian intermediate schools and the creation of a Ukrainian university in Lviv, and finally

---

10 The chairman of the Ukrainian Electoral Committee in Sanok was Fr. O. Konstantynovych, and the secretary V. Buchatsky, see V. Buchatsky, *Moskvofilstvo na Lemkivshchyni* [Moscophilism in the Lemko region], New York 1955, pp. 11–13; I. Winiarski, *Rusini w Radzie Państwa 1907–1908* [Rusyns in the Imperial Council 1907–1908], Lwów 1909, p. 8.

the division of Galicia into Polish and Ukrainian regions, with a separate executive branch and a Diet.

On balance the parliamentary elections of 1907 brought victory for the national movement, which obtained 20 seats, while the Moscophile–Old Rusyn camp got only five.[11] Nonetheless, Mykola Hlibovytsky and Dmytro Markov, confident in the support of Polish ND circles and supported by Tsarist diplomacy, undertook an attempt to open a Russian Club in the Viennese Parliament. They tried to open the way toward it through a *fait accompli*, with Markov making a speech in Russian on 9 July intended to lead to recognition of that language in the country. A week later the Moscophile party held a congress of "private agents" in Lviv, at which it was officially announced that Galicia was inhabited by "two peoples of Rus: Ukrainian and Russian,"[12] and a resolution was adopted calling deputies to resign from the Ruthenian Club (*Ruthenischer Klub*), the members of which were also in the national movement. The Moscophile–Old Rusyn camp was not unanimous, which in the end doomed Markov's activities to failure. Vasyl Davydiak, Mykhailo Korol and Volodymyr Kurylovych had considerably less radical views, though the first two finally agreed to the resolution's contents. The position of Kurylovych is remarkable, as a deputy from the Lemko region who in fact left the Ruthenian Club, but did not join Markov and Hlibovytsky. Markov's appearance in the Imperial Council and the congress of Moscophiles in Lviv in July 1907 revealed the goal and battle tactics of that camp. The Viennese government was able, however, to skilfully leave the matter as the Diet of Galicia's responsibility, considering that it was a local issue, not concerning the nation as a whole.

In 1908 successive political events strengthened the position of the pro-Russian camp. At the beginning of that year in elections to the local Diet Moscophiles got 10 seats, led by Dudykevych, while the stronger national movement members and radicals got barely 11. This was a visible result of the influence of the Polish right on internal Ukrainian political relations, which paved the way for an attempt on the life of governor Andrzej Potocki. In July, during the Slavic congress in Prague, a Polish-Russian rapprochement was reached in the form of the Dmowski–Bobrinski agreement, sealed by a banquet given in Lviv in honor of the Russian guests. The determination with which Russian circles and Moscophiles in the area sprang into action caused concern in the Moscophile–Old Rusyn camp itself, which – as mentioned earlier – was not unanimous and comprised within itself the attitudes of so-called Hard Rusyns, of anti-Ukrainian disposition, but not pro-Russian. This soon led to a break within the party. In 1909 the Old Rusyns remained with their old press organ, the *Halychanyn*, which espoused only "cultural unity" between Rusyns in Galicia and Russians. The group of radical Moscophiles, on the other

---

[11] Fr. V. Davydiak (Stryi), M. Hlibovytsky (Zolochiv), M. Korol (Rava Ruska), V. Kurylovych (Sanok), D. Markov (Brody); see K. Levytsky, op.cit., vol. 2, Lviv 1927, p. 444.

[12] Ibid., p. 453.

hand, assembled around the new publication, written in Russian literary language, entitled *Prikarpatskaia Rus'*. The historical literature generally designates the first as the *starokursnyki* (old course), representatives of an older orientation, while the first are called *novokursnyki* (new course), presenting a new course of action or new tendency. This division reflected the moods in the community. The "old" group predominated, led by Davydiak, but the "young" were very energetic, and therefore played a larger role in Galician politics in the years immediately preceding the outbreak of the First World War.[13]

Despite external support (from Russia and the Podolian ND) the Moscophiles did not dare to join in one mass with the Russian language. They launched a publication specially for the people, called *Holos Naroda* (Voice of the People), published in a dialect close to Ukrainian. One of the main representatives of the new strain, Marian Glushkevych, a Lemko by birth, summed up this direction of action in the following way: "If there isn't a war [...] there is nothing left but to join the Ukrainians."[14] The perspective of war and of the arrival of Russian armies on Galician territory marked the *novokursnyks'* political vision, and they skilfully found a basis for a pro-Russian campaign in Galicia, vigilantly observing the social and religious mood of the population there.

2.1. Russian Orthodoxy

The growth of Eastern Orthodoxy in Eastern Galicia and in the Lemko region in the early 20th century was part of a widespread political campaign executed by the Tsarist regime and the Holy Synod of the Russian Orthodox Church. The activity had two sources – North America and Russia. The center of action was Zhytomyr, capital of Volhynia province. In the years 1902–1914 that diocese was managed by Archbishop Antonii Khrapovitsky, and after he was transferred to Kharkov, by Archbishop Evlogii Georgievsky. The Pochaiv Monastery, directed by Archimandrite Vitalii Maksymenko, played a special role in the process. From there Russian emissaries set off for Galicia, and the monastery had developed a publishing operation which was wide in scale. Deliveries of the *Pochaiv Lystok* (Pochaiv Newsletter), sent out from Galician cities by Moscophile activists, came in the mail to the addresses of Rusyn peasants, including Lemkos. Russian propaganda proclaiming the slogan of "liberation" for Galician Rus' had particular power of influence. A zealous advocate of this program was Vladimir Bobrinski. Under his aegis branches of the Galician-Russian Association were established in Russia, and financial aid was sent

---

[13] W. Kołpaczkiewicz, "Na granicy wieków. Staroruski Guliwer na falach polityki wszechświatowej" [At the centuries' frontier. The Old Rusyn Gulliver in the sea of universal politics], *BP-U* 1938, no. 9, pp. 93–95.

[14] See S. Shakh, *Mizh Sianom i Dunaitsem* [Between the San and the Dunajec], Munchen 1960, p. 81.

to Galicia, along with periodicals and books for the purpose of reinforcing anti-Catholic and anti-Ukrainian convictions.

At the Slavic congress in Prague in 1908, at which delegates from Russia and Galician Moscophiles took part, Rusyns were officially recognized as Russians. This resolution energized pro-Russian circles in Galicia, who set about building up their institutions, i.e. the Kachkovsky Society, the Stauropegion Institute, and the People's Home in Lviv. In districts responsible to county jurisdiction so-called "private agents" were active. They functioned as liaisons between headquarters and propaganda centers located in Greek Catholic parishes, and transmitted correspondence and instructions, as well as money coming from Russia and from Russian centers in America. Aside from the secular intelligentsia, a significant percent of these agents were Greek Catholic clergy. In the case of the Lemko region the campaign was developed on the borderline of Gorlice and Jasło Counties. "Private agents" there were Yaroslav Kachmarchyk, lawyer and director of the *Lemkovska Kassa* (Lemko Savings Bank) in Gorlice and the following Greek Catholic priests: Teodor Durkot of Zdynia, Marian Myshkovsky of Rostajne and Mykhailo Yurchakevych of Czarne. In the counties of Krosno and Sanok agitators were grouped around Deputy Kurylovych, who in searching for his national identity straddled Dudykevych and Davydiak's groups.

Direct action in the area was undertaken by students visiting their home villages and local farm-hands induced by material gain. They made planned visits to local parishes and established Kachkovsky reading rooms there. One of the most energetic was Vasyl Koldra from Świątkowa Wielka. At mass meetings which he organized himself, he awakened anti-Polish feelings among Lemkos and called them to "endure in the struggle against Polishness and Catholicism." He posited the mighty power of Tsarist Russia and Russian Orthodoxy as the antidote to the threat from Poles and the Roman Catholic Church. He had portraits of Russian Tsars and princes, and patriarchs of the Russian Orthodox Church distributed in peasant huts.[15]

Having support in several regions in the area besides the Lemko region, and also in the counties of Brody, Kosiv, and Sokal, among others, Dudykevych's supporters undertook an attempt to use Orthodoxy as a means to implementing the program for unification with Russia. On 3 August 1911 a secret conference met in the Pochaiv cloister to discuss ways to spread Orthodoxy to Galician Greek Catholic parishes. The conference participants were: archimandrite V. Maksymenko, ministerial clerk for special affairs in the Russian government Razumovsky, Bobrinski's private secretary Bestuzhev, and guests from Galicia: Dudykevych and Markov, two editors of *Prikarpatskaia Rus'* and an associate of the publication *Novoe Vremia* (New Time),

---

[15] AP P, ABGK, ref. # 9445, *Istoriia pravoslavia v seli Hrabi pered svitovoiu viinoiu* [History of Eastern Orthodoxy in the village of Hrab before World War I], pp. 16, 43; ibid., ref. # 437, *Schizma – misje 1911–1914* [Schism – missions 1911–1914], pp. 81, 206, 207. Other students worked with Koldra, e.g. I. Vislotsky and I. Kushvara. Among farm-hands, an outstanding worker was 19 year-old K. Fedorko of Gładyszów.

Dmytro Verhun. During their conversations, the "Russian Galicians" declared that they would have no difficulty organizing 20–30 Orthodox municipalities in Galicia, if a demonstration were desired. They added, however, that the lack of Orthodox churches and local Orthodox clergy would deprive the movement of durability. The group jointly determined that the first order of business was making efforts to prepare cadres of Orthodox clergy in Russia from young men enlisted in Galicia. The Pochaiv conference's resolutions resulted in the Russian side allotting special funds to defray the expenses of Galician candidates, chiefly in the Orthodox seminary in Zhytomyr. The number of alumni from Galicia rose from year to year. In 1911 there were over 10 students at the Zhytomyr seminary, in 1912 about 20, and the press reported the acceptance of another 50 candidates. The majority were recruited in the border counties, while two came from the Lemko region: M. Deniovsky (Żegiestów) and Maksym Sandovych (Zdynia).[16]

The most favorable circumstances for the growth of Orthodoxy existed in those Greek Catholic parishes where there were ongoing disputes between churchgoers and rectors. That was the situation in the counties of Eastern Galicia (Sokal, Zolochiv) and in the West of the region. In the parish of Grab in Jasło County, the first center of Russian Orthodoxy in the Lemko region, a conflict had gone on for several years, fomented by Moscophiles, between the faithful and their rector, Fr. Fylymon Kysilovsky; the conflict arose from the costs of construction of presbytery buildings, church repair and other building works on parish land. The Moscophiles Vasyl Koldra and Ivan Kushvara, as well as parish recruits Mykhailo Hoshko, Sylvester Pavelchak and others, antagonistically disposed toward their rector, awoke an interest in a change of faith among the population, promising to build a new church and cover the costs of keeping an Orthodox priest for each parish.[17] The material issue was one of the most important factors in drawing people's sympathies to Russian Orthodoxy. Most applications for change of denomination which arrived at county offices in Galicia in the years 1911–1914 were filed by the economically poor population. The fact that the rectors had not addressed the populace's demand for their nationality to be noted with a double "s" (ss) in parish books, and for the word "Orthodox" to be used in the liturgy, demands rejected by many Greek Catholic priests, played an important role in this development.[18]

In the autumn of 1911 the ground for the development of Russian Orthodoxy in Galicia had been prepared. The first Orthodox priests, raised in Galicia, the sons of Greek Catholics and until recently Greek Catholic themselves, drawn into Russian Neo-Slavism as young boys, arrived from Russia. They included Fr. Yuliian Il-

---

[16] (X.Y.Z.), *Prawosławie w Rosji i jego podłoże w Galicji* [Orthodoxy in Russia and its foundations in Galicia], Lwów 1913, p. 7; J. Borodzicz, *Na Rusi galicyjskiej Schyzna się gotuje* [A Schism is being prepared in Galician Rus], Chrzanów 1911, p. 54.

[17] AP P, ABGK, ref. # 9445, passim.

[18] See *Chynnosty i rishennia provintsiialnoho Soboru v Halychyni 1891 r.* [Acts and decisions of the provincial Cathedral in Halychyna], Lviv 1894, p. 170.

echko, sent to Sokal County, Fr. Tsymbala to Zolochiv County, Fr. Ihnatii Hudyma, who had looked after the pastoral needs of the Orthodox faithful in Zaluch on the Cheremosh River, and Fr. Maksym Sandovych, returning to his native Lemko region. Sandovych's arrival in Grab on 2 December 1911 reinforced the position of Moscophiles there. His pious lifestyle (involving many long prayers) won over many parishioners, who clung more to the person than to the new church institution. According to contemporary reports, Sandovych was a deeply devout and humble man. His authority was built up through free distribution to believers of books, brochures and pictures on religious themes, presenting Russian churches and cloisters. Collections from church services were given to the poor, with the expectation in turn that they would not return to the Greek Catholic church.[19]

In December 1911 Jasło district authorities received over 200 applications for change of denomination, signed by residents of Grab and Wyszowatka. The application forms were distributed by "private agents." Campaigns collecting signatures for applications were carefully prepared. It sometimes happened that peasants refused to sign and were encouraged to convert with a bribe of money, or even – according to Greek Catholic sources – scared into doing so through the use of force.[20]

The immediately evident material benefits of conversion caused Orthodoxy to proliferate among Lemkos. The examples of Grab and Wyszowatka, where construction materials were bought with Russian money to build an Orthodox Church, and payment for pastoral services was not obligatory, encouraged the populations of neighboring municipalities to convert. In late 1911 and early 1912 the majority of residents in the villages of Czarne, Długie, Lipna, Nieznajowa and Radocyna in Gorlice County declared a change of confession. Groups of Russian Orthodox faithful appeared in other towns as well.

Made anxious by the rising importance of the *novokursnyki*, regional authorities set about taking steps to oppose them, which was easy since Russian Orthodoxy did not have legal status in Austria-Hungary. Furthermore, since Michał Bobrzyński's accession to the function of governor-general in Galicia, the politics of the region had changed. In relations with Ukrainians the new governor-general made an effort to reach an understanding with the national movement. That meant a sharpening of position toward Moscophiles, the more so as tension in Russo-Austrian relations was growing. A few conspicuous activists were arrested, including V. Koldra, acting in the western Lemko region.[21] The arrests also touched Orthodox priests. In April 1912 M. Sandovych was arrested on a charge of espionage in the service of Russia, and a few days later his deputy, Fr. Ivan Solovii.[22] The Przemyśl Greek Catholic ordinariate also reacted, initiating disciplinary proceedings against subordinate

[19]   AP P, ABGK, ref. # 437, pp. 49–50.
[20]   Ibid.
[21]   D.A. Markov, *Russkaia i ukrainskaia ideia v Avstrii* [The Russian and Ukrainian Idea in Austria], Moskva 1915, p. 60.
[22]   AP P, ABGK, ref. # 437, pp. 1, 90.

rectors, supporters of the pro-Russian orientation. The situation which had arisen threatened to bring the downfall of Russian Orthodoxy in Galicia and the failure of Dudykevych's party to fulfill its obligations toward its Tsarist protectors. The Russian Orthodox Church was saved at that moment by some Greek Catholic priests. Fr. Mykhailo Yurchakevych of Czarne was particularly active. Dressed in a Lemko costume he traveled many times throughout the surrounding area, providing pastoral services in secret. The situation created an atmosphere of Church persecution and bolstered community bonds among neophytes. The success of the Moscophiles did not, however, last. They managed to inculcate Orthodoxy in several regions of Galicia, which could give the impression of Orthodoxy growing, but departure from the Greek Catholic Church was not so much an expression of support for the *novokursnyki*'s political line as of allegiance to the traditional form of church services. Conversions to Orthodoxy generally were not the result of pro-Russian feelings.

A wave of arrests led to a political trial, known as the Bendasiuk trial, which took place on 3 March 1914 in Lviv. In the dock were Symeon Bendasiuk, Vasyl Koldra, and two Orthodox priests, Ihnatii Hudyma and Maksym Sandovych. They were accused of treason to the state and acting for Galicia's secession from Austria-Hungary. Two among the four accused were Lemkos. In the historical literature one may find comparisons of this trial with the Olga Hrabar affair from the previous century[23]. The key difference, however, lay in the fact that the 1914 trial showed the participation of Lemkos in the Moscophile political movement, a phenomenon which had not existed in 1882. This may constitute a basis for stating the drift of Moscophile tendencies from east to west and the existence of a relationship between the development of political movements in the Lemko region and the transformations taking place in Eastern Galicia.

Shortly before the outbreak of war, a group of Moscophile activists consisting of Semen Labensky (editor of *Prikarpatskaia Rus'*), Marian Glushkevych (a lawyer in Lviv), Mykhailo Sokhotsky (a lawyer in Sanok) and Yuliian Siokalo (a lawyer in Burshtyn – the elder brother of Yaroslav, a political activist in the western Lemko region), went to Russia and there created the Carpatho-Russian Liberation Committee (*Karpatorusskii Osvoboditelnyi Komitet*). The leaders of the newly created institution were Yuliian Yavorsky, a well-known Galician writer living in Kyiv. The Committee's purpose was "to inform the Russian community and the Russian army of liberation of the historical past and political situation of Russian Carpathia."[24] In reality it took shape in close agreement with the Russian authorities and was to help with the implementation of Russia's plans for Galicia. The Committee provided the

---

[23]   Her process of treason was held in 1882.
[24]   D. Doroshenko, *Istoriia Ukrainy 1917–1923 rr.* [History of Ukraine 1917–1923], vol. 1, Uzhhorod 1932, p. 5; J. Naumenko, "Ukraińskie formacje wojskowe w czasie wojny światowej (1914–1918)" [Ukrainian military formations during the World War (1914–1918)], *BP-U* 1934, no. 2, pp. 3–5; D. Solovei, *Vynyshchennia ukrainstva – osnovna meta Rosii u viini 1914 roku. Materiialy do istorii Ukrainy za chasiv pershoi svitovoi viiny*, Winnipeg 1963, pp. 55–56.

data needed for the development of a brochure entitled *Sovriemiennaia Galichina*, published by the Staff of the Kyiv Military District and intended for Russian officers and soldiers who had been sent to the Galician front. It was a peculiar kind of instruction manual/textbook. Russian soldiers were also provided with the proclamation of the Committee dated 29 July 1914, which spoke of the "liberation of Russian Halychyna territory and Russian Halych after 600 years of servitude."[25]

3. The World War and the Lemko Republics

The entrance of Russian armies into Galicia began the period of the region's occupation. The areas controlled by the Tsar's army were joined to Russia as "eternally Russian lands." Russian opinion journalism and native Moscophiles elaborated the justification for the action. As an example one may quote the following passage from an article by D. Verhun under the title "Chto takoe Galitsia (What is Galicia)," in which the author wrote:

> Red Rus is the cradle of the Russian people [...]. The names of rivers in particular sound homely and familiar to the Russian ear. Because after all the Poprad forming the boundary between Rusyn and Polish land obviously translates [...] with total and transparent simplicity as 'Pop – rad.' And thus is demarcated the difference between Western Slavdom, which calls the clergy priests, and Eastern, where they are called 'pop.'[26]

In order to spread Russian terminology in Galicia, a special Geographical Commission was established in November 1914, led by Pylyp Svystun. The members also included M. Hnatyshak, Y. Yavorsky and O. Markov. Officially the Tsarist regime was acting in defense of "the Russian population of Galicia." In reality it was pursuing a program of expansion into the West, joining territories to Russia that included not only ethnically Ukrainian areas, but ethnically Polish ones too.[27]

Novokursnyki obtained a great deal of influence on the organization of the new Russian provinces (*guberniia*). It should, however, be stressed that the Russian authorities removed the leader of that group, Dudykevych, from the highest administrative levels of government offices. Among well-known *novokursnyki*

---

[25] See *Sovriemiennaia Galichina. Etnograficheskoe i kulturno-politicheskoe sostoianie ieia k sviazi s na-tsionalno-obshchestvennymi nastroeniami* [Modern Galicia. Its ethnographic and culturo-political condition in relation to national-social moods], 1914. On the brochure, see S. Yefremov, "Do istorii Halytskoi Ruiny 1914–1915 rr." [Toward a history of the Halychyna Ruins, 1914–1915], *Ukraina* 1924, vol. 4, pp. 127–144; K. Levytsky, *Istoriia vyzvolnykh zmahan hatytskykh Ukraintsiv z chasu svitovoi viiny 1914–1918*, Lviv 1929, p. 42.

[26] Quoted from F. Przysiecki, *Rządy rosyjskie w Galicji Wschodniej* [Russian governments in Eastern Galicia], Piotrków 1915, p. 53.

[27] Four guberniyas were created from the occupied areas, with centers in Chernivtsi, Lviv, Przemyśl and Ternopil. The Przemyśl *guberniia* included ethnically Polish counties: Łańcut, Nisko, Przeworsk, Rzeszów and Tarnobrzeg. See F. Przysiecki, op.cit., pp. 26–27.

only M. Glushkevych made a political career during the occupation, as mayor of Przemyśl. Thus the Moscophile camp was effectively divided internally, as its own cadres were prepared for work in administrative offices of the local government. In September 1914 Yuri Bobrinski, brother of Vladimir, became governor of Galicia, and energetically worked at implementing the goal of fully integrating Galicia into Russia.

Introducing a Russian administrative division went hand in hand with transformations in the denominational structure. The occupation brought in its wake an inflow of Orthodox clergy from Russia and mass conversions from Greek Catholicism to Eastern Orthodoxy, which in many cases was forced by the replacement of the previous rector with a Russian one. It should nonetheless be underscored that voluntary conversions were also frequent. Starting from August 1914 ceremonies took place in Pochaiv celebrating conversions to Orthodoxy of visiting Greek Catholic peasants; these ceremonies were often officiated by the Bishop of Kremenets, Dionisii, later metropolitan of the Polish Orthodox Church. In February 1915 the Russian authorities made the decision to transfer the Archbishop of Volhynia, Evlogii Georgievsky, from Zhytomyr to Lviv, instituting a *de facto* province of the Russian Orthodox Church in Galicia. The number of Orthodox parishes then was approaching 200 and steadily growing. In December 1915 the Russian press wrote of 500 Orthodox parishes on the territory of occupied Galicia.[28]

The Ukrainian national movement found itself on the defensive. At the beginning of August the Ukrainians established two political organizations in Lviv under the names: Supreme Ukrainian Council (*Zahalna Ukrainska Rada*) presided over by K. Levytsky, and the Ukrainian Liberation Union, Volodymyr Doroshenko presiding. Under pressure from the approaching Russian armies, however, these organizations were evacuated to Vienna. The national movement activists who remained in their homes were subjected to repressions by the Russian occupying authorities. The metropolitan of the Greek Catholic Church, Andrei Sheptytsky, was also arrested and transported deep inside Russia. The situation saw a reversal after the front was broken through at Gorlice. The expulsion of the Russians from Galicia brought with it another wave of repressions, now of Moscophiles and Old Rusyns by the Austro-Hungarian government. Those arrested were placed in internment camps, of which the best-known was the camp in Thalerhof (in the province of Styria). The Austro-Hungarian authorities conducted planned arrests of those suspected of collaboration with Russian circles. The arrests were most frequently made on the basis of lists of organizations' members and subscription lists of Moscophile magazines prepared by districts of the Habsburg Empire before

---

[28]   Y. Petrovych, *Halychyna pidchas rosiiskoi okupatsii 1914–1915* [Halychyna during the Russian occupation 1914–1915], Viden 1915, p. 15; E. Pełczyński, *Prawosławie w Galicji w świetle prasy ruskiej we Lwowie podczas inwazji 1914–1915 roku* [Eastern Orthodoxy in Galicia in the Rusyn press in Lviv during the invasion of 1914–1915], Lwów 1918, pp. 20–21.

1914. The Austro-Hungarian military authorities had at their disposal what were possibly full lists even for the smallest towns.[29]

Victims of repressions looked for culprits among activists in the Ukrainian movement – in the milieux of their political opponents. The persecutions formed the legend of the martyrdom of the "Rusyns," built on hostility toward "Ukrainians" accused of denouncing them before the Austro-Hungarian authorities. This opinion was popularized by pro-Russian and old Rusyn political journalism, but as an over-simplification does not explain the truth of the matter. Cases of denunciations by national movement actors and reverse cases in the first phase of the war had a local dimension and we can judge that they resulted from conflicts between neighbors, from community problem, not in connection with larger political issues. The assertion that denunciations by national movement activists were the basis for the Austro-Hungarian repressions during the First World War is unfounded. Similar assertions appeared in Ukrainian journalism, when stories were published of national movement activists imprisoned at the Thalerhof camp because of denunciations by Poles and Jews.[30]

Still, the myth of martyrology out of which the Thalerhof legend grew had important consequences for the formation of political attitudes among those Rusyns who had not earlier embraced a Ukrainian national identity. This was true to an enormous extent for the population of the Lemko region, although it applied to some of the Subcarpathian Boikos and could also be encountered in Lviv. In the Lemko region the phenomenon had particular meaning since it concerned a compact, politically pristine region, whereas in Eastern Galicia the Moscophile and Old Rusyn clusters found themselves in the midst of the Ukrainian environment. The specific nature of the Lemko region was compounded by the fact that its peasant population, by nature conservative, found it hard to evaluate political events, which was probably due to the local and private focus of the interests of its small communities.

The political engagement of the pro-Russian and national-Ukrainian camps, growing since the late 19th century, accelerated the process of political self-definition among Lemkos. The rivalry transplanted to the Lemko region from Eastern Galicia defined the nature of the options for identity. Until the outbreak of the World War, both orientations interwove with each other, developing their agendas throughout the entire region. Centers of the Ukrainian and Moscophile movements stood in neighboring buildings both in Sanok and Nowy Sącz, drawing support from a broad group of Old Rusyns. The events of the war accelerated the polarization of positions, leading to an advantage for the Ukrainian current in the eastern part of the area, and Moscophilism in the western part.

---

[29] See P.J. Best, "Moscophilism amongst the Lemko Population," *Carpatho-Slavic Studies* (New Haven, Conn.) 1990, vol. 1, pp. 80–81, idem, "Moskalofilstwo wśród ludności łemkowskiej w XX wieku," in: *Ukraińska myśl polityczna w XX wieku* [Ukrainian political thought in the 20th century], ed. M. Pulaski, Kraków 1993, p. 145.

[30] See *Svoboda* 1930, no. 22, p. 4.

The divergence of political thought among Lemko activists in the East and West was a result of changing political conditions. The Sanok region gravitated towards Lviv economically, culturally and politically, hence the ease with which the Ukrainian idea became was diffused and the participation of the Sanok region in the Polish-Ukrainian war of 1918–1919. That war in fact appears to have been the event which decisively ensured the Ukrainian movement's advantage over Moscophilism. The Wisłok or Komańcza Republic bears witness to this.[31] The political fate of the western Lemko region took a different direction. The political involvement of Lemkos in Gorlice, Grybów, Jasło, and Nowy Sącz were influenced to a considerably higher degree than in the eastern region by Austro-Hungarian repressions and the ensuing legend of Thalerhof, which fostered the spread of anti-Ukrainian attitudes. Those feelings also led to the rise of the Florynka Republic.[32]

The course of the war in 1917–1918 directly influenced the rise of these republics. As a result of national liberation struggles, the Habsburg monarchy collapsed and its empire transformed into nation-states. The Lemkos struggled on different fronts in the war; for various reasons, their fates saw them scattered across Europe. In 1917 soldiers, prisoners and the formerly displaced returned to their homes, bringing experience acquired outside their homeland. Sometimes their prewar views had been fortified, while in others, these views faced challenges which caused a change to the opposite position. Those returning from Russia, who had faced "real Moskals," often rejected theories of the Russian origin of Lemkos.[33] Those returning from Austrian camps, however, had become firmer in their conviction of the rightness of continuing with the pro-Russian idea. The enlivening of political moods reached its zenith when news of the outbreak of war between Poland and Ukraine spread in November 1918.

Polish political thought at that time was the product of the traditions of the First Republic and the risings in the period of the partitions. The right of Poles to possession of Eastern Galicia was considered natural and historically justified. The regenerating Polish nation, however, met with strong opposition from the Ukrainians making claims to the same territory. Even before the fall of the monarchy, Ukrainian politicians in Vienna, referring to the demands made in 1848, came forward with proposals for dividing Galicia, delineating the borders of the future Ukrainian crown territory to include the Lemko region. The Ukrainians engagement in this struggle for their own nation-state meant a clash between two fully formed nations.

---

[31] The name "Komancza Republic" took shape as a result of the spread of information about the clamorous final battle between the Ukrainian militia and the Polish army which took place on 24 January 1919 in Komańcza. The political center of the eastern Lemko region was, however, Wisłok Wielki.

[32] See "Ruska Ludowa Republika Łemków" [The Rusyn National Lemko Republic], *Magury '88* (Warszawa) 1988, pp. 44–52; J. Moklak, "Republiki łemkowskie 1918–1919" [Lemko Republics, 1918–1919], *Wierchy* (Kraków) 1994, vol. 59, pp. 63–76.

[33] F. Kokovsky, "Lemkivski republyky v 1918–1919 rokah," *Istorychnyi Kalendar. Almanakh Chervonoi Kalyny na 1935 rik,* (Lviv) 1934, p. 115.

In contrast to the Polish faction, however, the Ukrainian movement did not encompass the whole Rusyn people. The Ukrainians had a weak position at the periphery of their ethnic region, a fact made manifest in the attitudes nursed in some places by Moscophiles and Old Rusyns. This phenomenon was particularly evident in the western Lemko region.

The proclamation in Lviv of the establishment of the Western Ukrainian National Republic (ZUNR, *Zakhidno-Ukrainska Narodna Respublyka*) had resounding echoes in the provinces. In the early days of November the Ukrainian National Council was created for Sanok County. In view of Polish troops being stationed in Sanok, Wisłok Wielki was chosen for the Council's headquarters. This action was initiated by the Greek Catholic rector of Wisłok, Fr. Panteleimon Shpylka together with the rector of Wisłok Niżny, Fr. Mykhailo Tesla.[34] On 4 November they called a mass meeting at which the manifesto of the Ukrainian National Council, printed in *Dilo*, proclaiming the establishment of the ZUNR in Lviv, was publicly read out loud. The next day an assembly in Wisłok Niżny gathered 70 representatives from the surrounding towns (two from each). The members of the Council in Wisłok were then chosen (all those present); the Council would comprise over 35 villages until the end of 1918.[35] The members of the Council board, in addition to Fr. Shpylka, included Teodor Shpylka (brother of Panteleimon), who was in charge of the executive organ; Hryhorii Sudomyr from Wisłok Niżny, a teacher, active in the administration and expansion of Ukrainian schooling; Andrii Kyr of Komańcza – a businessman, former Austrian officer, responsible for organizing the militia; Ivan Kucila (born in Kolomyia) – a judge who dealt with issues of settlements "in the name of the Ukrainian Republic"; Fr. Mykhailo Kril from Prełuki and Fr. Ivan Kovalchyn of Puławy. The Council took shape as a form of self-government and self-defense for local Ukrainians. For the purpose of maintaining public safety it created a militia which was composed of one man from each household.[36]

Armament and command cadres were seen as vitally important. The military and political goal was to take and hold Sanok. The Council strove to obtain aid from local ZUNR authorities in Stryi and Baligród, but the aid provided was not sufficient. At the beginning of December, at the last conference of the Council in Komańcza it decided to send deputies (Fr. Shpylka and a student, Nazarevych) to Hungary for the purpose of tracking down Ukrainian officers demobilized from the Austrian army. With the help of Yaroslav Biberovych, ZUNR representative in Budapest, 12 non-

---

[34] See P. Shpylka, "Vyzvolni zmahannia skhidnoi Lemkivshchyny v 1918 rotsi," *Lemkivskyi Kalendar, 1967* (Toronto–Passaic, NJ) 1966, p. 22.

[35] Balnica, Czystohorb, Darów, Dołżyca in the environs of Komańcza, Duszatyn, Jasiel, Jawornik, Kalnica, Karlików, Komańcza, Łupków, Maniów, Mików, Mokre, Osławica, Płonna, Polany, Prełuki, Przybyszów, Puławy, Radoszyce, Rzepedź, Smolnik, Solinka, Surowica, Szczawne, Szczerbanówka, Turzańsk, Wisłok Niżny and Wyżny, Wola Michowa, Wola Niżna and Wyżna, Wysoczany, Zubeńsko, Żubracze. AAN, MWRiOP, ref. # 474, p.n.n.

[36] P. Shpylka, op.cit., p. 24.

commissioned officers and financial help in the sum of 10,000 Austrian crowns were obtained.[37] The plan to storm Sanok was nonetheless rejected by Fr. Shpylka who considered the forces of the Wisłok Council too meager to hold the city.

Military action was carried out mainly on the Komańcza – Zagórz segment of the railway line. In January 1919 Polish divisions created from the ranks of militarized railwaymen from Zagórzany conducted an offensive in the direction of Komańcza, dissolving the Ukrainian National Council in Sanok County. Despite its short-lived existence the Council left an enduring mark on the consciousness of Lemkos in the region, fostering further growth of the Ukrainian idea, now built on hostility toward the victors, i.e. the Polish side.

Pro-Ukrainian feelings were also manifested in the western areas of the Lemko region, but did not lead to the national movement gaining an advantage there. In the towns of Gorlice, Jasło, and Nowy Sącz Counties, rallies were organized at which views were exchanged between proponents and opponents of joining the Lemko region to the ZUNR. On 17 November 1918 a rally was held in Świątkowa Wielka at which the Moscophile activist Dmytro Sobin spoke forcefully against joining the Lemko region to the western Ukrainian state. Moscophiles discussed strategies for action at the political conference in Świątkowa on 21 November. A few days later, on 27 November, they forced a resolution at a rally in Gładyszów that the Lemko region could belong only to Russia.[38] The meeting created a Council (the Russian Council, *Russka Rada*) with headquarters in Gładyszów, whose immediate goal was to make collections of funds to cover the costs of its delegate to the peace conference in Paris. The Council was to include five members from each village. Some sources call the Council convoked in Gładyszów the "Gładyszów Republic." A Greek Catholic priest from Czarne was elected chairman – M. Yurchakevych, known for his pro-Ortho-dox agitation among Lemkos before the war and during the Russian occupation.[39]

From the speeches of Lemko Moscophiles at local mass-meetings (e.g. in Gładyszów) it was evident that their political program still remained to be clearly defined. One of the speakers expressed the view that if the incorporation of the Lem-ko region into Russia were not possible, it should be joined to Bukovina or Serbia (sic!). The Gładyszów Council approved a series of resolutions concerning the or-ganization of community life, e.g. the removal of Ukrainian clergy from the Lemko region, the reintroduction of the word "pravoslavny" (Orthodox) into the Greek Catholic liturgy, and the introduction of the use and teaching of Russian language into schools. The Gładyszów congress's deliberations took place in an atmosphere heavy with the memory of the Thalerhof tragedy – paeans were read to the victims of the camp.[40]

---

[37] In the first phase of the search not a single officer could be recruited, it was only in the next phase that volunteers were found from the NCO camp. See P. Shpylka, op.cit., p. 28.

[38] O. Tarnovych, "Lemkivshchyna v chasi vyzvolnykh zmahan," *Svoboda* 1933, no. 271, p. 2.

[39] AP P, ABGK, ref. # 55, p. 299.

[40] Ibid., pp. 300, 301.

The decisions taken in Gładyszów received support from the residents of the surrounding villages, but there were nonetheless protests against imposing the pro-Russian orientation on the population. Ukrainian feelings dominated in such villages as, among others, Grab, Małastów, Muszyna, and Pętna. During the rally in Gładyszów Petro Kytchak, the representative of Grab, spoke against unions between the Lemko region and Russia. Kytchak played an important role in maintaining a high level of pro-Ukrainian feeling in Grab and Ożenna, villages which refused to send delegates to the Council in Gładyszów and displayed support for the ZUNR. In these towns Ukrainian militias were created.[41]

In November 1918 rallies were organized in the counties of Grybów and Nowy Sącz. They prepared the ground for the congress of delegates from individual villages in Florynka, which took place on 5 December of that year and constituted the Council (*Russka Rada*), to be led by Yaroslav Kachmarchyk of Muszyna. At the next assembly in Florynka on 12 March 1919 the incorporation of the Lemko region into Russia was approved, without specifying whether this meant White Russia or Bolshevik Russia. The *Russkii Uriad* (government) created at that time, whose members included: Fr. Dmytro Khylak of Izby, Mykola Gromosiak of Krynica, the earlier-mentioned Y. Kachmarchyk and Fr. Vasyl Kuryllo of Florynka. This body aimed to take control of the social and political life of the region, e.g. teachers were prohibited from filing "pledges of service" to the Polish authorities and Fr. Khylak ensured that the heading "Russian National Republic" appeared in official and public register documents.[42]

In attempting to outline the organizational scheme of these Councils it is essential to list the four political centers of the western Lemko region: Krynica for Nowy Sącz County, Florynka for Grybów County, Gładyszów and Czarne for Gorlice County, Świątkowa Wielka for Jasło County. This configuration was soon to disintegrate, however. On 28 January 1919 the Council in Krynica, chaired by the medical doctor Oleksandr Tykhansky, dissolved, most probably handing its affairs over to the management of the Florynka board.[43] More detailed information on the Council in Świątkowa is lacking. We may gather that it had ties to the center in Gorlice County, which at first was Gładyszów, and later Czarne. The Council remained longest in Florynka, which was probably the chief political center in the area.

Moscophile centers of power took shape throughout the entire southwestern area of the peripherally situated ethnic Rusyn strip, i.e. in the regenerated Polish nation-state and the Czechoslovak one being created. The crowning achievement of these endeavors was the narrowly pro-Russian memorandum passed at the congress of an

---

[41] Ibid., pp. 304, 306.

[42] See L. Hankevych, "«Lemkivska Republyka.» Odyn zabutyi protses," *Zhyttia i pravo* 1934, no. 2 (29).

[43] After the dissolution of the Krynica council, O. Tykhansky developed the work of the Carpatho-Russian National Council in Prešov, see Z. Peška, I. Markov, "Příspevek k ústavnin dejinam Podkarpatské Rusi," vol. V, *Bratislava* 1932, p. 532.

organization called the National Council of Russian Subcarpathia (*Narodny Soviet Russkago Prikarpattia*) in Sanok on 13 December 1918.[44] The congress gathered together representatives of Councils from the whole of Galicia and abroad (Slovakia and Bukovina). Sanok activists and representatives of the western Lemko region also took part in the congress.[45] Worthy of note is the phenomenon of the enfeeblement of Moscophile centers in the area of the former Eastern Galicia. There were, it is true, Councils in Zolochiv, Kolomyia, Buchach, Stanyslaviv and Przemyśl, but resolutions of a political nature were dealt with in Sanok or Prešov.

Faced with the fall of Tsarist Russia, the existing Moscophile conception lost currency. Furthermore, as the political situation stabilized in ethnic Polish areas, the administrative arm of the Polish government gradually encompassed Lemko villages in its reach. In search of a path to greater independence from Poland, Lemkos developed a pro-Czechoslovak orientation, a trend facilitated by the strong position Czechophile feelings had already achieved among Rusyns in Slovakia and Carpathian Ukraine.

In December 1918 the pro-Ukrainian Ruthenian National Council (*Ruska Narodna Rada*) in Prešov, under the influence of Anton Beskyd, former deputy to the Budapest parliament, changed to a pro-Russian orientation; then at the congress in Košice it took a pro-Czech stance.[46] Beskyd had close relations with Czechoslovak politicians, and under his influence a resolution to join Carpathian Ukraine to Czechoslovakia was passed, which was confirmed in Prešov on 7 January 1919. This idea found advocates among Czech emigrants in the US, led by Hryhorii Zhatkovych. Beskyd and Zhatkovych supported the Czechoslovak delegation's exertions over Transcarpathia at the peace conference in Paris.

There were several Lemko activists in Beskyd's milieu, e.g. Dmytro Vislotsky of Łabowa, political journalist and at that time editor of *Golos Russkago Naroda* – the press organ of the Prešov Council, as well as O. Tykhansky and D. Sobin. Cooperation between Lemko Councils and the Council in Prešov soon developed. Police reports to district government offices told of intensified pro-Czechoslovak activity in the Lemko region. The reports contained the names of some activists, e.g. Andreiko, Rusenko, Tykhansky, Vislotsky.[47] Close contact was also maintained with Beskyd by Fr. M. Yurchakevych, I. Kachmarchyk and V. Kurylovych. The plan to incorporate the Lemko region into Czechoslovakia was propagated by political journalism and

---

[44] CDIAL, f. 148, op. 2, case # 5, *Memorandum Narodnego Sovieta Russkago Prikarpattia*, 1918, pp. 1–2. See Z. Peška, I. Markov, op.cit., pp. 528–531.

[45] V. Bubniak, M. Gromosiak, Fr. M. Felenchak, Y. Kachmarchyk, Fr. T. Kachmarchyk, A. Koldra, Fr. V. Kuryllo, V. Kurylovych, Fr. R. Pryslopsky, O. Saviuk, Fr. Y. Siekierzhynsky, Y. Shatynsky, O. Tykhansky, O. Valnytsky, Y. Voitovych and Fr. M. Yurchakevych – chairman of the organization called *Russian National Council of the Lemko Region*, and D. Sobin – secretary of that organization. See Z. Peška, I. Markov, op.cit., pp. 528–531.

[46] K. Grzymała, "Ruś Podkarpacka" [Carpathian Ruthenia], *BP-U* 1937, no. 1, p. 8.

[47] APK, SP G II, ref. # 8, Political issues, espionage on behalf of Germany, Russia and Czechoslovakia 1919–1923, p.n.n.

more importantly contained in a memorandum to the government in Prague and to the Peace Conference. Beskyd obtained no support in this matter from either Minister Eduard Beneš, or Zhatkovych, who were opposed to expanding Czechoslovakia into the Carpathian Region.

Polish authorities at first passively observed the political involvement of Lemkos, attaching little importance to the pro-Ukrainian plans and even less to the pro-Russian ones. It was only with the appearance of these Czechophile tendencies that the state administration's concern was aroused. The Lemko region's entire southern segment adjoined the newly created Czechoslovak state. The southern slope of the Carpathian Mountains was also inhabited by Rusyns. Both groups spoke in dialects of the same language and with a few exceptions were members of the same Church. Czechophilism among Lemkos, in contrast to Moscophilism, was recognized as a danger to the Polish nation-state and provoked political reactions. The Polish population of the Nowy Sącz region also protested.[48]

The Polish reaction led to quick pacification of the Lemko region. The leading Lemko activists were arrested, and close surveillance of those at liberty was begun. The last echo of the events of 1918 and 1919 was the trial of members of the Council in Florynka (Khylak, Gromosiak, Kachmarchyk), which took place on 10 June 1921 before the District Court in Nowy Sącz.[49] The accused were defended by the lawyers Kyrylo Cherlunchakevych and Volodymyr Zahaikevych of Przemyśl and Lev Hankevych of Lviv. The defense successfully used an argument taken from American diplomacy which stated that the accused had acted according to Wilson's principles. After a trial lasting twelve hours, from 9:00 AM to 9:00 PM, the judges issued a verdict finding all of the accused not guilty. After sixth months under arrest they were freed and returned late at night together with their defense attorneys to Binczarowa, where they were guests of Fr. Teofil Kachmarchyk, father of one of the accused. L. Hankevych, a Ukrainian, remembered later that "Moscophiles and Ukrainian sat at one table and in perfect harmony discussed the fate of the Lemko region."[50] At that particular time, in the existing atmosphere of mutual hostility, such a meeting was surely an isolated incident.

The fate of both republics, in Wisłok and Florynka, reflected the path of the Lemko region's political development and the two-track tradition of national identity formation among Lemkos. There were significant differences between the activists

---

[48] In late January and early February 1919 a mass meeting took place in Nowy Sącz at which there were protests against "the Czech temptation and the Czech campaign in the Lemko region." See "Czesi na granicy słowacko-galicyjskiej" [Czechs on the Slovak-Galician Border], *Ilustrowany Kurier Codzienny* 1919, no. 33.

[49] The trial records have disappeared and it is now difficult to define the scope of action and number of members of the Florynka "government." In the records of Nowy Sącz District there is a copy of the court sentence, see AP K, SP NS, ref. # 85, Presidial records of the County District Office in Nowy Sącz 1918–1923, p.n.n. The copy of the sentence has been published, see J. Moklak, "Republiki łemkowskie" [The Lemko Republics], p. 69.

[50] L. Hankevych, op.cit., p. 6.

from the East and those from the West of the region. The Wisłok Republic, being pro-Ukrainian, had a clearly defined political program from the start. With regard to the reigning mood throughout the historical Lemko region, however, the historian encounters difficulties in assessing the interwoven approaches: i.e., the pro-Ukrainian, pro-Russian, Czechophile, and also pro-Soviet. Making assessments is rendered more difficult still by the fact that sources employ the terms "Council," "Soviet," or "Republic" interchangeably in reference to the same institutions.

The emergence of the so-called Lemko Republics should be considered the first political engagement of the Lemkos. They showed a desire to participate in building the future of the region on the foundation of the Byzantine Slavonic traditions cultivated there for centuries. This does not change the fact that the traditional divide into rival orientations beginning in the mid-19th century, the national (Ukrainian), Moscophile, and Old Rusyn, was maintained in the Second Polish Republic as well.

Chapter II: Moscophiles and Old Rusyns

1. Formation of the pro-Russian party

The development of Moscophilism and the Old Rusyn movement in the Lemko region during the interwar period was closely connected with political movements which developed in the Lviv, Stanyslaviv, Sambir, Zolochiv, and Rava Ruska areas, and in other cities scattered around the former Eastern Galicia. Lemkos did not have forms of social or political organization evolving exclusively from their local traditions. The organizations in which they actively participated took form mainly through the inspiration of Lviv activists. This was a natural state of affairs, considering that the centers of all of the more important and influential provincial institutions were located in Lviv. The processes through which the structures of such institutions developed in the Lemko region must therefore be presented in the context of the activity in Lviv's political centers.

The fall of Tsarist Russia and the emergence of the Polish state brought about a revaluation in the political consciousness of many actors – hence pro-Polish, pro-Russian, and pro-communist sympathies equally became visible. The accumulated archival documents do not allow us to precisely separate out the above political tendencies in the immediate postwar period, yet they did find a place in the party called the Halych-Russian National Organization, hereafter HRNO, formed in 1919, whose executive organ was the Russian Executive Committee (*Russkii Ispolnitelnyi Komitet*) in Stanyslaviv.[1] The chaos was aggravated by the fact that – as Ivan Kedryn attests – this Committee recognized the authority of the Western Ukrainian National Republic, which could signify the entry of the Moscophiles on the path of identification with the Ukrainian movement. According to Kedryn, this process showed the capacity for growth, but was interrupted by the fall of the Ukrainian state.[2]

Echoes of these changes were heard in the Lemko region as well. On 18 October 1922 at the pre-election assembly in Krynica, at which the delegates from Lviv (Gensiorsky and Pelekhaty) made speeches in the Ukrainian literary language in which they identified with the Russian Executive Committee, and a Regional Committee

---

[1] I. Kedryn, "W poszukiwaniu metryki... Kilka uwag i faktów z dziejów powojennego moskalofilstwa galicyjskiego," *BP-U* 1937, no. 15, p. 163; AAN, KGPP, ref. # 44, *Mniejszości narodowe w Polsce, teksty wykładów* [1935], p. 13.

[2] I. Kedryn, op.cit., p. 163.

was chosen for the Gorlice, Grybów and Nowy Sącz districts which included among its members Yaroslav Kachmarchyk and Metody Trokhanovsky. The former would later be linked with the Ukrainian current, while the latter would represent first the Moscophiles, and then the Old Rusyns.[3]

The variety of political currents present in the HRNO made the organization internally disharmonious. In 1921 two camps took shape: the right wing (V. Trush, M. Bachynsky and others) and the left wing – a group of Communist-leaning activists grouped around the journal *Vola Naroda*, which would later be part of the sphere of activity of the Communist Party of Western Ukraine.[4] Frequent mutual friction between the two camps led to a lasting break in 1923, brought on in large part by the decision of the Council of Ambassadors on 14 March of that year granting the former Eastern Galicia to Poland.

This decision placed the Ukrainian movement in Poland in an entirely new situation. Above all, parties working toward Ukrainian independence ceased to hope for support from the *entente*, and realistically-minded Ukrainian politicians set about working through available parliamentary means. The continuing negative disposition toward Poland led on the one hand to a nationalist conspiracy oriented toward Lithuania and Germany, while it inclined Western Ukrainian public opinion in the direction of the Ukrainian Soviet Socialist Republic on the other, in the process deepening the pro-Soviet sympathies among a part of the Moscophiles. The reactionary Moscophile right remained faithful to the pan-Russian idea, while the Old Rusyns declared still stronger loyalty toward the Polish state, without abandoning their (specifically understood) Rusyn national consciousness.

1.1. The Russian National Organization, 1923–1928

As a result of internal disunity in the HRNO, in May 1923 its right wing established the Provisional Russian National Committee (*Vremennyi Russkii Narodnyi Komitet*), which in November of that year was reconfigured as the Russian National Organization party (RNO, *Russka Narodna Organizatsiia*).[5] The RNO took a decidedly pro-Russian direction, which found expression in the resolutions of the party's first congress on 1 November. The congress brought together 342 delegates, who were united by a shared anti-Bolshevik stance and chose a 15-person supreme party organ – the Russian National Council (*Russkii Narodnyi Soviet*), whose members included the Lemko activist Orest Hnatyshak, at that time living in Przemyśl. The pan-

---

[3] AP K, SP NS, ref. # 85, p.n.n.
[4] M. Andrusiak, "Zarys historii moskalofilstwa wśród Ukraińców halickich," *BP-U* 1933, nos. 34–35, p. 6. See J. Radziejowski, *Komunistyczna Partia Zachodniej Ukrainy, 1919–1929. Węzłowe problemy ideologiczne*, Kraków 1976.
[5] *Russkii Narodnyi Siezd, 1 noiabria 1923 g. Rezolutsii Siezda i Ustav Russkoi Narodnoi Organizatsii s prylozheniem Rezolutsii Russkago Narodnago Soveta ot 2 fievrala 1924 g.*, Lvov 1924, p. 3; I. Kedryn, op.cit., p. 163.

Russian idea was strengthened within the RNO by the authority of Russian member Nikolai S. Sieriebrennikov (a deputy in the Polish *Sejm* – lower house of parliament), who was visiting Lviv with ever greater frequency. Under his influence a resolution was passed at the RNO Council meeting of 2 February 1924 endowing him with the right to represent the interests of "the Russian population" before county authorities and in the Polish parliament. The group was headed by Volodymyr Trush, principal of the state high school in Stanyslaviv, who fulfilled the function of RNO chairman.[6] The minority of Old Rusyns (M. Bachynsky and O. Lysiak) recognized the pan-Russian nature of the party.

Ties between RNO activists and activists for the Russian national minority from the Russian National Union (RZN) gradually became stronger. The RNO maintained influence over the M. Kachkovsky Society, the People's Home Institute (*Narodnyi Dom*), the Stauropegion Institute, the network of trade co-operatives concentrated around the institution of the Rusyn Auditing Union (*Russkii Revizyinyi Soiuz*) and the weekly *Russkii Golos* (Russian Voice) published in Lviv in Russian under the editorship of Ivan Shkirpan.[7]

The RNO Council was headed successively by V. Trush (1923–1925), Fr. Tytus Myshkovsky (1925) and Hryhorii Malets (1926–1928). Its political program accented the drive to obtain autonomy for "Russian lands in Poland." There were hopes for the development of Russian education, the creation of Russian language faculties at the universities in Lviv and Vilnius, and that, in the future, a separate Russian university would be secured. During the party congress in Lviv on 29 June 1926 Mykhailo Sokhotsky (a lawyer in Turka and Sanok) stated that "The most severe injury to those of Russian nationality living on Polish territory [referring to the Rusyns of Galicia] is the omission in the language laws of the rights of the Russian language."[8] The territory in which the RNO was active included the area whose centers were Brody, Kamionka Strumilova, Turka, Zboriv, Zolochiv and the three counties of the Lviv province inhabited by Lemkos: Krosno, Lesko and Sanok. Reports of the RNO's activities in the period 1923–1926 do not mention the counties of the Kraków province. The only representative of the Lemko region among the higher party authorities at the time was Fr. Kyrylo Chaikovsky from Mszana.[9]

Accounts by the starosts (district head) of RNO action in particular counties sent to the Lviv Province Office in July 1926 told of relatively low levels of activity. In many districts, e.g. in Jarosław, the party did not have a branch, while in others there appeared a phenomenon of Moscophiles and Old Rusyns moving to the Ukrainian camp, e.g. in the counties of Drohobych, Brzozów and Lesko. The starosts' accounts

---

[6] *Russkii Narodnyi Siezd, l noiabria 1923 g.*, pp. 3–4, 7–8, 11; DALO, f. 1, op. 58, case # 581, *Otchiety o siezdakh i sobraniakh chlenov russofilskogo obshchiestva "Russkaia Narodnaia Organizatsiia," 1926–1927*, p. 1.

[7] AAN, MSW, microfilm 25607, p. 10.

[8] DALO, f. 1, op. 58, case # 581, p. 3.

[9] AAN, MSW, microfilm 25607, p. 11.

also contained information about the Polonophile movement in some provincial branches of the RNO, e.g. in Sokal, though these always had neighboring groups of activists connected with Sieriebrennikov.

Sieriebrennikov's political flirtation with top-level Lviv Moscophiles quickly brought the desired results. Slogans from the propaganda he put out had their effect on the resolutions taken by the RNO Congress in Lviv on 29 June 1926. After Sieriebrennikov's speech, in which he spoke of "the spirit of the true Russian nation," Malets spoke. He stated that the Russian world, by virtue of its greatness and culture, held a magnetic power over the tribes of "Rus," and spoke out against the Polish government, accusing it of supporting "Ukrainian and Byelorussian separatism." The course of the congress's deliberations strengthened Sieriebrennikov in his conviction that the Polish congress of the RZN (Russian National Union) could be held in Lviv. The participation of the RZN and RNO in a joint congress was to create a broad front of political struggle for Russians in Poland. The congress was planned for 4 December 1926, but met two months later, on 2 February 1927.[10]

The main host and organizer was Malets. The preparatory work and debates were actively participated in by B. Lelavskii, M. Sokhotsky, A. Polishchuk (a merchant from Brody), and others. The Lemko region was represented by Fr. Chaikovsky, who read a welcoming telegram "from the Lemko region." Resolutions passed by the congress spoke of agrarian reform which would take into consideration the rights and needs of the "Russian population." The calls for faculties of Russian language and literature as well as Russian history at the universities of Lviv and Vilnius were repeated. A great deal of space was devoted to religious issues, above all the Eastern Orthodox Church, which was represented at the congress by, among others, Fr. Mikhail Ivaskov, a Russian from Volhynia, active in the development of Eastern Orthodoxy in the Lemko region in the late 1920s. The assertion, already made at the RNO congress in June 1926, that the RZN stood in defense of "the [Orthodox] Church's independence from Rome and rulers," was repeated. The congress's deliberations were conducted in Russian.[11]

Participation in the congress of the RZN was a test of the political attitudes of RNO leaders. The congress confirmed the traditional division existing within the party, i.e. between extreme Moscophiles and pro-Polish Old Rusyns. Moreover, doubts emerged among some supporters of Sieriebrennikov as to the wisdom of spreading the Russian idea in the Lviv region. The head Moscophiles, V. Trush, A. Syvuliak, and M. Tretiak, did not take part in the congress, nor did Old Rusyns with pro-Polish connections.[12]

The integration of the top leadership of the RNO and RNZ which took place in February and March brought in its wake significant results for both organizations.

---

[10] SN 1927, no. 1, p. 62.
[11] Ibid., no. 1, p. 62 and no. 2, p. 180.
[12] DALO, f. 1, op. 58, case # 581, pp. 66, 67.

Both organizations, formally independent, energized their activity in many areas of social and political life. According to the report on RNO activity filed by Mykhailo Marko at the congress in Lviv on 16 June 1927, the organization had county branches in Kamionka Strumilowa, Krosno, Sambir, Sanok, Sokal and Zhovkva. Its operations were not limited to the area of the Polish Republic. In the period referred to in the report (29 June 1926 to 16 June 1927) the RNO sent delegates to the congress of the League of National Minorities in Geneva.[13]

1.2. The Russian Peasant Organization, 1928–1939

On 7 June 1928 the RNO General Council called a nationwide congress in Lviv. The congress was participated in by 129 delegates from the southeastern voivodeships. At the petition of Roman Durkot from Kulikovo, the congress approved the change of the party's name to the Russian Peasant Organization (RSO, *Russka Selianska Organizatsiia*); this party entered into the composition of the Russian National Union (RZN) as an autonomous unit.[14] The resolution was a product of the ideology of Galician Moscophiles, which postulated the existence of one pan-Russian nation, divided into subordinate nations: Russian, Ukrainian, and Byelorussian, and the existence of only one literary language for that nation – the Russian language. In the thought which formed this conception, the Ukrainian language had the right to exist as the language of part of the Russian population, as a regional language or – from a philological perspective – as a dialect of Russian language, while the Ukrainian people had the right to their own state, but did not have the right to a *gosudarstvo*, or superstate, which could only be Russian.[15] As a result of lively program discussions with the participation of Sieriebrennikov, a series of resolutions indicating the pro-Russian and pro-Orthodox character of the party, its opposition to the Polish Republic and hostility to Ukrainian factions, was passed.

The most important resolutions at the congress stated:

- the RSO's demand that the Russian population be given free rein to develop as a nation, since "the Polish constitution does not divide citizens into categories";
- the congress's recognition of deputy Pavel Korol [voted in 1928] as the one representative of the Russian population in the Sejm and refused to accept representation from deputies of any Ukrainian party, calling Ukrainians "murderers of Rusyns";
- the congress's protest against the policy of crediting state banking institutions who denied credit to the Rusyn Auditing Union (*Russkii Revizyinyi Soiuz*) in Lviv;

---

[13] Ibid., p. 83.
[14] The contents of the statement declaring accession to the RSO began with the words: "Please accept me, according to my nationality as a citizen of the Russian countryside…" Quoted from CDIAL, f. 394, op. 1, case # 7, *Blanky zaiav pro pryiom w chleny Ruskoi Selanskoi organizatsii*, pp. 1, 2, 3.
[15] I. Kedryn, op.cit., p. 164.

- the congress's call for Old Rusyns loyal to the Polish Republic to subordinate themselves to the RSO;
- the congress's branding of the actions of the head authorities of the Greek Catholic Church in Lviv as "narrowly partisan, chauvinistic and unworthy of the teaching of Christ."[16]

It was decided that the press organ of the RSO and also temporarily of the RZN (a decision testifying to the low level of active participation by ethnic Russians) would be the Russian-language *Russkii Golos*, published in Lviv, while the periodical *Zemlia i Volia* printed in a language closer to Ukrainian was designated for the rural population. The RSO recognized the following Lviv cultural, educational, and economic institutions as belonging to it: the Stauropegion Institute, the *Narodnyi Dom* Institute (which, however, remained in the possession of Old Rusyns) and the Rusyn Auditing Union. The Kachkovsky society, however, would exist as a separate institution, indirectly linked to the Central Council of the RSO through Malets and Tsebrynsky.

The congress appointed the first supreme authorities of the new party. Illia Vynnytsky from Drohobych became Council Chairman. The Lemko region was represented in the Council by five representatives: Semen Vozniak of Krosno, Osyp Hukevych of Sanok, Teodor Voitovych of Uście Ruskie, Teodor Fedak of Polan (in Krosno County) and Fr. Chaikovsky.

In the Lemko region RSO chapters first appeared in the Lviv province, in the counties of Sanok and Krosno. The circumstances in which the party developed were different, however, and the social background of its members also differed. While the RSO in Krosno County was founded mainly by peasants, in Sanok it was composed of the intelligentsia. There were also important confessional differences: in Krosno County the majority were converts to Eastern Orthodoxy, while in Sanok they were Greek Catholics.

Already before, in the period when RNO structures were being built in Krosno County, confessional conflicts among Lemkos had been taken advantage of. Political rallies were organized among Orthodox believers. One of the first was the rally in Tylawa held on 16 November 1926, which attracted about 900 participants, mostly inhabitants of Tylawa and Trzciana. The presence there of prominent Lviv Moscophiles R. Vavrik, M. Tsebrynsky, and Sieriebrennikov, indicates the political importance of the meeting. In their speeches, they spoke out in harsh terms against the Ukrainian idea and the Greek Catholic clergy. The rally's first resolution spoke of the necessity for Lemkos to recognize only one party, the RNO, predecessor of the RSO.[17]

---

[16] CDIAL, f. 130, op. 1, case # 39, *Rezalutsii kraievoho zizdu delehativ Halytsko-ruskoi natsionalnoi orhanizatsii – "Russka selianska organizatsiia" vid 7 chervnia 1928 r. pro politychne stanovyshche moskvofiliv*, pp. 1–2.

[17] AAN, MWRiOP, ref. # 928, *Sprawy osobowe księży. Antypaństwowa działalność kleru greckokatolickiego w Małopolsce*, p. 322.

One of the most active Orthodox priests was Mikhail Ivaskov, delegated by Metropolitan Dionizy to the post of administrator for Tylawa. Together with Teodor Fedak he organized local RSO congresses in Ciechania, Mszana, Myscowa, Olchowiec, Polany and Tylawa. As a result of Ivaskov and Chaikovsky's operations, and those of local operatives M. Bankovsky, T. Fedak, P. Haida, P. Kashchak and I. Viityk, a county congress of the RSO was organized in Tylawa for 30 December 1928.[18] Over 70 delegates from over a dozen villages in Krosno County attended the congress. The program speakers were Fr. M. Ivaskov and T. Fedak. The congress selected the RSO County Committee with Ivan Yadlovsky from Tylawa as chairman.[19] Resolutions passed at the congress placed a duty upon members to broaden the party's influence in the region by forming new local committees and libraries named for Kachkovsky. Through ties with Eastern Orthodoxy, the RSO developed its agendas in the Kraków province and in the counties of Grybów, Gorlice and Jasło as well. To a small extent this process occurred in Nowy Sącz County also.

The situation was completely different in Sanok County, where Eastern Orthodoxy was prominent in only two places, Lipowiec and Czeremcha. The Sanok region in many aspects of its social and political life gravitated toward Lviv. In Sanok since the second half of the nineteenth century the Lemko and Boiko elements of the Old Rusyn intelligentsia, who after the outbreak of world war stood faced with a choice of national identity, were quite numerous. The Polish-Ukrainian War of 1918–1919 tipped the scales in favor of the Ukrainian national movement, eliminating to a considerable extent the old pro-Russian and Old Rusyn spirit there. The process mainly involved young activists, while the older ones either did not want to or could not break away from the ideas with which they had grown up, and remained faithful to Moscophilism or to the Old Rusyn idea.

The peasant population participated in the creation of local RSO centers above all for pragmatic reasons, expecting an improvement in living conditions, improved social organization, a higher level of civilization in the region, etc. Local exponents taking action in agreement with the Central Council of the party came out against such expectations. The first RSO congress for the entire Lemko region, which took place in Sanok on 2 February 1929, had as its slogan the struggle "for political cultural and economic rights for Lemko Rus." The organizers of the congress expected participation of delegates from eight counties, but in view of unfavorable climatic conditions (severe frost, -33°C) delegates came from only four nearby counties. The proceedings were opened by Yevhen Shatynsky, chairman of the RSO District Com-

---

[18] The RSO committee in Tylawa elected at the meeting of 9 December 1928 consisted of: I. Kyrpan – chairman, I. Liitsyshyn – secretary, M. Kukuliak – treasurer. The committe in Mszana consisted of: T. Broda – chairman, A. Grabsky – secretary, A. Bankovsky – treasurer, O. Hidnyk and M. Baly – members. See *Zemlia i Volia* 1929, no. 52, p. 4.

[19] The remaining members of the committee were: P. Petryk (Zyndranowa) – deputy chairman, I. Kyrpan (Tylawa) – secretary, S. Fedak (Mszana) – treasurer, I. Dytko (Polany), P. Baran (Trzcianne) and H. Glovatsky (Barvinok) – members. See *Russkii Golos* 1929, no. 6, p. 3.

mittee in Sanok. Discussion was preceded by program papers delivered by delegates to the Central Council: Yurchakevych and Hrabets. Activists from Sanok also took the floor: Y. Shatynsky, M. Muzychka, D. Gensiorsky. There were protests against the Ukrainian movement, chiefly UNDO (the Ukrainian National Democratic Alliance), and accusations against Ukrainian politicians of working to eliminate the concepts of "Rus" and "Rusyns" from public life. In view of the absence of delegates from the Kraków province, it was resolved to call an all-Lemko peasant congress from the whole Lemko region in Sanok in March 1929.[20]

The party's local structures in the Kraków province developed parallel to those in other voivodeships. The first local RSO committees to spring up were in Grybów County. Among the most industrious activists were Yurii Khokholak and Yuliian Halkovych of Bogusza, Vasyl Didovych of Binczarowa, and, from Śnietnica, Sofron Krynytsky and Zakhar Stavysky. These also worked actively on behalf of legalizing the institutions of Eastern Orthodoxy developing on its parallel track. In the spring of 1930 this led to the establishment of the first RSO structures in Grybów County. The congress of delegates from particular villages took place in Florynka on 27 April and brought into being the County Committee for Grybów County. Just as had occurred at the Sanok congress, one of the program speeches was given by A. Batenchuk, visiting from Lviv, delegate to the Central Council, a Lemko from Węglówka (Vanivka). Aside from political issues, he spoke penetratingly on economic matters, which dominated the discussion.[21]

The organizational development of RSO encountered difficulties from the BBWR (Non-partisan Bloc for Cooperation with the Government), in collaboration with which activists from the Old Rusyn milieu worked. After the experience of the 1928 elections, which gave the Lemko region no representative in parliament (Korol, elected in that cycle, was from Biała Podlaska), a large number of Lemkos, hitherto sympathetic to the RSO, tended increasingly towards supporting the BBWR. It comes as no surprise, therefore, that the RSO lost the 1930 elections, in spite of an active campaign in the Lemko counties. Nevertheless, even in places where the party's organizational structure was relatively feeble, i.e. in Nowy Sącz and Gorlice counties, local RSO election committees were formed.[22]

The first period of the RSO's development was ended by the deliberations of the Second Nationwide Congress of the organization, which took place in Lviv on 25 December 1931. M. Marko, rapporteur from Lviv, spoke of the more than three years of RSO activity and revealed a total of 116 RSO local committees throughout the area of the three southeastern Polish voivodeships. In the case of the Lemko region only

---

[20] *Russkii Golos* 1929, no. 7, p. 3; *Zemlia i Volia* 1929, no. 54, p. 4.
[21] The Grybów committee consisted of V. Dubets and H. Habura (Florynka), Y. Drozhdzhak (Królowa Ruska), H. Kosovsky and Z. Stavysky (Śnietnica), Y. Porutsidlo (Czyrna), V. Rydzanych (Banica), M. Kuziak (Wawrzka), D. Trokhanovsky (Binczarowa), P. Slyva (Bogusza) and M. Zhuk (Kamianna). See *Zemlia i Volia* 1930, no. 18, p. 3.
[22] AP K, UWKr, ref. # 272, *Sprawozdania sytuacyjne wojewody krakowskiego (1930)*, p. 77.

the Lemkos in the Nowy Targ and Jasło counties did not have separate County Committees. The delegates from the Lemko region, Ivan Bankovsky of Mszana, Semen Handiak of Świerzowa Ruska, and E. Mokrytsky of Sanok, underscored the importance of economic issues in the shaping of Lemkos' political attitudes. These remarks were applied in the formulation of content of congress resolutions on the matter of solutions and methods for further development of party structures in the provinces. To this purpose the five-person Initiative Commission was formed, in which the Lemko region was represented by Ivan Basalyga of Kunkowa. The congress chose the new Central Council, which once again included several representatives from the Lemko region. Fr. Chaikovsky and S. Vozniak kept their places in the Council, while Voitovych and Fedak were replaced by other peasants: I. Basalyga and Vasyl Dubets of Florynka. The district of Sanok was represented by Andrii Madeia.[23]

Before 1932 the RSO did not deal with the Lemko problem as a separate issue in its organizational work. The terms "Lemko" and "the Lemko region" are used in party documents, it is true, but this resulted rather from respect for regional autonomy than political reasons. Because in 1932 the first signs of the nation's regional policy were already visible, and the Lemko question was raised with increasing frequency by Ukrainian circles, discussions of Lemko region issues also appeared in the pages of the Moscophile press. The RSO central authorities saw symptoms of separatism in some Lemko milieux as early as 1930, when elections were held e.g. on the County Committee in Gorlice. The editors of *Zemlia i Volia* were informed of the existence of separatist tendencies among Gorlice activists by an anonymous letter, but after the note was printed the leading activists in the county (D. Bubniak, K. Bodak, M. Yurkovsky, V. Maletsky, Y. Siokalo, T. Voitovych) resolved at a County Committee meeting to send a clarification to the editors denying the Gorlice group's secession from the RSO.[24] Sending the clarification could be a tactical move demonstrating the desire to continue relations with the RSO despite growing Old Rusyn tendencies within it, which just then were finding support from state administrators. This attitude among leaders of the Lemko movement may show that they were caught between the Scylla of the Polish Republic authorities and the Charybdis of the RSO, endeavoring to attain the most advantageous position for themselves.

The issue of Gorlice's secession was strongly felt in Lviv RSO circles. In the aftermath of that event, the Central Council took steps toward strengthening the organizational movement in Gorlice and in other counties of the Kraków voivodeship. The campaign was directed on behalf of the Council by Fr. Chaikovsky and Volodymyr (vel Kornel) Kutsii, residents of Gorlice. The first link of the planned enterprise was the congress of delegates from the Grybów area called by Kutsii for 22 May 1932 in Florynka. The congress, chaired by Fr. Chaikovsky, gathered around 400

---

23   DALO, f. 1, op. 51, case # 1231, *Dielo obshchestva im. Mikhaila Kachkovskogo vo Lvovie*, vol. 4, 1930–1931, p. 9.

24   The author of the report was said to be I. Kachmarchyk of Męcina. See *Zemlia i Volia* 1931, no. 12, p. 3.

people from the surrounding area. Representatives of the Gorlice region Y. Siokalo, S. Krushynsky, and S. Tsiuryk also took part.[25] The discussion touched on a series of problems relating to economic, cultural, educational, confessional and political issues. The discussants: M. Kuziak (Wawrzka), T. Shlakhtych, V. Dubets and H. Vilchansky (Florynka), and especially S. Krushynsky (Gorlice), talked of the harmful nature of social and religious conflicts, taking up the energy of Lemko society and making a consolidation of forces impossible.[26] In order to complete the integration of the Lemkos associated with the RSO, Kutsii exhibited in his speech the tragic moments in the life of the Rusyns in the 19th and 20th centuries, drawing particular attention to the Talerhof. The congress chose the Broader Committee including the Grybów region and neighboring regions.[27] The committee was given the task of carrying out a propaganda campaign, wide in scope, in the counties of Gorlice and Nowy Sącz. It is difficult to evaluate the results of the congress from today's perspective, all the more since according to police reports the population "did not show interest and reacted to the speakers' arguments with pessimism."[28]

Despite different attitudes among peasants toward RSO ideology, the congress confirmed the durability of the organizational structure in the Kraków voivodeship. The leading representatives of the Grybów Committee undertook the mission of creating a Gorlice center closely linked with the Lviv center. V. Dubets and D. Voitovych were active participants in the congress specially organized for that purpose in Smerekowiec on 12 June 1932. About 200 peasants and members of the intelligentsia took part. A program speech was made by Sofron Krushynsky of Gorlice. After his speech the congress voted to make itself fully subordinate to the Central Council of the RSO. The discussion also dealt with economic problems of the countryside, and T. Voitovych answered numerous questions on this subject. At the end a new County Committee was chosen for Gorlice County with headquarters in Gorlice. Yaroslav Siokalo, who in late 1928 moved his law chambers from Borynia in Turka County to Gorlice and became involved in Lemko political life, was named chairman of the committee.[29]

---

[25] AP K, UWKr, ref. # 277, pp. 172, 173.

[26] Ibid., ref. # 352, *Sprawozdania sytuacyjne tygodniowe, miesięczne Starostwa Powiatowego w Nowym Sączu 1930–1933*, p.n.n.

[27] The Broader RSO Committee in Grybów consisted of: V. Didovych (Binczarowa), M. Dubets, V. Dubets and H. Habura (Florynka), Y. Dolupko and S. Durkot (Polany), H. Kosovsky and S. Krynytsky (Śnietnica), M. Kuziak (Wawrzka), V. Kysilovsky and D. Voitovych (Brunary Wyżne), Y. Porucidlo (Czyrna), M. Skarlosh (Królowa Ruska), P. Slyva (Bogusza), M. Zhuk (Kamianna). See *Zemlia i Volia* 1932, no. 22, p. 1.

[28] AP K, UWKr, ref. # 352, p.n.n.

[29] The full membership of the Gorlice RSO Committee: S. Tsiuryk (Smerekowiec), M. Duda (Skwirtne), T. Dziamba (Zdynia), S. Felenchak (Bartne), S. Yachechak (Nowica), I. Kachmarchyk (Męcina), V. Maletsky (Klimkówka), D. Shkirpan (Małastów), P. Vanko (Czarne) and S. Krushynsky, Y. Siokalo and T. Voitovych. See *Zemlia i Volia* 1932, no. 25, p. 3.

Summer and autumn of 1932 were a time of intensive development of the RSO in the Gorlice and Grybów regions. Its local committees were particularly active in Bartne, Brunary Wyżne, Czarne, Florynka, Królowa Ruska, Męcina Wielka, Smerekowiec, Śnietnica and Uście Ruskie. The most energetic actors in the area were I. Basalyga, Y. Khokholak, V. Dubets, S. Felenchak, S. Krushynsky, S. Krynytsky, V. Kutsii, Y. Mokhnatsky, Y. Siokalo, D. Voitovych and T. Voitovych.[30]

Toward the end of 1932 the RSO Central Council in Lviv prepared a multitiered plan for organizational work in the Lemko region. The plan was presented during the congress comprising the entire region convoked expressly for that purpose in Gorlice on 15 October, gathering delegates from the counties of Gorlice, Jasło, Krosno and Nowy Sącz.[31] During the first part of the meeting a program speech was delivered by Fr. Chaikovsky, expressing the important role of the Lemko region as a "Rusyn stronghold" in the political struggle in which the RSO was engaged. He proposed that a special organ in charge of all matters of public life be established for the Lemko region. Chaikovsky's plan, developed beforehand in the narrow confines of the Central Council, reflected changes from the previous RSO stance toward the Lemko region. The Lviv authorities recognized the specific nature of the Lemko region and created a separate Lemko organizational unit within the party. It was clear that with regard to the regional policy conducted by state authorities, nurturing Lemko separatism and bringing the Lemkos closer to the BBWR, there was some probability that the ranks of the RSO would be dissolved. The Central Council took the view that maintaining political influence on the Lemko region depended on recognizing its distinct culture and taking that into consideration in the party structure.

The plan presented by Chaikovsky was approved with satisfaction by the congress participants, since it corresponded to the delegates' expectations. The newly created organ was designated the Lemko Committee and enjoyed considerably greater acceptance than the RSO District Committee in Sanok or the RSO Broader Committee which covered the Lemko community in the Kraków province. Its popularity was apparently decided by the use of the term "Lemko" in the name. This tactical move by the Central Council testified to their being well-informed on Lemko issues and the importance which the RSO attributed to the Lemko region. The committee was made up of one representative from each county inhabited by Lemkos: Orest Hnatyshak (Nowy Sącz County), Dmytro Voitovych (the former Grybów County)[32], Yaroslav Siokalo (Gorlice County), Lev Stakhursky of Hałbów (Jasło County), Stepan Herenchak of Tylawa (Krosno County). No representative from Sanok County was chosen, but a place was reserved for one on the commit-

---

30 *Zemlia i Volia* 1932, no. 35, p. 2 and no. 37, p. 3.
31 No representatives of the Sanok region took part in the congress. See *Zemlia i Volia* 1932, no. 43, p. 2.
32 Though Grybów County at that point no longer existed, recognition was given to the party structures established before its dissolution (1932).

tee. On the other hand, no place was allotted for representatives of the Lemkos in the counties of Brzozów, Lesko and Nowy Targ, despite the fact that the committee represented their interests as well.[33]

The committee's task was to give assistance, broadly understood, to the Lemko region in its economic, cultural, and educational development. For this purpose, the committee committed to establishing official connections with Lemko emigrant communities in North America. Chaikovsky went so far as to present a list of 30 persons residing in the United States, to whom special letters requesting their cooperation were sent. The committee's work program contained four separate sections, corresponding to four departments: finance (S. Krushynsky, Y. Siokalo), cooperation (I. Bankovsky, I. Basalyga, V. Kutsii), culture and education (S. Durkot, S. Krushynsky, P. Masara) and schooling (I. Rusenko, M. Trokhanovsky, O. Vislotsky).

The finance department's task was the collection and disbursement of funds. The department of cooperation was appointed to form trade cooperatives and mutual aid funds. It supervised the inspectors of the Auditing Union of Rusyn Cooperatives (RSRK, *Revizyinyi Soiuz Russkich Kooperatyv*), who fulfilled the function of instructors. At the Gorlice congress it was resolved to create three permanent inspector positions, to be maintained by the RSRK and with money obtained from voluntary taxation of the Lemko population.[34] The funds collected in this way were also used for the work of the cultural and educational department, which mainly was responsible for the promotion of reading and the duties of the school commission.

The main figure in the latter institution was Metody Trokhanovsky, who reported on the state of education in the Lemko region. At his proposal, the task of developing and introducing into schools a primer in the Lemko idiom was officially undertaken. Fr. Chaikovsky, as representative of the Lviv authorities, supported the project, a measure of common ground in the struggle against Ukrainian schooling. One of the congress resolutions addressed to the state school authorities was devoted to this question. Shortly thereafter Trokhanovsky joined the Old Rusyn camp.

Chaikovsky's project relating to the development of journalism in the Lemko dialect had an important place in the discussions of the congress. This attests to the desire to keep the Lemkos in the RSO sphere of influence even at the price of recognizing Lemko separatism. In previous years, readers of *Zemlia i Volia* had voiced proposals for creating a separate section of the paper in the Lemko dialect. True, there had been opposing voices among Lemkos themselves, underscoring the difficulties due to significant existing differences in the dialects of different regions, but the RSO judged that staunch opposition on this issue could expose the party to the risk of losing the support of many Lemkos, especially since the idea of a Lemko newspaper was not a new one. In 1928 there was an irregularly published newspaper

---

[33] *Zemlia i Volia* 1932, no. 43, p. 2.
[34] The monthly tax figures were: intelligentsia 2–5 zloty, peasants – 10 groszy.

called *Lemko*, issued to meet the needs of the BBWR's electoral campaign; in Ukrainian circles as well, the thought of issuing a Lemko periodical had been gestating.

The creation of a superordinate organ of the RSO for the Lemko region, such as was the Lemko Committee in Gorlice, went in tandem with the further build-up of county structures. The main concern was the counties of Nowy Sącz and Jasło. Two weeks after the Gorlice congress, on 23 October, the RSO county congress for Nowy Sącz County met in Krynica Wieś. The program principles of the RSO were enunciated by V. Kutsii – representative of the Central Council. S. Krynytsky spoke in the name of the Committee of the Grybów Region. The congress, in which approximately 200 delegates participated, created a new County Committee for Nowy Sącz under the leadership of Antin Stanchak of Andrzejówka.[35] The Krynica congress approved the program of the Gorlice Lemko Committee.[36]

The furthest behind in the development of RSO structure was Jasło County. Despite the participation of that county's delegate in the all-Lemko congress in Gorlice, there was no county committee there. Delegates from several local committees who had taken part in the congress in Czarne on 18 September 1932 undertook to create a party structure in Jasło County. However it was only after the Gorlice congress that, due to Chaikovsky and Kutsii's efforts, the process culminated in a county RSO congress in Świątkowa Wielka (6 November), at which the resolutions of the Gorlice congress were confirmed. Execution of the party's tasks was entrusted to the newly chosen County Committee for Jasło County under the chairmanship of Danylo Yankovych of Świątkowa Wielka.[37]

In autumn of 1932 the entire area of the Lemko region was covered by the RSO structure – from local committees through county and regional committees as well as the Lemko Committee in Gorlice. RSO centers in the Jasło and Krosno counties were loosely connected with the Gorlice center. The Lemko population in this latter gravitated more towards the Sanok center.

In late 1932 and early 1933 a confrontation erupted between the two centers. Sanok had a longer tradition of Moscophile activity, a larger intelligentsia and better-organized socioeconomic life, as well as more cultural and educational associations. For these reasons it claimed precedence in the role of cultural and political center. The formation of the Lemko Committee in Gorlice, however, which in the intent

---

[35] The full membership of the committee: K. Tykhansky (Wojkowa), H. Gromosiak (Krynica Wieś), Y. Harbera (Mochnaczka Niżna), L. Krainiak (Złockie), S. Kulanda (Łabowa), P. Kuzma (Nowa Wieś), Y. Petryk (Krynica Wieś), I. Pyroh (Milik), B. Rusyniak (Wierchomla Wielka), M. Senko (Tylicz), A. Stanchak (Andrzejówka), A. Venhrynovych (Powroźnik). See *Zemlia i Volia* 1932, no. 44, p. 2.

[36] AP K, UWKr, ref. # 352, p.n.n.

[37] The full membership of the committee: S. Dytko (Pielgrzymka), D. Yankovych (Światkowa Wielka), F. Kasych (Jaworze), V. Komanetsky (Światkowa Mała), F. Mishko (Świerzowa Ruska), Y. Sosenko (Desznica), F. Sydoryk (Kotań). See *Zemlia i Volia* 1932, no. 42, p. 3.

of the resolution constituted co-optation of the representatives of Sanok County, clearly shifted the center of RSO political life from Sanok to Gorlice.

This state of affairs continued for barely four months. Toward the end of December 1933 plans were made in Sanok RSO circles to hold a congress of the "shop-stewards" of that organization from the Sanok district, i.e., from Brzozów, Krosno, Lesko and Sanok counties, for the purpose of discussing the party's duties in relation to the attempts of the Lemko elite in the Kraków province to establish its independence. The congress took place on 18 February 1933 in Sanok.[38] Fr. Chaikovsky, representing the RSO Central Council, one of the creators of the Committee in Gorlice, took part. His presence at both congresses was a reflection of Lviv activists' attitudes toward Lemko matters; they undoubtedly had some misgivings about accepting the existence of two separately acting committees. At the beginning of the deliberations Chaikovsky put forth a petition for the convocation of a Galicia Broader Lemko Committee to unite the Gorlice and Sanok centers, and to be tightly connected with the RSO Central Council in Lviv. Implementation of this idea turned out to be impossible due to the absence of delegates from the Kraków province. Of the members of the Lemko Committee in Gorlice, only S. Herenchak of Tylawa came to Sanok, but he represented local RSO branches in Krosno County.

In view of the absence of delegates from the western region, the congress decided to establish a Committee for the Eastern Lemko Region with headquarters in Sanok, simultaneously recognizing the Gorlice Committee as representing the Western Lemko Region. The board of the newly chosen committee included: Andrii Madeia, Emanuil Mokrytsky and Lev Yavorsky of Sanok, Yosyf Perelom of Dukla, Yosyf Sobolevsky of Kostarowce, Yosyf Fedak of Srogów Górny, Mykola Hnizdur of Olchowiec and Ivan Halyk of Czerteż. The appointed committee divided its members into three departments: finance, cooperation, and culture and education. The congress empowered the Sanok committee to negotiation with the Gorlice center for the purpose of appointing an all-Lemko National Committee.[39]

In contradistinction to the resolutions of the Gorlice congress of 15 October 1932, the Sanok congress stood much more firmly on a foundation of pan-Russian ideology. The delegates at the congress, in contrast to the situation existing in Gorlice, did not concern themselves at all with the question of teaching the Lemko dialect in schools or printing periodicals in that dialect. In matters of language, the Sanok congress took a firm position in favor of teaching the Russian literary language in popular schools and called for the establishment of a faculty of Russian language at the University of Lviv.[40] A separate resolution dealt with party discipline and un-

---

[38] *SN* 1933, no. 1, pp. 77–79. E. Mokrytsky was elected chairman of the congress, Y. Sobolevsky – deputy chairman, and sekretaries – T. Stefanyshyn and I. Halyk (student). See *Zemlia i Volia* 1933, no. 11, pp. 1–2.

[39] *SN* 1933, no. 1, p. 78.

[40] Ibid.

derscored the necessity for the cooperation of all social organizations in the Lemko region with the RSO central headquarters in Lviv.

Significant changes in the political life of the Lemko region occurred in 1933. The party structure of the RSO was destabilized by the activation of the Old Rusyn current. In December of that year the Old Rusyns created an organization bearing the name of the Lemko Association (*Lemko Soiuz*), whose membership included representatives of the RSO Lemko Committee in Gorlice. In view of this, the plans to establish a unified all-Lemko national committee within the party by joining the Gorlice and Sanok committees were laid to rest.

Considering the importance which the RSO central authorities attached to the Lemko Region as one of the few regions which held onto its former Rusyn consciousness, the Lemko question was one of the main issues under discussion during the Third Nationwide Congress of the party in Lviv on 26 December 1933. This congress brought approximately 80 delegates from 32 counties, including members of the Gorlice committee as well, who were at the same time members of the Lemko Association, officially standing opposed to the pan-Russian ideology. What is more, certain leaders of the Association, such as Orest Hnatyshak and Serhii Durkot, became members of the newly appointed RSO Central Council.[41] The Gorlice committee representatives' attitude may attest to their still-unformed political consciousness or to a pragmatism which led them to look for the most profitable solution possible.

At the Third Congress of the RSO, loosening the party structure was broadly discussed. The creation of the Lemko Association was pronounced a sign of the violation of party discipline. Sofron Krynytsky of Śnietnica, a member of the RSO county committee, spoke publicly against the Lemko Association and the *Lemko* newspaper. Blame for the state of affairs which had arisen was placed not on the Lemko activists of Gorlice, however, but on the Polish government, which was accused of conducting a regional policy of "wrecking the unity of the Rusyn nation."[42] It appears this is explicable in terms of the continued presence of the founders of the Lemko Association among the ranks of the RSO.

The subsequent Fourth Congress of the RSO which took place in Lviv on 26 December 1934 appointed other active members of the Gorlice and Nowy Sącz committees to the Central Council: Yaroslav Siokalo of Gorlice and Semen Kulanda of Łabowa. Hnatyshak was again appointed for another term. Kulanda in his speech assured the congress participants that the Lemko population condemned the press organ of the Lemko Association, *Lemko*. Other delegates from the Lemko region spoke words of harsh criticism directed at the Old Rusyn activists. Yuliian Halkovych of Bogusza spoke in no uncertain terms: "The entire Rusyn peasantry of the Lemko region stands with the RSO. Grounds for suspicion of separatism can be pro-

---

[41] In addition to Hnatyshak and Durkot, the Lemko region was represented by K. Bodak (Rozdziele), Fr. K. Chaikovsky (Mszana), A. Shuflat (Węglówka), V. Maletsky (Klimkówka), and Y. Shatynsky (Sanok). See *Zemlia i Volia* 1934, no. 3, p. 2.

[42] *Zemlia i Volia* 1934, no. 15, pp. 2–3.

vided only by the local *Lemko Soiuz*, but among the peasants no one has taken part in its creation nor belongs to it." Yosyf Fedak of Srogów, on the other hand, said that: "We Lemkos are insulted by the fact that we stand accused of Lemko separatism. We were Russian and such we will remain."[43] One of the resolutions approved by the congress declared struggle against "Ukrainian, Rusyn and Lemko" separatisms.[44] There was a nod to the side of Lemko autonomy in the form of the creation of a separate Lemko section of the RSO press organ designated for the people, *Zemlia i Volia* (Land and Liberty).

Despite the RSO's internal organizational difficulties, it maintained full local structures in both the Lviv and Kraków voivodeships until the end of the interwar period. Organizational changes consisted only in the relocation of the headquarters of certain county committees, e.g. from Gorlice to Uście Ruskie in the case of Gorlice County.[45] The nationwide RSO congresses held in 1935 and 1937 confirmed the active involvement of Lemkos in executing the statutory goals of the party. A declaration which was pro-Russian in content was framed in local committees as well. One illustration of these moods may be, for example, the resolutions accepted by the committees in Gorlice and Nowy Sącz in 1936. The resolution of the RS conference in Kwiatoń, passed on 2 August, stated that: "We feel ourselves to be Russians and categorically protest against being called Lemkos in a national sense."[46] Speeches were made against the "Lemko language" and Trokhanovsky's primer in Banica, Bogusza, Kwiatoń, Leluchów, Smerekowiec and many other places, postulating the introduction instead of a "Galician Rusyn" [Russian] primer.[47] The resolutions passed at the conference in Bielanka on 18 August were also against "Lemko separatism" and the proper noun "Lemko," stating that Lemkos belonged to the "great 160-million-strong Russian nationality."[48] These slogans were also repeated in resolutions of other local committees in various counties and were always reflected in the resolutions of RSO congresses.[49]

For the Lemko population, the idea of economic, cultural and educational activity coordinated by the RSO was highly attractive. Intensively organized courses in farming drew peasants in. Rural farming courses for women were also conducted.

---

[43] CDIAL, f. 394, op. 1, case # 2, *Protokoly zboriv "ruskykh selanskykh orhanizatsii" u Horlytskomu, Zborivskomu ta Sianotskomu povitach (1935)*, p. 3.

[44] M. Baczyński, *Kwestia mniejszościowa oraz rola i metody opozycji mniejszościowej w odrodzonej Polsce*, Lwów 1935, p. 10.

[45] CDIAL, f. 182, op. 1, case # 459, *Hazetni povidomlennia, zvity i inshi materiialy pro orhanizatsii-nu, finansovo-hospodarsku ta propahandystsku diialnist chytalni v seli Kvitoni, Horlytskoho povitu, 1934–1939*, p. 35.

[46] Ibid.

[47] *Zemlia i Volia* 1936, no. 29, p. 3.

[48] CDIAL, f. 182, op. 1, case # 479, *Hazetni povidomlennia pro vidkryttia, diialnist chytalen ta protydii z boku ukrainskykh natsionalistiv, 1934–1939*, p. 40.

[49] Ibid., f. 394, op. 1, case # 5, *Lysty chleniv ruskykh selanskykh orhanizatsii v Stanyslavovi, Sianoku, Peremyshli pro sklykannia zizdiv tsykh orhanizatsii, kilkist ioho uchasnykiv, 1935*, pp. 1, 2.

The economic sphere of activity included courses to meet the needs of developing the trade cooperative movement, setting up and coordinating the operations of cooperatives which since the late 1920s had come into being even in the most far-flung Lemko areas. Thanks to such initiatives as these a considerable portion of Lemkos recognized the RSO as belonging to them. Consequently Lviv economic institutions which served the party were also acknowledged as their own.[50]

The party achieved even greater popularity among Lemkos due to its fostering of military traditions, especially the martyrology of the Lemkos placed in Austro-Hungarian internment camps. An object of particular commemoration was the camp in Talerhof. "Talerhof congresses," organized in many localities, reminded Lemkos of their wartime sufferings. These congresses automatically became platforms for RSO ideologues, who took advantage of the fertile ground for agitation provided by hostility to the Ukrainian movement. Their contribution to the universalization among Lemkos of a feeling of otherness toward Ukrainians was considerable.

The springboard for the Ukrainian movement was the Eastern Byzantine-Slavonic Rite Church. The Ukrainian Eastern Rite historical tradition was not taken into account. In fact, many Ukrainians stood opposed to the Eastern Orthodox faith as un-Ukrainian. The lack of an unobstructed perspective on the confessional question, one unimpeded by the context of political rivalry, gave rise to the formation of politico-religious camps: Moscophile-Orthodox and Ukrainian-Greek Catholic. Nonetheless, considering the increasingly embittered denominational conflicts which were arising mainly in the form of property disputes and leading to ever greater divisions within the Lemko community, voices were raised in criticism of interdenominational relations. Some party members pointed to the harmful effects of these conflicts, their paralyzing of community-wide enterprises, particularly economic ones, which harmed the development of the Lemko countryside. Sofron Krynytsky's speech at the RSO congress in Florynka on 22 May 1932 was characteristic of this vein. On that occasion Krynytsky, himself an adherent of the Orthodox faith, spoke, according to the report of the correspondent from *Zemlia i Volia*, thus:

> Religious conflicts have called forth a great many misunderstandings among our people in the Lemko region. So we need to put a lot more work into wiping out the differences between the Orthodox and the Uniate Lemko, and convince all [Lemkos] that religion should not pose the slightest obstacle when the common business of the Rusyn nation is at hand. The Rusyn population of the Lemko region must understand that the *Russka Selianska Organizatsiia* unites the Rusyn peasants [...], with no thought for whether they belong to the Orthodox or the Uniate faith.[51]

The issue of the RSO's attitude toward Eastern Orthodoxy appeared with increasing frequency in the pages of the press. Interdenominational conflicts were officially condemned, with reference to the threat they posed to the social and economic pro-

---

50   AAN, KGPP, ref. # 44, p. 13.
51   Quoted from *Zemlia i Volia* 1932, no. 26, p. 2.

gram of the RSO, being implemented for the benefit of the Greek Catholic faithful as well.[52] This attitude, as distinct from the one presented by the party in the late 1920s, resulted from the national question taking precedence over the religious one. The Russian idea, it is true, was close to Eastern Orthodoxy, but the Greek Catholics were a majority in the RSO ranks. There was support for Eastern Orthodoxy in the beginning phase of its formation, and the pro-Ukrainian authorities of the Greek Catholic Church were sharply criticized at that time, but there were no pronouncements against the Greek Catholic faith itself. What is more, the RSO supported the Apostolic Administration of the Lemko Region and even endeavored to have the Administration elevated to the rank of diocese. Furthermore, it produced a plan to establish a Greek Catholic diocese for the "Russian" population inhabiting the area of former Eastern Galicia, with a separate consistory and ecclesiastical seminary, in order to free Moscophile Greek Catholics from the Ukrainian ecclesiastical hierarchy.[53]

On the question of Eastern Orthodoxy, matters came to a head with a polemic between party authorities and the Eastern Orthodox metropolitan of Warsaw. Eastern Orthodox Church authorities in Warsaw were accused of showing a lack of engagement in legal regulation of many Orthodox institutions' activities and their property issues: lands, presbyteries, churches.[54] The RSO's relationship with the local Orthodox clergy was also dependent on the social engagement of the priests. Property disputes and attempts to register institutions went on, and construction of sacral sites, whether churches or chapels, was carried out, until priests actively took part; and the RSO supported their engagement in social issues. Criticism began to be voiced at the beginning of the 1930s, when the interdenominational situation normalized and some of the priests withdrew from village community life, concerning themselves strictly with their pastoral ministry. The RSO then protested against their "asocial" stance. The Ukrainian press also wrote about it, e.g. about Fr. Chaikovsky's speech to the all-Lemko congress in Gorlice on 15 October 1932, where he "scolded the three Orthodox priests there present for not engaging in educational activity."[55]

The RSO's attitude toward matters of faith was derived from its political and socioeconomic program. That was the only way for the party to be sure of support from Eastern Orthodox and Greek Catholic milieux. The aforesaid program line brought certain results in the area of expanding the local structure, but exposed the party to accusations from adherents of both denominations. At the general party congress of 14 February 1937 efforts were made to develop a program which would lead to the consolidation of the Lemko community around the RSO – since the party

---

[52] "RSO i pravoslavnyi rukh na Lemkivshchyni," *Zemlia i Volia* 1932, no. 43, p. 1.

[53] *Oriens* 1937, no. 2, p. 56.

[54] This accusation did not correspond to reality, since the authorities of the Warsaw metropolitan were making efforts toward legalizing as many affiliates and parishes throughout the Lemko region as possible.

[55] *Zemlia i Volia* 1934, no. 12, p. 3; *Dilo* 1932, no. 284, p. 4.

was losing influence, chiefly among youth. The increasingly frequent criticism of the RSO's educational and interdenominational policies did not lead to any reduction of the party's social and political importance, however. Until the end of the interwar period the party remained the strongest and best-organized political party in the Lemko region.

2. Transformations in the Old Rusyn movement

As has already been mentioned, in the first years after the war, chaos reigned in the Moscophile-Old Rusyn milieu of the former Galicia. The essence of this chaos was the presence of Moscophiles and Old Rusyns in the same organizational structures. Nevertheless, immediately after the war the Old Rusyns who were opposed to the Russian and Ukrainian ideas and closer to the idea of Polish nationhood, made several attempts to break away.

The first manifestation of these tendencies was the convocation by a small group among the intelligentsia of a rally in Lviv on 29 June 1920. The rally gathered approximately 200 people, and their deliberations took place under the slogan "Let us be ourselves." The discussion underscored the differences between "Lesser Rusyn" culture and the Ukrainian and Russian cultures. The purpose of the rally was to ratify the recognition of Polish statehood by Rusyns, which was supposed to ease the attainment of concessions on the development of the community's cultural, educational, and economic life.[56] Next, the Committee for the Affairs of Old Rusyn Institutions and Associations was created on 29 June 1922, with whose help it was intended to reactivate and take over the Lviv association *Rada Ruska* (Rusyn Council), an old Moscophile institution from the times of Ivan Naumovych. The committee included the later leaders of the Old Rusyn party: Fr. Ivan Kostetsky, Ivan Sas Liskovatsky, Oleksandr Lysiak and Teodozii Zaiats.[57] The attempt to reinvigorate that nineteenth-century institution failed, however.

In the years 1919–1923 government circles took no interest in the Old Rusyns. The authorities' actions moved in the direction of weakening the Ukrainians politically, and they found a counterweight in the Moscophile current, without becoming fully informed as to the internal situation of that movement. Government milieux clearly perceived the pro-Russian majority, whereas the pro-Polish (Old Rusyn) minority escaped their attention. This must explain the transfer of the People's Home in Lviv to the Moscophiles, over which disputes continued throughout the entire interwar period; as well as the Stauropegion Institute, of which the government com-

---

[56] AP R, AKL, ref. # 72, *Współpraca z Czerwińsko-Ruską Organizacją "Zgoda,"* list O. Łysiaka prezesa *Ruskiej Agrarnej Partii do ks. Łukaszkławicza z 25 XI 1929 r.*, p. 1.

[57] DALO, f. 1, op. 55, case # 383, *Dielo o registratsii rusofilskoho obshchestva "Russkaia Rada" vo Lvovie*, p. 1.

missioner became the well-known Lviv Moscophile Mykola Tretiak.[58] In the Lemko region this phenomenon occurred with even greater force, to the extent that the administrative authorities repeatedly made inaccurate assessments of social moods, labeling Old Rusyns as Moscophiles or vice versa.

2.1. The Rus Agrarian Party, 1928–1931, and the Rus Agrarian Organization, 1931–1939

Before the Old Rusyns finally decided to create a separate political party, the group twice made changes to the internal organization of the RNO. The first secession took place in 1926. At that time, they formed an association called the Agrarian Union (*Rolnychii Soiuz*), which had been charged with the task of coordinating rural economic development in the southeastern voivodeships. The Agrarian Union existed until the end of 1927. At the beginning of December of that year, while preparing for the parliamentary elections, the Old Rusyns constituted the Provisional Organizational Agrarian Committee with the task of developing a charter for a political party.[59] It also published a press organ in Lviv entitled the *Holos Naroda* (Voice of the People).[60]

The initiative group was made up of activists concentrated around Lev Cherkavsky. On 3 January 1928 they convoked a congress of the Agrarian Union in Lviv, attended by over 60 delegates, each from a different branch.[61] Cherkavsky's committee submitted a draft of the party program, which was to represent the interests of poor Rusyn peasantry. The congress also appointed the highest executive authority of the newly created Rus Agrarian Party (RAP) – the Council, numbering 16 members, including three representatives from the Lemko region: I. Kachmarchyk, T. Voitovych and T. Yadlovsky. This last fulfilled the function of secretary during the congress. Oleksandr Lysiak was selected as president.[62]

The creation of the Old Rusyn party was connected with the pre-election campaign. The primary goal of the Old Rusyns was to put deputies from their list into parliament. This idea was struck down at the meeting on 26 December 1927, in which delegates from the Agrarian Union took part with Cherkavsky and Bachynsky leading; the latter henceforth was unambiguously pro-Polish, abandoning the Russian idea. Nonetheless it was resolved to go to the 1928 elections together with the Russians. O. Lysiak shed light on the matter of the Agrarian Union's renouncement of a separate list and the RAP's participation in the elections together with

---

[58]   I. Kedryn, op.cit., p. 163.
[59]   AAN, MSW, ref. # 961, *Sprawozdanie Wydziału Spraw Narodowościowych MSW z życia mniejszości narodowych, XII 1926–XII 1927*, p. 296.
[60]   AP R, AKL, ref. # 72, p. 2. See J. Moklak, "Political Orientations among the Lemkos in the Inter-War Period: 1918–1939," *Carpatho-Slavic Studies* (New Haven, Conn.) 1990, vol. 1, p. 18.
[61]   *Holos Naroda* 1928, no. 2, p. 2.
[62]   AP R, AKL, ref. # 72, p. 2.

the RZN in a letter to Fr. Yuliian Lukashklavich on 25 December 1929. According to Lysiak, Bachynsky, in his function of government commissioner at the *Narodnyi Dom* Institute in Lviv, received an order from the Lviv province authorities to join the RAP to the Russian list. In said letter Lysiak explained that the RAP arose at the behest of the administrative authorities, fearful of the loss of influence on *Narodnyi Dom,* which after the change in Bachynsky's political orientation remained under the influence of the Old Rusyns.[63]

That was the first attempt by the Old Rusyns at making an entrance onto the parliamentary stage as an independent force, and did not succeed due to the position of the state authorities. Lysiak – in the letter mentioned above – even addressed some critical words to the authorities, accusing them of supporting Moscophilism and simultaneously limiting the development of the Old Rusyn movement, a movement loyal to the state. He even stated that in the context of its attitude toward the RAP, the government's policy was harmful to the nation. He wrote:

> A fair agreement and beneficial solution of the Rusyn question depends not on us, but on the Polish government and society. The Rusyn question is so important for the Polish State and Nation that it should not be made light of or passed over in silence, so that some day in the future the saying 'A Pole is wise after the damage is done' will not be vindicated.[64]

In fact, in the years 1926–1929 the government authorities cut off a series of economic initiatives undertaken by the Old Rusyns, several times refusing them financial credits. The head of the Nationality Bureau of the Ministry of the Interior, Henryk Suchenek-Suchecki, was also negatively disposed toward the RAP; in 1929 he welcomed the Moscophile movement and spoke ill of the RAP's demands. In 1928 due to the failure to obtain credits for property reform, the RAP was on the brink of self-liquidation. To interest the state authorities in their operations, RAP leaders were forced to resort to a public declaration of loyalty printed in a popular Polish newspaper and public speeches featuring paeans to Józef Piłsudski.[65]

In issue 307 of the *Ilustrowany Kurier Codzienny* on 9 November 1929, an open letter written by Oleksandr Lysiak and Dmytro Yablonsky, president and secretary of the RAP, addressed to government circles, appeared. The authors of the letter took as the basis for their assertions an article by the former governor of Lviv, Piotr Dunin-Borkowski, entitled "Starting point in the Ukrainian issue in East Lesser Poland," printed in the publication *Droga* (The Road). They agreed with Borkowski that the consciously Russian movement might be dangerous for Poland,[66] but denied that the Rusyn movement was illusory – Borkowski perceived Ukrainians rather than

---

[63] Ibid.

[64] Ibid., p. 1.

[65] AAN, MSW, ref. #1038, *Wiadomości Ukraińskie* 1929, no. 15, p. 6. The first such declaration was M. Bachynsky's speech at the ceremony for the unveiling of the Piłsudski monument in Kolomyia.

[66] See P. Dunin-Borkowski, "Punkt wyjścia w sprawie ukraińskiej w Małopolsce Wschodniej," *Droga* 1929, no. 6, pp. 561–572.

Rusyns in the nationality aspect of the movement. The authors of the letter appealed to the government to combat the Ukrainian as well as the Russian movement, and to support the Rusyns of the RAP.[67] A couple of weeks later, Lysiak, in a different letter to Fr. Lukashklavich, wrote that: "We [the RAP] bared our national soul before our elder brother, i.e. the Polish nation, and now it is the elder brother's turn to offer us his hand [...] we desire a fight neither with the government nor the people of Poland, and will fight neither."[68] RAP activists did not take on the question of separate Rusyn statehood, seeing the Polish Republic as their fatherland.

Public declarations of loyalty to the nation and the undermining of the legitimacy of the existence of Russian and Ukrainian nationals in southeastern Poland brought forth a wave of reactions in the Moscophile and Ukrainian press. The press of each group had traditionally been hostile to the other, but this time they lashed out in similar tones at the Old Rusyns, accusing them of enclosing themselves within an allegedly anachronistic Rusyn national consciousness.

Until the end of 1929 the RAP developed strictly through its own powers. Over the three years of the party's existence 26 regional centers had been set up, referred to in some sources as branches. For the needs of the trade cooperatives the RAP possessed a credit institution called the Central Cooperative Association, supporting 102 dependent cooperatives. During this period, a difficult one for the party, there could be no talk of its resilient development. In reality it had influence only in the counties of Lviv, Kolomyia and Stanyslaviv, but even there remained in the shadow of the pro-Russian party.[69]

The situation in the Lemko region was similar. In 1928 RAP created local Lemko Election Committees there. Still, here too it would be hard to posit a broad local party structure. Almost all individuals connected with the RAP cooperated simultaneously with the RSO. This happened because of the convergent common ground between party programs – both parties claimed to represent the interests of Rusyn peasants and employed the same terminology. The general lack of comprehension of the political differences between the two parties vying for the same electorate caused many Lemkos to acknowledge the fact of the RNO-RSO and RAP's formation of one bloc in the 1928 election as a natural development.

The press organ of the Old Rusyns, *Holos Naroda*, attained considerable popularity in the Lemko Region with its reports on the progress of the electoral campaign of 1928, and henceforth established its position among other periodicals which reached the Lemko region. As the popularity of Old Rusyn slogans grew, the editors of *Holos Naroda* acquired a gradually increasing circle of associates. In 1930 the editors' correspondents were Lemkos living in the counties even furthest from Lviv: Nowy Sącz, Grybów and Gorlice.

---

[67]   AAN, MSW, ref. # 1038, p. 6.
[68]   AP R, AKL, ref. # 72, p. 3.
[69]   *SN* 1929, no. 6, p. 815.

Beginning in November 1929 a change occurred in the attitude of the government authorities toward the RAP. It was perceived in government milieux that the Old Rusyns' declared loyalty to the state could lead to the rise of a strong pro-Polish party in southeastern Poland, which fit its concept of national assimilation proposed a few years earlier by Prime Minister Władysław Sikorski. The earlier mentioned open letter of Lysiak and Yablonsky published in the *Ilustrowany Kurier Codzienny* linked the RAP with government circles, and more closely with the BBWR, the pro-government political bloc which since that time had tried to take control over the socio-economic and political life of the Old Rusyns. The consequences of this rapprochement were the results of the 1930 election. From the BBWR list the Old Rusyns gained two seats in the Sejm, for Mykhailo Bachynsky and Fr. Yosyf Yavorsky.[70] To a considerable degree, the election was decided by the votes of Lemkos, who in cooperation with state authorities expected to solve many problems in the life of their region. If in 1928 both Moscophiles and Ukrainian politicians could indulge in statements undermining the RAP's political influence in the community (e.g. deputy V. Mudry at the Third Congress of UNDO in December 1928, speaking of RAP, stated that it was "a fictional party"[71]), then in 1930 such accusations had no justification, although the local structure of RAP remained feeble.

A year later the RAP changed its name to the Rus Agrarian Organization (RAO, the *Russka Agrarna Organizatsiia*), which took place at the general meeting of the party in Lviv on 25 February 1931, led by Fr. Yevhen Montsibovych.[72] It is difficult to unambiguously elucidate the reasons which led to the change in party name. It would appear that the reasons were propagandistic in nature. The intention was probably to obtain some share of supporters from the pro-Russian milieu (the new name sounded similar to RSO), considering the great differentiation in political attitudes among Rusyn peasants.

The RAP congress on 25 February had real significance for the further crystallization of the Old Rusyns' political program. In the first resolution of the congress, the group affirmed its loyalty to the Polish Republic: "We Rusyns of Red Rus,[73] gathered at the general assembly of the Rus Agrarian Organization, declare firmly and decidedly that the Republic of Poland is also our nation and we declare decisive and permanent loyalty to her."[74] Subsequent resolutions expressed protest against the policies of the Moscophiles and the Ukrainian parties, judging their activities to

---

[70] AAN, MSW, ref. # 945, p. 8.

[71] V. Mudry, "Ukrainske Natsionalno-Demokratychne Obiednannia i ioho natsionalne seredovyshche," in: *III Narodnyi Zizd Ukrainskoho Natsionalno-Demokratychnoho Obiednannia v dniakh 24 i 25 hrudnia 1928 r. (Zvit zlozhenyi na pidstavi stenohrafichnoho protokolu)*, Lviv 1929, p. 89; *Holos Naroda* 1929, no. 23, p. 1.

[72] *SN* 1931, no. 1, p. 102.

[73] "Red Rus" is a historic term used since medieval times to refer to the area known today rather as Eastern Galicia or Western Ukraine.

[74] *SN* 1931, no. 1, p. 102.

be attacks on the values of Rusyn culture. In matters interdenominational, they expressed aversion to the clergy, who were accused of "using the Church for Ukrainian political propaganda hostile to Rusyns and the Nation."[75]

In spring of 1931 the RAO central authorities set about expanding the local structure through creating county party committees. In April successive district congresses took place in Zolochiv (15 April), Ternopil (22 April), Halych (25 April), Sokal (26 April), Kolomyia (27 April), Kalush (28 April) and Sanok (29 April).[76] The Sanok congress drew approximately 200 delegates from 20 villages situated in the counties of Brzozów, Lesko and Sanok. Among them, a considerable portion were Lemkos, and two, Petro Kozak of Besko and Yosyf Sobolevsky of Kostarowce held the highest functions in the congress presidium – chairman and deputy chairman.[77]

The district congresses led to the general RAO congress, held in Lviv on 2 May 1931, which gathered 160 representatives from the Lviv, Stanyslaviv and Ternopil voivodeships. Sanok district was represented by Ivan Fedorenko, Emanuil Mokrytsky, Yakov Mytsko, Yosyf Perelom and Petro Zapotochny. Among the issues touched upon was the question of reaching the widest possible masses of peasants through the party's sphere of action. Focusing on peasants who self-identified as Ukrainian could be a tactical operation calculated to take the peasant voting electorate away from the Ukrainian parties. The programmatic concept of the party would not be changed, launching the slogan "absolute loyalty to the Polish state"[78] and striving to enhance Rusyn rather than Ukrainian national consciousness among the peasants. This was the program promoted by Bachynsky and Yavorsky during their journeys as party spokesmen.[79]

The work begun in 1930 on behalf of building local RAO structure and elevating its political importance brought the anticipated results. In the period 1930–1931 the party developed much more formidably than during the period 1926–1930. This change took place as a result of Bachynsky and Yavorsky's efforts: they developed a detailed RAO program of activity and presented it to the Lviv voivodeship in May 1931. In this plan they proposed designating a paid farming instructor for each county (if necessary, one instructor for two or three counties) in order to increase the number of the trade cooperatives they owned and the inclination of cooperatives subject to Ukrainian institutions to subordinate themselves to RAO. The plan also anticipated the creation of a permanent position for a political organizer with the task of "[…] founding reading rooms and creating in each village a […] [cell] consisting of at least five dedicated people."[80] Both deputies attached a warning to the plan presented to the voivodeship in which they cautioned that the success of

---

[75] Ibid., p. 103.
[76] DALO, f. 1., op. 5t, case # 1231, pp. 50, 51.
[77] Ibid., p. 51.
[78] Ibid., p. 53.
[79] AP K, UWKr, ref. # 352, p.n.n.
[80] DALO, f. 1., op. 5t, case # 1231, p. 55.

the party's development in the area depended on "purely financial factors" and presented a request for subsidizing of the RAO by the BBWR and the government.[81]

Only in provinces with weak Ukrainian influence could the RAO count on meaningful successes. One of the regions which met this criterion was the Lemko region, which more or less at the same time was encircled by a program of operations, wide in scope, implemented by the Ukrainian movement. It should suffice to note that in 1932 the Lemko Commission appointed by *Prosvita* developed its activities spreading Ukrainian national consciousness among Lemkos. In view of the intensifying struggle – which from the perspective of the passage of time and the transformations which have since taken place can be called intra-Ukrainian – government circles faced the necessity of taking a definite position in agreement with Polish *raison d'etat* and surrounded the RAO with full political and financial protection.

2.2. Lemko Association (*Lemko Soiuz*), 1933–1939

The formal proposal for the creation of a Lemko Association (*Lemko Soiuz*) was announced at the RAO congress in Sanok on 8 December 1933, attended by approximately 200 delegates from the counties of Gorlice, Grybów, Krosno, Lesko, Nowy Sącz and Sanok and by representatives of the party's central authorities: deputy Bachynsky and Ivan Sleziuk – director of the People's Home (*Narodnyi Dom*) Institute in Lviv.[82]

Bachynsky and Sleziuk arrived in Sanok with a prepared plan for creating a new Lemko organization whose program and sphere of activity were accepted by the BBWR and discussed with Lemko leaders Hnatyshak and Trokhanovsky.[83] The nature of Bachynsky and Sleziuk's mission is confirmed by the content of their speeches, which had many criticisms of Ukrainian political parties and the Greek Catholic clergy representing the Ukrainian movement.[84] As a result of the discussion of Bachynsky's program paper, the congress took a series of resolutions in which it addressed the government with an appeal for the quickest possible resolution of the most pressing problems for the Lemko community, indicating the necessity of creating a Greek Catholic bishopric independent of the Przemyśl hierarchy for the Lemko region, the issuance of a ban on "dissemination of harmful agitation in school or churches" by teachers or Ukrainian clergy, and taking care to ensure that vacant positions were filled by candidates of Old Rusyn orientation. The congress's fifth resolution contained the decision to start a Lemko Association with headquarters in

---

[81] Ibid.

[82] M. Baczyński, op.cit., p. 29; *SN* 1933, no. 6, p. 697; J. Moklak, "Political Orientations among the Lemkos," pp. 19–20.

[83] The personal relationship of Hnatyshak and minister B. Pieracki with the starost of Nowy Sącz, M. Łach, is worthy of note – they were classmates in school at the Nowy Sącz middle school. See Homo Politicus (I. Kedryn), *Pryczyny upadku Polszczi*, Kraków 1941, p. 117.

[84] *SN* 1933, no. 6, pp. 696–697.

Sanok, which would face the task of supervising socioeconomic and political action throughout the entire Lemko region. In the last resolution the congress approved in its entirety the policy direction theretofore pursued by deputies Bachynsky and Yavorsky and expressed "loyalty and deep obeisance to Mr. President of the Republic of Poland and Mr. Marshal Piłsudski."[85]

At the end of the congress the board of the newly founded organization was selected, with 11 regular members. The majority were members of the intelligentsia: O. Hnatyshak (Krynica), M. Trokhanovsky (Krynica), Y. Siokalo (Gorlice), L. Yavorsky (Sanok), Y. Perelom (Sanok) and E. Mokrytsky (Sanok). Two were involved in trade: the merchant Mykhailo Muzychka (Sanok) and managing director Beskydu Teodor Stefanyshyn (Sanok). Peasants were represented by: D. Halytsky, Y. Fedak and O. Ivanysyk. Bachynsky, Yavorsky and Sleziuk were chosen as honorary members.[86]

The Lemko Association owed its existence entirely to Bachynsky and Sleziuk, who – starting from the assumption that RAO (despite the recent change of name) was not a popular party in the Lemko region and yielded in popularity to the RSO – created it with the intention of putting the Lemko population in the column of citizens loyal to the Polish state. Executing this goal depended on the effectiveness of the operations carried out in order to tear the Lemkos away from the RSO, which is why from the very beginning of the Association's formation, its program was shaped in opposition to the pro-Russian orientation.[87] Important ideological differences between the RSO and the Lemko Association frequently led to conflicts between them, which were usually registered in the press of both organizations. Local and regional RSO congresses repeated their protests against the activities of the Lemko Association in their resolutions, accusing it of Lemko separatism.

At the Fourth Nationwide Congress of RSO delegates on 26 December 1934, Mykhailo Muzychka justified his accession to the Lemko Association by his conviction that the organization had been created for the purpose of strengthening the Rusyn intelligentsia, promoting the development of the level of teaching, letters, etc., about which one of the founders of the Association, Metody Trokhanovsky, spoke at a closed session before the congress in Sanok. Meanwhile – as Muzychka expressed his indignation – the term "Rusyn" was quickly eliminated from use and replaced by the term "Lemko." The Association's press organ, *Lemko*, originally published in Krynica, was intended to be called *Rus Lemko*. The change in terminology defining membership in an ethnic group had the purpose of gradually eliminating the feeling of Rusyn consciousness among Lemkos, a development calculated to make a lasting break of ties with the Moscophile movement. Muzychka spoke in the name of the wider group of participants in the Sanok congress and stated that: "We were

[85]   Ibid.

[86]   AP K, UWKr, ref. # 279, *Sprawozdania sytuacyjne miesięczne wojewody krakowskiego, I–XII, 1933,* p. 404; *SN* 1933, no. 6, p. 697.

[87]   AAN, MSW, ref. # 945, M. Baczyński, op.cit., p. 20.

deceived. All of Lemko Rus protests against the Lemko Association, which has only a few individuals remaining with it."[88]

In the wake of the nationwide RSO congress's resolutions, criticism of the Lemko Association spread throughout the provinces. Lemkos themselves protested against being called Lemkos in a national sense, and against the introduction of the "Lemko language" in schools.[89] The Lemko Association was denied the right to represent the Lemko region to the outside world, and was accused of Polonizing the Lemkos. Typical of these reactions were the resolutions of local RSO congresses in several localities in the counties of Gorlice, Jasło, and Sanok. For example, resolution no. 5 at the RSO congress in Kwiatoń announced: "We definitively condemn the political activity of the Gorlice Lemko Association, which is leading only to intensification of the Polonization of the Lemko region, and we simultaneously state that the Lemko Association has not the slightest right to represent us outside our community."[90]

The protests advanced against the Lemko Association did not hold back the development of that organization. Its activists conducted their campaign in the area, winning over new associates with promises of developing the cultural, educational, and economic activity of the Lemko region. At the meetings organized in many places, the Association's charter was talked over. It was asserted that the Lemko Association was not a political organization, but rather, like the Kachkovsky Society, was working for the "welfare of the Lemko countryside," and was not in opposition to Moscophilism, but that its members had full freedom of choice whether to join the RSO or not.

A basic method for arousing the interest of Lemkos in the activities of the Lemko Association was organizing different types of courses in the area of husbandry. They were conducted in cooperation with the Kraków and Lviv Agriculture Chambers and district farming associations in Nowy Sącz and Sanok. Lemkos were encouraged to take part in various disciplines of arts and crafts: sculpture, masonry, etc. especially in health resort areas visited by recovering patients and holidaymakers.

Until 1936 the Lemko Association engaged in dynamic cultural, educational and economic activity. As long as it had full support from state actors, it could compete with the RSO, and also with the Ukrainian movement. Among the important successes of the organization was the introduction of Trokhanovsky's primer into schools everywhere, designated for teaching in the Lemko dialect. The Rusyn Dormitory (*Ruska Bursa*) in Gorlice remained under the influence of Lemko Association activists and fulfilled an important role in the formation of Lemko youth.[91] A whole row of other achievements (of local significance) on behalf of raising the

---

[88] *Zemlia i Volia* 1935, no. 4, p. 4.
[89] CDIAL, f. 182, op. 1, case # 459, p. 35.
[90] Ibid., case # 479, passim, and case # 459, p. 35.
[91] The Dormitory's Board in 1933–1934 consisted of Y. Siokalo – chairman, M. Yurkovsky – deputy chairman and the following members: T. Yadlovsky, O. Vislotsky, K. Bodak, V. Maletsky and E. Fedorchak. See "Ruska Bursa w Horlytsiakh," *Holos Naroda* 1928, nos 36, 43, 44, 45; T. Kuryllo, "Nashi

civilizational and cultural level of the Lemko region could also be counted among the organization's successes.[92]

Beginning in 1935, however, the importance of the Lemko Association in the Lemko community decreased noticeably. At the general meeting in Gorlice on 22 December of that year, led by Lev Yavorsky (a notary from Bukowsko), M. Trokhanovsky, summarizing the results of the previous work of the Association, stated that they were unsatisfactory. Searching for the reasons behind this phenomenon, he pointed to the weak level of activity among members of the organization, but also spoke of the external difficulties which the Lemko Association encountered in its statutory work, indicating the Ukrainian movement and the RSO. Trokhanovsky's statement, and those of other speakers in the same vein, revealed the actual position of the Association in the Lemko region. It soon became apparent that it was an elite organization, gathering mainly members of the Old Rusyn intelligentsia, and, in spite of many efforts to do so, unable to compete with the RSO which predominated in the area. Nonetheless, despite the organizational difficulties referred to during the discussion, a program of further social initiatives was drafted and a new Executive Board selected. Orest Hnatyshak was again made chairman.[93]

The decline of the social and political importance of the Lemko Association had begun as early as the run-up to the parliamentary elections of 1935. A general weakening of the Old Rusyn movement as a result of Polish-Ukrainian agreement occurred at that time – the compromise with the Polish government known as "Normalization." Toward the new course of government nationality policy, the role theretofore played by Old Rusyns was now to be taken by Ukrainian groupings loyal to the government. The Old Rusyn question gradually lost its political dimension, which meant that the Lemko Association lost its previous privileged position. This course in government policy was decisively defined in the speech of Prime Minister Marian Zyndram-Kościałkowski in January 1936 at the meeting of the Committee on Nationality Issues, at which it emerged that the area of the Lemko region, since it belonged to ethnically Polish lands, was to be designated for the implementation of assimilation policy, i.e. Polonization.

The change in the position taken by government circles toward Old Rusyns put a question mark over the future of the Lemko Association, since its previous initiatives had been executed with the acceptance of state actors. The visible lack of

---

bursy," *Kalendar "Lemka"* (Lviv) 1936. See P. Fetsitsa, "Povernuty nam Rusku Bursa," *Nashe Slovo* 1994, no. 24, p. 4.

[92] See *Lemko* 1936, no. 1, pp. 1–2.

[93] The full membership of the Executive Board of the *Lemko Soiuz* in 1935: O. Hnatyshak – chairman, Y. Siokalo and Y. Perelom – deputy chairmans; members: S. Barna, K. Bodak, L. Yavorsky, O. Kantsler, V. Maletsky, I. Poliansky, V. Telesnytsky, M. Trokhanovsky, Y. Valevsky, Y. Venhrynovych, T. Voitovych, S. Vozniak, and L. Zhelem; deputy board members: S. Tsiuryk, O. Ivanysyk, I. Lakus, E. Mylanych, M. Tylka, V. Zviryk. The Controlling Commission consisted of: T. Yadlovsky, H. Fedorchak, Ms. Kuryllo-Haidova, O. Mylanych, M. Perelom. See *Lemko* 1936, no. 1, p. 2.

support from the state deepened the internal crisis of the organization. In order to enliven its activities, a congress of Lemkos from Nowy Sącz County was convoked and took place on 19 April 1936 in Muszyna. BBWR deputy Jakub Bodziony was invited to the congress and handed the resolutions passed consequent to the discussion, with a request that he push for them in government circles. One resolution stated that "the Polish government has not kept its promises, in view of which the population of the Lemko region was supposed to be given their own representative, in whose place they got a Ukrainian. The congress demands that in the next elections the Lemko region be given a Lemko representative in both houses."[94] Further, the congress protested against the "usurpation by Ukrainian deputies of the right to represent the Lemko region," and demanded teaching posts "in all Rusyn villages" be offered first to Lemko teachers, and the creation of a Pedagogical High School in Gorlice for the purpose of shaping Lemko cadres of teachers for the Lemko region. Among the chief authors of the contents of these resolutions was M. Trokhanovsky.

Resolutions passed at the congress in Muszyna made the Lemko Association a party opposed to the government's nationality policy. The Association also found itself at a disadvantage because of deepening conflicts with the RSO, which for a while had continued to operate with the argument of the Lemko Association's amical relations with the state. Soon, however, the RSO drew conclusions from the new political situation in which the Lemko region found itself, and in the summer of 1936 it intensified its agitation there. It was counting in particular on the part of the undecided population which since the early 1930 had oscillated between the Lemko Association and the RSO.[95]

It is remarkable that until the fall of the second Polish Republic, i.e. until September 1939, the Lemko Association opposed the campaign conducted by the RSO and simultaneously looked for support among government circles, despite the state's known position on the Lemko issue. In autumn of 1936 the Executive Board of the Lemko Association developed a memorial to the state authorities in which it directed some criticism at the RSO, accusing it of undermining the Association's authority among the Lemko population and discrediting its organizational activities. From the government's point of view the rivalry between the Moscophiles and Old Rusyns was accepted to the extent that it paralyzed the possibilities of political development on both sides. This fit the theses of nationality policy announced by Prime Minister Kościałkowski.[96]

As a result of government and administrative circles withdrawal of support and the constant presence of the RSO and Ukrainian movement in the Lemko region, the Lemko Association's work was practically defunct as early as 1937. Trokhanovsky, Hnatyshak, and others – although they remained faithful to the Association and

---

[94]   *Lemko* 1936, no. 17, pp. 2–3.
[95]   AAN, MSW, ref. # 963, *Sprawozdanie Wydziału Narodowościowego MSW, z życia mniejszości narodowych za kwartały, IV 1935, I, III, IV 1936*, p. 316.
[96]   Ibid.

at the general meeting of the organization in Sanok on 14 May 1938, with approximately 40 delegates participating, demanded the restoration of school textbooks drawn up "in the Lemko spirit" in their resolutions[97] – still remained members of the RSO. They took part in the Lviv congresses of that party, joining its highest organs, i.e. the Central Council, and simultaneously reached an understanding with government actors whenever they perceived even a minimal chance of obtaining concessions on economic or cultural and educational development of their region. RSO headquarters looked favorably on this position, recognizing that exclusion of Lemko separatists from the party could lead to the weakening of its influence in the Lemko region. Despite many opinions to the contrary, it must be admitted that the Lemko Association had the support of a part of the Lemko community and the RSO central authorities appreciated that state of affairs, taking no steps which could cause the group's loss of favor.

The positions of Hnatyshak and Trokhanovsky mentioned earlier were not exclusively held by those two. Other members of the Lemko Association, e.g. Siokalo, Vozniak, and Yavorsky also represented those views. The phenomenon of double allegiance to the two organizations, grown from one seed but ideologically opposed, had been seen earlier; it occurred in the RNO (1923–1926), and in the years 1928–1933 certain members of the RAP and RAO were simultaneously members of the RSO, e.g. P. Kozak, E. Mokrytsky, Y. Mytsko, Y. Perelom, and T. Voitovych. Accession to ideologically opposing organizations was undergone for reasons common in the provinces. Peasants took part in enterprises which brought concrete benefits for their households, rarely getting involved in rivalries at the level of the central authorities. The intelligentsia's intentions were undoubtedly similar – both groups underscored the necessity to raise the level of the Lemko countryside. Still, unlike the simple peasant population, the intelligentsia gathered around the Lemko association took upon itself the weight of forming relations with the state authorities, and also with Moscophile and Ukrainian organizations. In the course of these relationships the political maturity of the Association's leaders took shape. In the organization they definitely saw a guarantee for the development of local Lemko values. For this reason the initiative of its creation, though executed by Bachynsky and Sleziuk in agreement with the BBWR, must have had deep underpinnings in the mood of the local intelligentsia.

---

[97] AAN, MSW, ref. # 1058, p. 56.

3. The Kachkovsky reading rooms – developing local structure

These reading rooms were run by the central authorities of the Kachkovsky Society in Lviv. During the interwar period, as in earlier periods, they were closely linked with the pro-Russian movement. They attracted a great deal of interest in the community, grouping around themselves all who were willing, regardless of ideological differences existing between the Old Rusyns and Moscophiles and of the members' religious denominations. A separate issue is the participation in the work of the reading rooms by adherents of the Ukrainian idea, which had, it is true, an incidental character, but happened especially in areas where the *Prosvita* Ukrainian local structure was weak, or for the purpose of taking over reading rooms by national activists.

Beginning in summer 1921, the first attempts were made to reactivate the work of the reading rooms, which had declined during the war. The residual preserved source materials allow for the inference that the initiative of restoring the reading rooms came from the residents of particular villages, former reading room members. In 1925 the reading rooms in Węglówka and Wróblik Królewski were revived. By 1926 four reading rooms had been revived in the Lemko region, though efforts were undertaken toward reviving others in several other places.[98]

The first such efforts were spontaneous. The systematic development of the reading room movement was only opened by the congress of the Kachkovsky Society which met in Lviv on 8 December 1925.[99] The congress stood decisively on the platform of the Russian idea, producing a plan for introducing a double "s" ("ss") in the Society's documentation,[100] which was related to the general activation of Moscophile forces in the southeastern voivodeships. Among the resolutions passed at the congress were also some which drew attention to the necessity to actuate the development of reading rooms in the area. The congress chose a new Society chairman, Marian Glushkevych.

---

[98] CDIAL, f. 182, op. 1, case # 272, *Hazetni povidomlennia, zvity ta inshi materiialy pro* [...] *diialnist v seli Vanivtsi, Korosnivskoho povitu, 1925–1939*, p. 9 and case # 284, *Hazetni povidomlennia, zvity ta inshi materiialy pro* [...] *diialnist v seli Voroblyku Korolivskym, Korosnivskoho povitu, 1925–1939*, p. 35; case # 290, *Hazetni povidomlennia, zvity ta inshi materiialy pro* [...] *diialnist v seli Mshana, Korosnivskoho povitu, 1925–1938*, p. 1.

[99] DALO, f. 1, op. 51, case # 1229, *Dielo obshchestva im. Mikhaila Kachkovskogo vo Lvovie*, vol. 2, 1922–1927, pp. 127, 128.

[100] MSW rejected a plan calling for use of the double "s" ("ss") due to political considerations. See DALO, f. 1, op. 51, case # 1230, *Dielo obshchestva im. Mikhaila Kachkovskogo vo Lvovie*, vol. 3, 1929, p. 141.

In 1926 the number of reading rooms grew slightly. The four reading rooms in Florynka, Krynica Wieś, Radocyna and Uście Ruskie were revived.[101] It is noteworthy that while the reading room in Florynka was being renovated, the initiators of that enterprise, Vasyl Dubets, Hryhorii Habura, and Vasyl Kuryllo in a letter to the executive board of the Society in Lviv dated 5 February 1926 made a proposal for the revival of the Kachkovsky Society branches (not reading rooms) in Krynica, Grybów, and Gorlice. In view of the scant number of reading rooms at that time, however, the plan was not implemented.[102]

In summer 1927 the board of the Society released a plan for statutory changes, justifying their position by the necessity for adapting the organization to new socio-political conditions. The plan posited resignation from Kachkovsky's patronage and endowing the Society with the name "Nauka" (Study), an idea which was, however, rejected. Furthermore, statutory goals regarding the "Russian people" were clearly enunciated, to be achieved with the help of "Russian-language" publishers. A new statute expanding the zone of the Society's activity to the entire area of the Polish Republic was approved at the general assembly on 1 November 1928, and confirmed by the Lviv Province Office on 2 August 1929.[103]

The most extensive development of Kachkovsky reading rooms in the Lemko region took place in 1927 – 12 such institutions were founded during that year.[104] In the years that followed, during the presidency of Symon Bulyk,[105] the number of reading rooms founded decreased slightly: in 1928 only five were founded,[106] in 1929 – eight,[107] and in 1930 – seven.[108]

In August 1929, after direct observation of the reading room movement in the Kraków province by the board of the Society, the Lemko region was set aside as a distinct region of influence. This was because it turned out that the number of reading rooms founded in the Lemko region surpassed areas in the former Eastern Galicia. However, the year 1930 closed this propitious stage in its development. In 1931 barely two reading rooms were founded.[109]

Beginning in 1932 and up until 1935 the number of reading rooms founded yearly began to grow again. This was connected to the favorable attitude of state administrative organs, which acted according to government guidelines and favored the Kachkovsky reading rooms ahead of the *Prosvita* reading rooms. In 1932 eight

---

[101] CDIAL, f. 182, op. 1, case # 230, *Lystuvannia, hazetni povidomlennia ta inshi materiialy pro orhanizatsiinu, finansovo-hospodarsku diialnist chytalni v seli Ustia Ruske, 1921–1938*, p. 3.

[102] Ibid., case # 306, pp. 2, 5.

[103] DALO, f. 1, op. 51, case # 1232, *Dielo obshchestva im. Mikhaila Kachkovskogo vo Lvovie*, vol. 5, p. 58.

[104] Bartne, Binczarowa, Bodaki-Przegonina, Gładyszów, Grab, Hańczowa, Kamianna, Milik, Polany (Grybów County), Ropki, Śnietnica, Tylicz.

[105] AAN, MSW, ref. # 961, p. 225.

[106] Królowa Ruska, Kunkowa, Olchowce, Rozdziele, Wierchomla Wielka.

[107] Andrzejówka, Bogusza, Desznica, Mochnaczka Niżna, Mszana, Myscowa, Skwirtne, Tylawa.

[108] Bartne, Czyrna, Nowa Wieś, Powroźnik, Smerekowiec, Świątkowa Wielka, Zdynia.

[109] Wierchomla Wielka and Krynica Zdrój.

reading rooms were opened,[110] in 1933 – 10,[111] in 1934 – 15[112] and in 1935 – 16[113] reading rooms.

Among the reading rooms founded in the years 1922–1935, many failed, largely through lack of member activity. Frequently it happened that not long after the founding, a second opening took place, as took place in the case of Bartne (1927 and 1929), Bodaki-Przegonina (1927 and 1935), Florynka (1926 and 1935), Gładyszów (1927 and 1932), Kamianna (1927 and 1935), or sometimes there were even three openings – as happened in Wierchomla Wielka (1928, 1931 and 1935), Mszana (1929, 1932 and 1935) and Śnietnica (1927, 1932 and 1935).[114]

After 1935 the number of newly founded reading rooms diminished. In 1936 five institutions were founded,[115] in 1937 – only one (in Brunary Wyżne), and in 1938 – two reading rooms.[116] This phenomenon resulted from the policy called "normalization" in Polish-Ukrainian relations, which were affected the development of the network of Kachkovsky reading rooms negatively. The amplitude of their development over the course of the two decades between the world wars is shown in Figure 1.

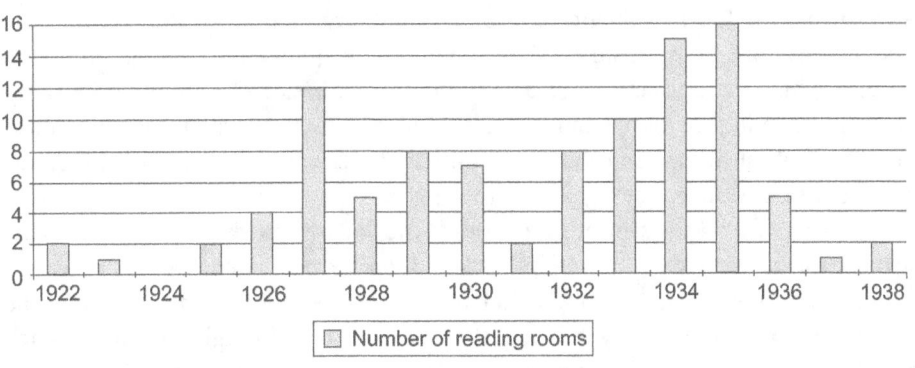

Figure 1. The number of Kachkovsky reading rooms founded in the years 1922–1938

Source: CDIAL, f. 182, op. 1, many pages.

---

[110] Gładyszów, Klimkówka, Nowica, Radocyna, Śnietnica, Tyrawa Solna, Zawadka Rymanowska, Złockie.
[111] Banica, Czarne, Kostarowce, Łabowiec, Łosie (Nowy Sącz County), Polany (Krosno County), Szczawnik, Wapienne (re-opening), Wojkowa.
[112] Bieliczna, Końskie, Kotów, Kwiatoń, Lipowiec, Maciejowa, Mochnaczka, Muszynka, Pietrusza Wola, Radoszyce, Ropki, Trepcza, Trzciana, Zyndranowa, Żydowskie.
[113] Bodaki-Przegonina (re-opening), Ciechania, Długie, Florynka, Izby, Jaszkowa, Kamianna (re-opening), Kożuszne, Królik Wołoski, Mszana (re-opening), Pętna, Roztoka Wielka, Sieniawa, Śnietnica (re-opening), Uhryń, Wierchomla Wielka (re-opening).
[114] *Zemlia i Volia*, various numbers from the years 1927–1935.
[115] Czarnorzeki, Hyrowa, Jastrzębik, Nieznajowa, Słotwiny.
[116] Szklary and Zboiska.

The scheme of the Moscophile reading room movement development outlined thus far demands to be filled in by establishing the intensity with which reading rooms developed in particular counties. From the very beginning they did not develop at an even pace. The new reading rooms appeared mainly in the western and central parts of the Lemko region – rarely in Sanok County, as a result of the greater popularity of the Ukrainian *Prosvita* reading rooms in that region. In Sanok, moreover, many Kachkovsky reading rooms had naturally died out in the 1920s. In 1930 the county authorities conducted a campaign of eliminating them from the register of associations. Most often this occurred due to a lack of public engagement of the institutions, which since 1914 did not conduct statutory work.[117] The reading rooms closed down in this fashion included those in Czeremcha, Czerteż, Olchowce, Osławica, Prusiek, Sanoczek, Sanok, Siemuszowa, Stróże Wielkie, Surowica, Tarnawka, Trepcza and Tyrawa Solna.[118] To justify the closing, the Sanok starost (district head) gave several reasons, e.g. in the case of Sanoczek he wrote that the reading room there "has been completely out of service since 1914, has no members, does not hold board elections, and does not reveal its existence in any other way, so that the local population has completely forgotten about the fact that the association at one point existed."[119] The content of the quoted justification shows the process, which took place starting at the end of the nineteenth century, of pushing Moscophile influence away from centrally situated areas of former Eastern Galicia toward the West, to provincial areas minimally touched by the Ukrainian regions, which Sanok no longer belonged to in the 1920s.

In spring of 1934 the central authorities of the Society in Lviv named a special instructor for the Lemko region with the task of monitoring reading rooms' condition, finances, and meeting protocols. Volodymyr Kutsii (perhaps Kornel?) became the first instructor.[120] The Society's work in the area was done through the intermediacy of delegate-organizers (who were simultaneously inspectors) acting within counties. They included: A. Batenchuk, M. Tsebrynsky, Y. Yanovytsky, O. Yaskov, Yuliian Yurchakevych, A. Kopystiansky, V. Kutsii, O. Lutsyk, D. Protsyk and V. Vavryk.[121] They visited the Lemko region many times, gave program speeches, explained the Society's statutory goals, and encouraged people to participate in education outside of schools. In the activities performed they cited the nineteenth-century leaders of the pro-Russian current: Ivan Naumovych and Adolf Dobriansky. They also traded on Kachkovsky's name despite his not having been a Moscophile but rather one of the "hard-line Rusyns."[122]

---

[117] DALO, f. 1, op. 54, various numbers.
[118] Ibid., nos.: 7603, 7604, 7606, 7608, 7611, 7614, 7617, 7618, 7619, 7620, 7624, 7626.
[119] Ibid., case # 7611, p. 2.
[120] *Zemlia i Volia* 1934, no. 18, p. 7.
[121] DALO, f. 1, op. 51, case # 1230, p. 20; *Lystok* 1939, no. 2, p. 17.
[122] AP K, UWKr, ref. # 51, [p.n.n.] On Kachkovsky's political stance, see J. Moklak, "Mychajło Kaczkowśkyj i czytelnie jego imienia na Łemkowszczyźnie," *Magury '87* (Warszawa) 1987, pp. 53–64.

The activists from the Lviv authorities of the Society mentioned above had ties with the RSO. What is more, Tsebrynsky and Yurchakevych belonged to the party's Central Council. The Society's personal connections with the RSO at the highest levels permit the inference that the network of Kachkovsky reading rooms developed in the Lemko region was intended to supplement the influence of the pro-Russian party and to some extent was subordinate to it.

The "shop-stewards," who generally belonged to the intelligentsia and lived in the cities and towns of districts, acted as liaisons between the Lviv headquarters and local centers of the Kachkovsky Society. In Sanok County these were E. Mokrytsky, M. Muzychka, and Y. Perelom; in Krosno, S. Vozniak; in Gorlice, S. Krushynsky, R. Maksymovych, Y. Mokhnatsky and Y. Siokalo; in Grybów and Nowy Sącz, S. Durkot, O. Hnatyshak and M. Trokhanovsky.[123] They looked after the supply of books and periodicals to reading rooms and promoted particular titles. Aside from *Nauka*, which was the Society organ edited by Tsebrynsky, they provided *Zemlia i Volia*, the RSO organ, *Lemko*, the Lemko Association organ, and *Holos Naroda*, the RAO organ. It should be noted that the Society received a small subsidy from the MWRiOP (the Ministry of Religious Denominations and Public Education) for the distribution of books in its libraries.[124]

The largest group of Society associates in the area consisted of teachers, priests, and many farmers, who actively participated simultaneously in building RSO structure in their localities. On their shoulders lay the task of establishing libraries and conducting statutory activities.

In the 1930s the Moscophile reading room movement reformed its organizational structure, creating affiliated branches of the Kachkovsky Society. The first branches took shape in the late 1930s in Brody, Sambir, Sokal and Zhovkva; and in 1931 in Stanyslaviv and Zolochiv.[125] The locations of the first branches to be revived indicate that the area of the former Eastern Galicia was the main focus of the Lviv authorities' interest; it was there that they first made an effort to reconstruct the Society's prewar substance. It was soon revealed, however, that those branches were rather keeping alive smouldering pro-Russian sentiment than developing it in a forward direction. On the other hand dynamic growth of the number of Kachkovsky reading rooms was observed in the areas west of the San River, culminating in the establishment of branches in Ustrzyki Dolne (4 March 1934) and Sanok (23 March 1935).[126]

---

[123] AP K, UWKr, ref. # 279, p. 84. Numerous mentions in *Zemlia i Volia*.

[124] CDIAL, f. 182, op. 1, case # 422, *Hazetni vyrivky z statiamy V.R. Vavryka*, p. 3.

[125] *Nauka* 1931, no. 4, p. 105.

[126] The founding assembly took place several months before legal registration (1 November 1934). The first Board was then elected, consisting of Y. Perelom as chairman, I. Tylka of Tyrawa Solna as deputy chairman, V. Mikhnovsky of Olchowiec as secretary, Y. Shatynsky and Y. Fedak as members and L. Yavorsky of Bukowsko and O. Ivanysyk of Łukowe as deputy members. See CDIAL, f. 182, op. 1, case # 470, *Hazetne povidomlennia, zvity i inshi materiialy* [...] *pro diialnist chytalni w misti Sianoku*, pp. 4, 6, 7; DALO, f. 1, op. 54, case # 7610, *Filia russofilskogo tovarishchestva im. Mikhaila Kachkovskogo v Sanokie, 1935*, p. 1.

The Sanok branch was in charge of the reading rooms in the counties of Krosno, Lesko and Sanok and the single branches in Brzozów County (Jabłonica Polska and Końskie) and Dobromyl County (Kreców). The reading rooms in the area of the Kraków province had a separate affiliate structure – their governing authority was the reading room in Gorlice founded in 1933.[127]

At first the reading rooms were located in private homes, and it happened that some householders donated unused buildings for the purpose. Some rooms were leased from municipal authorities for a rental fee. In other cases they were located in church buildings. The wealthier reading room branches built their own buildings, fully adapted for execution of statutory goals, with a library, a theatrical stage, and rooms for holding each type of husbandry course, etc. In the first half of the 1930s the state administration encouraged these initiatives, though the reading rooms acquired funding themselves. Often it came in contributions from the more affluent intelligentsia, e.g. O. Hnatyshak donated 100 zloty to the fund to build a reading house in Krynica,[128] and sometimes the practice of self-taxation among reading room members was invoked. A particularly important source of financial support was the group of Aid Committees organized by Lemko emigrants in North America. Aid also came from organizations and individuals in Czechoslovakia.[129]

The essence of the Kachkovsky reading rooms' success among Lemkos was based not so much on the Society program as the concrete social benefits which the reading rooms brought the population. Generally speaking, they developed the cultural and educational life of the countryside. The academies and occasional evenings they organized demanded the preparation of an artistic program. Many reading rooms had their own choirs. To ensure a high level of artistic quality, top-notch instructors were brought in. For example, in Krynica the reading room members taxed themselves and thus acquired the means to maintain an instructor-conductor, a post filled by Oleksandr A. Ropytsky from Lviv.[130] In Żegiestów, the choir and orchestra were conducted by Izydor Iacenyk, a student of Ropytsky, who conducted the choir in Andrzejówka.

In the 1930s amateur theater circles also grew increasingly active. Plays featuring multiple acts were even mounted, some written by Fr. K. Chaikovsky and I. Lutsyk. Preparation of theatrical productions featuring amateurs, most of whom were acting for the first time in their lives, demanded a great deal of work from the instructors.[131]

---

[127] The board of the first reading room in Gorlice consisted of Y. Bishko as chairman, S. Baidovych, M. Yurkovsky, E. Kuryllo, P. Seifert, Y. Siokalo, I. Siokalo, and O. Vislotsky. See *Karpatorusskii Kalendar Lemko-Soiuza na god 1954* (Yonkers, NY), p. 59.

[128] AP K, UWKr, ref. # 352, p. 171.

[129] *Zemlia i Volia* 1933, no. 3, p. 5.

[130] CDIAL, f. 182, op. 1, case # 462, p. 9.

[131] The instructors were O. Gromosiak in Kamianna, I. Hychko in Trepcza, T. Yadlovsky in Smerekowiec, I. Yurkovsky in Skwirtne, S. Varkholiak in Wróblik Królewski, M. Voloshynovych in Królik Wołoski. See *Lemko* 1936, no. 39, p. 3.

Theatrical circles achieved recognition not only from the Lemko public, but also in surrounding Polish cities, e.g. the group from Wróblik Królewski had successful performances in Iwonicz and Łężany. The theatrical shows dealt with topics relating to the Lemko tradition, but also fulfilled propaganda functions. Beside homegrown creations, works of Russian poetry were recited. At the ceremony in honor of the Kachkovsky reading room in Węgłówka's silver jubilee on 25 October 1931, the repertoire included Aleksandr Pushkin's tale of the golden fish. The Kachkovsky reading rooms in Florynka and Czarne, for their part, organized a special ceremony for the centenary of the death of Pushkin, "the greatest Rusyn poet."[132] Interest in the art of acting grew relatively quickly, and by 1935 there were 37 reading rooms with their own theater groups.[133]

Despite the enormous success of the Kachkovsky reading rooms among Lemkos, sources also reveal a weak side of their work. There were reading rooms burgeoning with activity, such as those in Andrzejówka, Jabłonica Polska, Pielgrzymka, Tylicz, Węglówka, Wróblik Królewski, and Zawadka Rymanowska, but a considerable number of reading rooms showed scanty involvement. The reports of inspectors monitoring the execution of reading room statutory obligations, Y. Yanovytsky and N. Kohut, often contained language stating a lack of activity, e.g. "the reading rooms exist only on paper" or "there is no sign of life." The inspectors enumerated a series of violations of the duties of reading room boards: no registers of members, no protocols of meetings, no cashbooks, and others.[134]

The inspectors also recorded the prevailing conditions in supervisory units, i.e. Society branches. Inspection of the Sanok branch brought to light the same defects observed in many reading rooms. Lutsyk, arriving in Sanok on 17 April 1937 with the goal of making an inspection, stated in a letter to headquarters in Lviv that "conducting an inspection is impossible, because the branch shows no activity whatsoever […], does not keep a register of members […], books of meeting protocols […], cashbooks […], a list of library books […]."[135] The same day, 17 April, as a result of harsh criticism of the chairman of the board of that branch, Yosyf Perelom, he resigned from his the post he had theretofore filled, and Fr. Volodymyr Venhrynovych of Kostarowce was appointed chairman.[136] This disorder in documentation to a greater or lesser degree was evident in all of these institutions, but the reasons for

---

[132] *Zemlia i Volia* 1931, no. 45, p. 2.
[133] Andrzejówka, Bieliczna, Bogusza, Desznica, Florynka, Gładyszów, Hańczowa, Jabłonica Polska, Klimkówka, Kostarowce, Krynica Wieś, Królowa Ruska, Królik Wołoski, Kunkowa, Labowa, Łosie, Milik, Mochnaczka Niżna, Mochnaczka Wyżna, Nowa Wieś, Nowica, Pietrusza Wola, Powroźnik, Radocyna, Regetów, Rozdziele, Skwirtne, Smerekowiec, Świątkowa Wielka, Trepcza, Wapienne, Węglówka, Wojkowa, Wysowa, Zdynia, Złockie, Zyndranowa. See CDIAL, f. 182, op. 1, case # 542, *Vidomosti pro naiavnost hurtkiv bibliotek pry chytalniakh, 1938–1939*, pp. 5–6.
[134] CDIAL, f. 182, op. 1, case # 475, *Zvity instruktora tovarystva Osypa Yanovytskoho pro svoiu robotu ta lystuvannia z nym, 1934–1938*, p. 13.
[135] CDIAL, f. 182, op. 1, case # 470, p. 27.
[136] Ibid.

the phenomenon should be identified not as aversion to the Society or the reading rooms, but rather a lack of organizational discipline.

In general, beginning in the mid-1930s, a crisis descended upon the development of Kachkovsky reading rooms in the Lemko region. The Moscophile publication *Russkii Golos* issued a proclamation to the Society on 27 September 1936 in which we read:

> The crisis and the financial state of our Society are not allowing us to develop our cultural and educational operations as is needed [...]. Meager resources keep the Society from implementing the plan for reviving and expanding its operations among the broad masses of the Russian population. The work of the Society cannot take on broad dimensions and for that reason the plans remain [mere] plans.[137]

An appeal was made for contributions to the community and October 1936 was declared Kachkovsky Society Month throughout the entire country. Ukrainian publications commented on this fact as a testimony to the decline of the Moscophile idea in the Lemko region and in Poland.

Nonetheless the Kachkovsky Society was an institution which penetrated deeply into the consciousness of the Lemko population, because it did not foist on its audience the Russian idea outright (in contrast to Ukrainian institutions[138]), but operated according to values accepted by the peasants and tried to defy their social and economic expectations. Among Moscophile and Old Rusyn institutions, the Kachkovsky Society thanks to the reading rooms had the furthest-reaching organizational structure, surpassing even the extremely well-organized RSO in this aspect.

The Kachkovsky reading rooms were used by both Moscophiles and Old Rusyns. The attitudes among Lemko members of the reading rooms varied. The decisive majority took part in the work of the rooms from practical incentives and the need to develop culture and education in rural areas, and were politically indifferent. A determinant related to political criteria was their ties to the Rusyn tradition, which, however, was often understood as a cultural or religious value; hence Lemkos' difficulty with national identification.

4. Orthodox faith and political consciousness

Both the Eastern Orthodox and Greek Catholic clergy played important roles in the development of Lemko confessional and political consciousness. The majority of Greek Catholic priests supported the development of Ukrainian socioeconomic and political institutions, but a certain number promoted the Old Rusyn dispensation, and even a few the pro-Russian one. Orthodox clergy appointed by the Orthodox

---

[137] Quoted from *Dilo* 1936, no. 226, p. 1.
[138] Y. Tarnovych, *Ilustrovana istoriia Lemkivshchyny*, Lviv 1936, pp. 246–247.

Metropolitan in Poland, Dionizy Valedinski, to come to the Lemko region had a significant influence on the development of Moscophile institutions.

Conversions of Greek Catholics to Orthodoxy began in late 1926 in the central Lemko region, and next spread to the western part. As a result of Metropolitan Dionizy's efforts, the first centers of Orthodoxy were legalized by the MWRiOP in March and April 1928.[139] Though it is true that state authorities did not immediately accept the convert community, responding negatively to the Metropolitan's subsequent requests, but in the end – recognizing the durability of the Orthodox faith in the Lemko region – they established six permanent Orthodox affiliates, of which five: Czarne, Desznica, Mszana, Radocyna and Tylawa were subordinate to the Lviv parish, and one (Bogusza) – to the parish in Piotrków.[140] Table 1 contains a statistical comparison of Orthodox believers in those affiliates.

The structure of the Eastern Orthodox Church in the Lemko region, established in 1928, did not at the time of its approval include all of the areas immersed in Orthodox faith. In a letter to the MWRiOP dated 21 September of that year, Archbishop Feodosii put forward a plan to make many changes to the structure. He proposed developing affiliates in Bogusza, Czarne, Desznica, Mszana and Radocyna and establishing a new affiliate of the Lviv parish in Świątkowa Wielka. He even tried to institute a parish (not an affiliate) for Bartne and Przegonina.[141] The authorities of the Warsaw Metropolia made a fruitless effort to obtain the status of parish or affiliate for many other localities, including some only partly comprised by Orthodox believers.

In the second half of May 1935 at the meeting of the Missionary Commission of the Warsaw–Chełm Orthodox diocese, which was chaired by Metropolitan Dionizy, the decision was taken to modify the structure of the Orthodox church in the southeastern voivodeships. The entire area was divided into two districts: the Eastern Galician district, which coincided with the Greek Catholic Przemyśl diocese (not including the Lemko region), under the leadership of archimandrite F. Narko, and the Lemko district, coinciding with the AAL (Apostolic Administration of the

---

[139] AAN, MWRiOP, ref. # 1086, *Miesięczne listy dotacji dla parafialnego duchowieństwa i służby cerkiewnej: woj. lwowskie i łódzkie, 1928–1933*, pp. 5, 25.

[140] The approval process for the Orthodox Church in the Lemko region took place in two stages. In the first stage, in its rescript of 3 March 1928 MWRiOP established permanent affiliates in Desznica, Czarne and Radocyna (parish in Lviv) and affiliates in Bogusza (parish in Piotrków). In the second stage, by the decision of 26 April 1928, two further affiliates were established, in Tylawa and Mszana, which were joined to the Lviv parish. See AAN, MWRiOP, ref. # 1049, *Wykazy parafii i filii etatowych i nieetatowych oraz etatów duchowieństwa według diecezji*, pp. 15, 162, 177. See J. Moklak, "Kształtowanie się struktury Kościoła prawosławnego na Łemkowszczyźnie w Drugiej Rzeczypospolitej," in: *Przez dwa stulecia, XIX i XX w.*, ed. S. Pijaj, Kraków 1993, pp. 51–77.

[141] Feodosii proposed joining Bartne and Przegonina to the affiliate in Bogusza, showing a lack of familiarity with the geography of the Lemko region – it was considerably closer from there to Czarne, Desznica or Radocyna, see AAN, MWRiOP, ref. # 1043, pp. 194–195, 217.

Table 1. The structure of the Eastern Orthodox Church in the Lemko region as determined by MWRiOP in 1928

Eastern Orthodox parish affiliate	Parish	County	Affiliate location	Number of Eastern Orthodox adherents
Bogusza	p	Grybów	Bogusza	539
			Królowa	697
Czarne	l	Gorlice	Czarna	280
			Wołowiec	187
			Nieznajowa	131
			Lipna	160
Desznica	l	Jasło	Desznica	200
			Świątkowa Wielka	400
			Świątkowa Mała	250
			Świerzowa Ruska	350
			Hałbów	100
Radocyna	l	Gorlice	Radocyna	353
			Długie	176
Mszana	l	Krosno	Mszana	800
			Smereczne	200
			Wilsznia	280
Tylawa	l	Krosno	Tylawa	700
			Trzciana	540

Abbreviations: p – Piotrków, l – Lviv.

Sources: AAN, MWRiOP, ref. # 1043, pp. 185–186; ibid., ref. # 1075, [p.n.n.]. Another statistical configuration prepared in the Jasło district provides the following number of Orthodox believers in the respective municipalities of Świątkowa Wielka – 350, Świątkowa Mała – 150, and Świerzowa Ruska – 225. See ibid., ref. # 1043, p. 219.

Lemko Region), under the leadership of Fr. Yurii Pavlyshyn, provost of the affiliate in Czarne.[142]

---

[142]   J. Moklak, "Kształtowanie się struktury Kościoła prawosławnego," pp. 65–66.

From then on the Warsaw metropoly conducted a separate mission campaign among Lemkos, but until 1939 the Orthodox church structure in the Lemko region remained unchanged, and the number of adherents of Orthodox faith recruited from Greek Catholic parishes oscillated within the environs of 19,000.[143]

The tendency shown by Lemkos to convert from the Greek Catholic confession to the Orthodox was a direct result of the ministerial methods of the Greek Catholic clergy. Since the late nineteenth century the term "ortodoxus" (*pravoslavny*, true-believing) had been deleted from the liturgy and replaced with the word "ortopistos" (*pravovirny*, true-faithful). These acts had a political basis, and were explained by the desire to eliminate mental associations with Russian orthodoxy, which functioned as a political actor in internal and foreign policy in Russia, among the faithful. Thus young Greek Catholic priests in particular fostered an attitude toward Orthodoxy built on feelings of an external Russian threat. This behavior did not, however, have canonical justification, and contravened the resolutions of the Holy See of 19 May 1887, as well as the position of the Lviv provincial synod of 1891, which clearly underscored the words addressed to the faithful by the deacon: "All of you Orthodox Christians (*Vsikh vas pravoslavnykh Khristiian*)."[144]

A direct cause of conversion was the liturgical question. The population, accustomed to a fixed mode of worship, expressed its dissatisfaction with the clergy, who omitted the word "Orthodox" from the liturgy. The attachment to this word was so strong that when the rector introduced it into the liturgy at the request of the faithful, e.g. at Christmas, an immediate healing of relations with parishioners occurred. One priest who permitted this described his impression thus: "[…] in order to make people happy, I said 'All of you Orthodox Christians.' And truly, the joy this caused was tremendous. Since that time people began to take a liking to me, and this in spite of my distinct political and party convictions."[145]

Religious feeling in the Lemko region was closely observed by the Greek Catholic consistory in Przemyśl. Signs of conflicts between believers and some Greek Catholic clergy had been flowed to the diocese since the beginning of the 1920s. The prevalent mood among the faithful in Tylawa and Trzciana before the conversion was known in Przemyśl. The Orthodox movement in the interwar period had begun in those villages and quickly spread to the other parts of the Lemko region.[146] Father Ivan Poliansky, an Old Rusyn faithful to the Greek Catholic church, chancellor of

---

[143] The statistical configuration for 1933, prepared for the needs of the Polish government, gives the number 18,022, see AAN, MSZ, ref. # 5219, *Komisja Kresów Wschodnich. Materiały programowe i organizacyjne*, p. 3.

[144] See *Chynnosty i rishennia provintsialnoho Soboru w Halychyni 1891 r.*, Lviv 1894, p. 170.

[145] I. Polianskii, "Perebih sporu o slovo «pravoslavnyi» v Tylavi, ta jeho vyslid: vybukh relihiinoho rozdoru na Lemkivshchyni," *Visti Apostolskoi Administratsii Lemkivshchyny* 1936, vol. 10, p. 148.

[146] See A. Kruhelsky, *Tylavska skhizma na Lemkivshchyni, ii istoriia i teperishnyi stan*, Lviv 1933; J. Moklak, "Życie polityczne i religijne ludności łemkowskiej powiatu krośnieńskiego w latach 1918–1939 (na tle całego regionu)," in: *Krosno. Studia z dziejów miasta i regionu*, vol. 3, S. Cynarski, Rzeszów 1995, pp. 206–208.

the AAL, stated that the Przemyśl ordinariate could with relative ease hold back the development of Orthodoxy in the Lemko region through some concessions of a terminological nature. According to Poliansky, it would suffice to reintroduce the word "Orthodox" in Greek Catholic liturgy in order to effectively master the mood of the population leaning towards conversion. The diocesan visitation to Tylawa conducted on 17 July 1926, three months before the conversion, did not resolve the conflict, however, despite the parish administrator's efforts to secure the visitor's agreement to introduce the word "Orthodox" into the liturgy.[147] The absence of a compromise between parishioners and diocesan authority in the matter was effectively used by Moscophile activists in other places too, and for a long time constituted a barrier which prohibited the defusing of growing religious conflicts.

A convergence of events seizes the scholar's attention. On the one hand strenuous efforts by Metropolitan Dionizy to increase the importance of the Orthodox Church in southeastern Poland were taking place, while on the other the pro-Russian RSO reorganized, establishing ever closer contact with the Russian National Union. It is difficult to definitively state how closely the Metropolitan circles cooperated with the RSO. It seems that lasting associations existed only at intermediate levels: between the Warsaw Metropolia and the RZN, and between the RZN and RSO.[148] In the former relationship, the common ground was Orthodox confession understood as a pan-Russian idea, in the latter – coinciding political and confessional programs resulting from obeisance to Russia and hostility to the Ukrainian movement. Hence the RSO at first supported the development of Orthodoxy, and its activists also included Greek Catholic clergy. Attitudes to the denominational issue would change only in the 1930s, when the RSO approved a resolution on the necessity of preventing religious disputes.[149]

Before that came to pass, however, conversions to Orthodoxy became a mass phenomenon and nurtured the strengthening of the pro-Russian current. They were accompanied by public speeches against the Greek Catholic church and Ukrainian secular institutions. Several times the mood grew to such a pitch of fanaticism that people were incited to commit crimes.

The first social conflicts in a religious context occurred in the summer of 1927. They were initiated by the so-called "attack of the women," which was conducted in Tylawa on 3 July 1927, and consisted in the demolition of the Greek Catholic presbytery by a group of irate women. The attacker' fury only subsided when "a bed that was too big would not fit out the window."[150] The women served an ultimatum on the Greek Catholic rector, Fr. Ivan Shkilnyk: he had 14 days to leave Tylawa or they threatened to repeat the assault. The women's storming of the presbytery was calculated to avoid repressions from the authorities, but further attacks were begun

---

[147] I. Polianskii, op.cit., pp. 151–152.
[148] AAN, MSW, ref. # 961, p. 228; *SN* 1927, no. 3, pp. 289–290.
[149] *SN* 1935, no. 6, p. 651.
[150] A. Kruhelsky, op.cit., p. 30.

without deception. During a repeat attack the police intervened, as property belonging to the Greek Catholic Church (goods and real estate) were legally protected by a concordat concluded between Poland and the Vatican in 1925. Henceforward the watchfulness of Police posts in regions threatened with interdenominational conflicts was intensified. In subsequent years, as a result of numerous attacks on Orthodox churches from which liturgical objects were spirited away, the police often had to intervene.[151]

Some Orthodox priests got involved in campaigns whose aim was the seizure of Greek Catholic parish property: church buildings and presbytery. In Krosno County Fr. Mikhail Ivaskov, appointed to Tylawa by Metropolitan Dionizy in January 1927, played an inspiring role. He replaced Fr. Panteleimon Rudyk, who returned to his position of rector in Lviv. In one of his reports to the MWRiOP Lviv governor Piotr Dunin-Borkowski wrote on the basis of dispatches from the starost of Krosno:

> the Orthodox population of these municipalities [Hyrowa, Mszana, Trzciana, Tylawa] is consumed with religious fanaticism fomented by the priest responsible for shepherding the Tylawa flock, Fr. M. Ivaskov, and by his minions. That population, as a rule unintelligent and ill-informed, lives in the belief that it is persecuted for having converted, and that because it considers the property of church and parish to be its own [...] and is of the opinion that the authorities are acting illegally by not transferring that property to the Orthodox faith, since the whole village has gone over to Orthodoxy.[152]

Attempts to seize Greek Catholic property occurred in municipalities where civil tension was at its highest and where the priest's approach was to excuse such efforts or even give them his blessing. They included cities and towns in the Gorlice and Jasło counties, where energetic pro-Orthodox activity was led by Fr. Mykhailo Hrytsai. In autumn of 1927, at his initiative, and often with his participation, the converts made a series of attempts to seize Greek Catholic churches in Świątkowa Wielka, Radocyna, Długie, Czarne and other places.[153] The tension among the embittered population was so great that threats to burn down churches and presbytery buildings were made, and Gorlice district saw fit to set up a permanent National Police Post in Nieznajowa with the task of maintaining public order in municipalities populated largely by Orthodox believers.[154]

In the spring of 1928 social conflicts once again broke out, leading for the first time to an interventionist reaction from the government. On the eve of the Easter holiday, 12 April, the Orthodox populace of Świerzowa Ruska and Kotań took over

---

[151] AP K, UWKr, ref. # 278, *Sprawozdania sytuacyjne miesięczne wojewody krakowskiego, I–XII, 1930*, p. 61; see ref. # 279.

[152] AAN, MWRiOP, ref. # 1043, p. 33.

[153] Ibid., pp. 27, 31, 43, 48, 57–60. The starosta of Gorlice, A. Ricci, in a letter to the Kraków governor L. Darowski defined the activitis of Fr. Hrytsai as "intensive agitation" on behalf of Eastern Orthodoxy, adding that "instead of having a calming influence on the excited minds of the population, he uses his sermons to incite the population to take the church by force."

[154] Ibid.

the Greek Catholic church buildings in both places by force. The church in Kotań, robbed of its liturgical objects, was soon abandoned, while in Świerzowa ceremonial night watches were organized. The rector of the local Greek Catholic parish, Fr. Petro Kalamunetsky, lost whatever influence he had had on the course of events. The problem reached the MWRiOP in Warsaw as a matter of professional duties. A hastily organized expeditionary unit consisting of about 30 police functionaries set off for Desznica late at night in a truck. Jasło County starost Antoni Zoll took part in the operation, as did Commissioner Stańko, representative of the National Police Headquarters in Kraków, armed with tear-gas canisters. From Desznica the unit went on foot to Świerzowa and Świątkowa Mała. The next day order was restored in both places, and the Greek Catholic churches sealed shut.[155]

In the first years of Orthodoxy's growth, the clergy in their organizational work placed priority on their pastoral duties. Nonetheless some of them actively participated in developing Kachkovsky reading rooms and maintained contact with the RSO. Among those involved in this current were Fr. Stepan Pashkevych, who revived the reading room in Grab in 1927 and for a certain time fulfilled the function of chairman of the board, Fr. Oleksandr Ivanovych and his wife (took part in the revival of the reading rooms in Królowa Ruska in December 1928 and Bogusza in June 1929), Fr. Kostiantyn Sheremeta – provost of the Orthodox affiliate in Mszana (beginning in summer 1928 personally ran the Board of the Kachkovsky Society in Lviv and the effort in Krosno district to legally register the reading room in Mszana), and M. Ivaskov, who organized a network of libraries "for the enlightenment of the Lemko region."[156] There were some incidents of sociopolitical journalism engaged in by Orthodox priests (e.g. M. Dolnytsky, M. Ivaskov, P. Shvaika).[157] During this first period of the spread of Orthodoxy, social engagement, especially of a political type, was trumped for most priests by efforts on behalf of strengthening the Orthodox faith and the structures of the Orthodox Church in the Lemko Region.

Things were different in the 1930s. The active involvement of some priests in the reading room movement increased. There were several factors contributing to this change. Firstly, the fascination with Orthodoxy had weakened and interdenominational conflicts were becoming less and less frequent. The clergy were forced to look for new areas of dialogue with the population. After the wave of socio-religious upheavals, there now began the term of trial, which would show how capable the Orthodox clergy were of participating in the daily life of the Lemkos. Among over 40 priests[158] working in affiliates or outposts before 1939, a certain number were engaged

---

[155] AP K, UWKr, ref. # 32, *Sprawy wyznaniowe. Prawosławie na Podkarpaciu*, p.n.n.

[156] CDIAL, f. 182, op. 1, case # 363, *Hazetni povidomlennia, zvity i inshi materiialy pro [...] diialnist chytalni v seli Tylava, Korosnivskoho povitu, 1929–1938*, p. 1.

[157] CDIAL, f. 129, op. 3, case # 269, *Rukopysy statei, vidozv, povidomlen ta in. nadeslani z Lemkivshchyny do redaktsii pravoslavno-tserkovnoho zhurnalu "Voskriesienni" a u Lvovi*, pp. 86, 99, 117, 158–163.

[158] Priest's (incomplete) statement, see J. Moklak, "Kształtowanie się struktury Kościoła prawosławnego," pp. 76–77.

in village issues. These priests, opposed to the Greek Catholic Church which supported the Ukrainian movement, stood with the pro-Russian orientation, or much less frequently the Old Rusyn one. There were exceptional cases of participation by Orthodox priests in the Ukrainian movement, e.g. Fr. Volodymyr Okhab of Mszana.

The Orthodox clergy's involvement caused certain Kachkovsky reading rooms to become an integral part of the Orthodox mission in the Lemko region. In many cases they were located in Orthodox parish buildings, e.g. in Czarne. In the reading rooms themselves, which were statutorily interfaith, the cult of Maksym Sandovych spread. Reading rooms took active part in the mourning ceremonies in honor of the Talerhof dead. The ceremonies in Czarne, organized jointly on 1 September 1935 by the local reading room and the Orthodox affiliate, gathered over 8,000 participants from 27 villages. Several Orthodox priests took part in them (A. Krynytsky, V. Lutkevych and Y. Pavlyshyn).[159]

Beginning in the mid-1930s, the RSO and Kachkovsky Society central authorities influenced their local chapters in the area for the purpose of neutralizing the interdenominational conflicts smouldering in some places. The aim was to gain Greek Catholic converts of Old Rusyn orientation. Above all they proposed to organize general assemblies with the involvement of clergy from both confessions. The idea was to prevent religious disputes and "unite on the soil of cultural and educational activities."[160] Thanks to preserved archival records, we are well-acquainted with the course of inspections conducted by Y. Yanovytsky at the Kachkovsky reading room in Czyrna in May 1936. The inspection revealed that the reading room's operations had ceased due to religious disunity in the village. As inspector, Yanovytsky bound the reading room officials to renew its activity with the help of clergy from both denominations: Orthodox – Fr. Stepan Pashkevych of Piorunka, responsible for Czyrna, and Greek Catholic – Fr. Stepan Kuzyk.[161]

In the 1930s the most active involvement in the Moscophile movement's development was shown by Fr. Yurii Pavlyshyn. He fulfilled the function of provost at the Orthodox parish affiliate in Czarne, with authority over Lipna, Nieznajowa and Wołowiec. Pavlyshyn led the Orthodox mission campaign in the Lemko region, which consisted of, among other things, founding the Sandovych Orthodox Brotherhoods and supporting Moscophile reading rooms. He set in motion particularly energetic operations in the area of his affiliate, especially in Czarne, where he was chairman of the Kachkovsky reading room.[162] He represented the strictest Russian orientation. In public appearances he often used the Russian literary language, and he conducted his correspondence with the central board of the Kachkovsky Society

[159] CDIAL, f. 182, op. 1, case # 427, pp. 21, 26.

[160] Ibid., case # 383, *Informatsiia, zvity i inshi materiialy pro* [...] *diialnist chytalni v seli Chyrnii, Novosanchivskoho povita, 1930–1936*, p. 13.

[161] Ibid., p. 11.

[162] *Zemlia i Volia* 1934, no. 45, p. 4. The following local farmers actively cooperated with Pavlyshyn: D. Baisa, V. Baisa, S. Barna, Y. Motyka, Y. Pryslopsky, P. Pryslopsky, P. Zhydiak.

in Lviv entirely in Russian.[163] Thanks to his involvement reading rooms took shape in the local vicinity, e.g. in Pętna – an area with strong Ukrainian influence.[164]

Among the many Kachkovsky reading rooms in the Lemko region, only one was explicitly denominational, formally enunciating its statutory goals in terms of Orthodox religious values. This was the reading room in Bartne, which took the official name: Kachkovsky II Orthodox Reading Room in Bartne.[165] Its inception was the result of interdenominational conflict between Orthodox and Greek Catholic members of the previous reading room. On 23 April 1930 the members of Orthodox faith finally seceded, having chosen as their leader Stepan Felenchak. The reading room's split into two separate units had ideological and confessional significance largely at the local level, because elsewhere, despite equally dramatic interconfessional conflicts, the phenomenon did not recur. The Society's central authorities in Lviv recognized that reading room as Orthodox, but neither it nor its predecessor engaged in statutory activity. The conflict was motivated rather more by the desire to exhibit attitudes than different views on methods of social action, its scope or goals. The reading room in Bartne was finally revived by the Orthodox priest Balyk in 1936.[166]

An important role was also played in the development of the pro-Russian dispensation by the Greek Catholic clergy. Old Rusyn sentiments within the Greek Catholic church lived on into the 1930s, despite the tendency toward nationalization (Ukrainization) in the Church since the mid-nineteenth century. There were considerably fewer Moscophiles among the Greek Catholic clergy than Old Rusyns, but they played a more prominent role. With regard to the years 1911–1919 it is worth remembering the activities of Fr. Yurchakevych. In the interwar period the leading figure was Fr. Chaikovsky, who had a high function in the central RSO and Kachkovsky Society authorities. He was a self-declared Russian, a member of the RZN (Russian National Union). He had no hesitation, publicly, about working together with Orthodox clergy, when at issue was the development of the pro-Russian idea.[167] A politician, social and religious activist, and sociopolitical journalist, he achieved fame through his feuilletons printed over the years in *Zemlia i Volia*. Particularly well-known were his articles written under the pseudonym "Dido Torochylo," in which he showed great journalistic talent, familiarity with reader psychology, and ease in acquiring the reader's sympathy. He had no equal in his own camp and very few in the Ukrainian camp could measure up to him. He himself, however, was not a Lemko – he came from the Boiko region. In 1933 by order of the tutelary authorities in Przemyśl he was transferred to the environs of Staryi Sambir.[168]

---

[163] CDIAL, f. 182, op. 1, case # 427.

[164] Ibid., case # 470, pp. 7, 8, 9; *Nauka* 1935, no. 1, p. 12.

[165] CDIAL, f. 182, op. 1, case # 349, *Hazetni povidomlennia, zvity i inshi materiialy pro [...] diialnist chytalni v seli Bortne, Horlytskoho povitu, 1930–1937*, p. 3.

[166] Ibid., pp. 27, 28.

[167] Ibid., case # 290, p. 8. On the list of Kachkovsky reading room members in Mszana he was preceded by the Orthodox priest Sheremeta.

[168] *Zemlia i Volia* 1933, no. 1, p. 4.

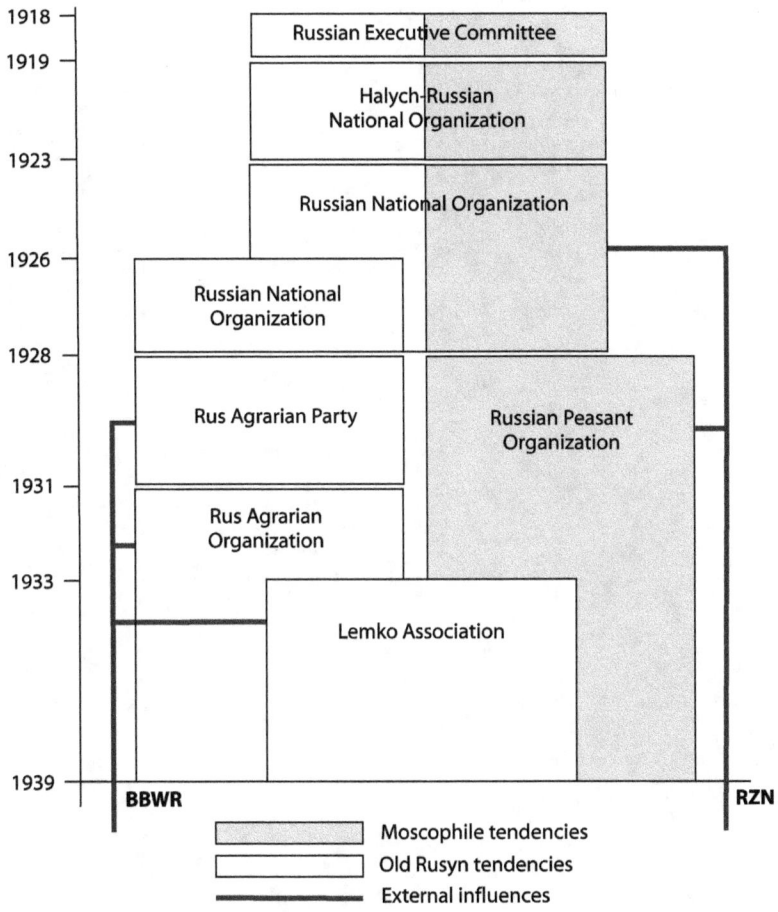

Figure 2. Diagram of Moscophile and Old Rusyn organizations

Author's study

Chapter III: The Ukrainian national movement

The period immediately following the war furthered the development of the Ukrainian movement in the Lemko region. The collapse of the ZUNR (Western Ukrainian National Republic) in June 1919 caused migrations of the Ukrainian intelligentsia, mainly teachers, from Eastern Galicia to the western part of the region, where Polish-Ukrainian relations were not as strained. School authorities were eager to hire Ukrainians in Lemko schools, fearful of political provocations above all from the Moscophile intelligentsia. In these more favorable circumstances, the western Lemko region acquired great numbers of Ukrainian teachers, who were able to regenerate the pedagogical organization which had existed there before 1914.

The ranks of the secular intelligence were reinforced by military men. In autumn of 1918 a group of soldiers and officers from Ukrainian infantry regiments stationed in Nowy Sącz and Zakopane, which had been disarmed by the Polish authorities in the early days of November settled in the Lemko region.[1] Furthermore, the postwar period was also characterized by an inflow of the younger generation of Greek Catholic clergymen, whose national consciousness had matured in confrontation with the Ukrainian struggle for nationhood. The secular and clergy intelligentsia shaped the substance of organizational work, took command of cultural, educational, and economic institutions, and represented the Ukrainian movement in the political life of the Polish nation.

1. The *Prosvita* Society and the Lemko Commission

The strongest Ukrainian cultural and educational organization in the Lemko region was the *Prosvita* Society. In the Galician era branches of this organization had already been established in Nowy Sącz (1902), Sanok (1903) and Jasło (1903). The outbreak of war in 1914 interrupted their statutory activities, but after the war the reading rooms independently revived their activities and in 1923 the prewar

---

[1]   See Y. Tarnovych, *Ilustrovana istoriia Lemkivshchyny*, Lviv 1936, p. 257. Tarnovych refers to the recollections of Mykola Filts, contained in his work *Z dorohy zi Zakopanoho do Lvova* (no date or place of publication).

number of reading rooms was corroborated by a list made at the recommendation of the Executive Board in Lviv – it mentioned 30 reading rooms in three branches. It is highly probable that the number of reading rooms was in fact higher, since other sources refer to seven branches in 1923. Besides those mentioned, there were branches in Krosno with six reading rooms, Brzozów – with three, Gorlice – with nine and Grybów – with two reading rooms.[2] Among the first to be revived were the reading rooms in Besko, Komańcza, Krempna, Odrzechowa, Ożenna and Wisłok Niżny. The number of members of each reading room varied from about one dozen to several dozens.

In the years 1918–1923 the Ukrainian movement had explicitly anti-Polish aspects, which remained in connection to the unregulated political status of Eastern Galicia. After the March 1923 decision of the Council of Ambassadors in the matter of Galicia, which went against the strivings of Ukrainian pro-independence circles, some activists went underground. Others took to the path of legal struggle, declaring their recognition of the Polish state. Another option was chosen by activists in cultural and educational institutions, who were faced with the task of maintaining and promoting Ukrainian national consciousness in Poland. This was the path taken by *Prosvita*, undertaking a campaign to rebuild its local structures.

As early as 1923, the Executive Board of *Prosvita* came forward with a plan for educational work in Volhynia, the Chełm Region, Pidlashia, the San River Region, and the Lemko region, but at that time focused its attention mainly on the Chełm Region and Volhynia. The work of the Executive Board then revolved around collecting books and sending them to the reading rooms there for the purpose of breaking through the so-called Sokal border.[3] They turned their attention to the issue of the Lemko region in October 1925, but specific preparatory work was undertaken in the spring of 1926.

Interest in the Lemko region followed from the Society's statutory program, which mandated educational activity in provincial areas, especially where the survival of Ukrainian consciousness demanded support from central hubs. Furthermore, the intelligentsia scattered about the Lemko region and the activists of the Executive Board in Lviv perceived the activities of Moscophiles and Old Rusyns, who found support in the Lemko region and there built their own institutions to the extent that they were losing influence in the southeastern voivodeships. Older members of *Prosvita* could still remember the prewar era, typified by the delayed (relative to the Moscophiles) activity of the Ukrainian movement, which allowed the rival Kachkovsky reading rooms to gain the sympathies of the Lemko population.

---

[2]   CDIAL, f. 348, op. 1, case # 6350, *Knyha rejestratsii filiialiv tovarystva i iikh chytalen z danymy pro zasnuvannia, zvity statutiv ta iikh likvidatsii, 1924–1932*, p. 2; ibid., case # 6351, *Adresna knyha chytalen tovarystva z danymy pro zakhody po vidnovlenniu iikh diialnosti, 1924–1938*, pp. 36, 38, 50, 70, 148.

[3]   CDIAL, f. 348, op. 1, case # 10, *Prohrama poshyrennia diialnosti tovarystva na Volyn, Lemkivshchynu, Nadsannia, Pidlashshia, Polissia i Kholmshchynu, 1926*, p. 1.

As a result, the political consciousness of many Lemkos took shape in an atmosphere hostile to the Ukrainian idea. The national activists were aware of the effects of neglecting the provinces, hence their pronounced interest, beginning in 1923, in those areas.

For their part local activists, acting independently of Lviv headquarters, took initiatives to revive the reading room movement. In abundant correspondence with the Board of *Prosvita* they drew its attention to school and economic issues. The correspondence kept in the Lviv archives permitted general directives to be determined involving the expansion of activities in the Lemko region. A tentative list of those willing to work in the area was established, above all teachers in popular schools and Greek Catholic clergy. In Gorlice County alone over 30 local activists were counted. They also included students and emigrants from Dnieper Ukraine, e.g. the Horkovych brothers, residents of Wysowa.[4]

On 27 April 1926 an educational survey was begun. The program paper was given by Mykhailo Halushchynsky – the chairman of *Prosvita*. He reminded the audience of the Commission on Lemko Matters which had been active before the war, created under the auspices of the Executive Board, and whose activities had been cut short by the war. Addressing the problem of peripheral ethnic areas, he said: "In our situation there is no house on the side, there is only the entirety of the organism and that entirety demands our heightened and focused attention."[5] Halushchynsky proposed a two-stage timeline for the campaign. The first stage would consist of developing the cooperative movement, the Village Society (*Silskyi Hospodar*) circles, fire brigades, and, later, the *Prosvita* reading rooms and *Ridna Shkola* circles. He correctly observed that Lemkos who had been drawn into the Moscophile and Old Rusyn movement felt antipathy toward the Ukrainian movement, so it was necessary, in his view, first to use the trade cooperatives accepted by Lemko society. Obviously the *Prosvita* reading rooms would continue to engage in their activities, and the founding of new institutions entered the scope of the normal rhythm of *Prosvita* Society activity. Halushchynsky judged the most important task at hand to be registration of all pro-Ukrainian intelligentsia currents in the Lemko region.[6]

Halushchynsky proposed to divide the area covered by the campaign into regions containing partially Lemko counties: 1) Jasło, Krosno, Lesko and Sanok, 2) Gorlice,

---

[4] Teachers and school principals: S. Batiuk (Wysowa), M. Gyzha (Wysowa), O. Hryvna (Gładyszów), D. Lytvyn (Rychwałd), O. Mulokevych (Pętna), H. Pylypchak (Wołowiec), H. Sembrat (Regetów), K. Tkhir (Nieznajowa), V. Zarivny (Uście Ruskie), H. Zhydiak (Łosie); teachers without administrative functions: S. Tsebushnyk (Leszczyny), S. Tsymbalisty (Łosie), M. Hladyk (Uście Ruskie), Ts. Kneiova (Bednarka), Kostiuk (Kunkowa), Y. Muzyka (Konieczna), Ms. Poloshynovych (Krzywa), I. Seifer (Zdynia); Greek Catholic priests: V. Ardan (Zdynia), A. Bardakhivsky (Wołowiec), O. Lalovych (Nowica), O. Mentsinsky (Małastów), O. Steranka (Gładyszów), I. Tytar (Hańczowa), T. Zeleny (Doliny). See CDIAL, f. 348, op. 1, case # 5, *Administratyvna karta Lemkivshchyny ta informatsii i vidomosti pro ekonomichni i suspilni vidnosyny, ustanovy, toshcho, 1913–1933*, p. 40.

[5] Ibid., case # 10, pp. 3–4.

[6] Ibid., p. 7.

Grybów, Nowy Sącz, and Nowy Targ, and the city of Kraków would be allotted its own branch. He proposed creating centers in cities and towns with favorable transportation connections in which Ukrainian lawyers and doctors could settle.

With regard to the western Lemko region, Halushchynsky spoke of Nowy Sącz as the central hub of the Ukrainian movement, with its material base: a dormitory for boys (*Bursa*), an apartment for the *Prosvita* branch, and a church. He proposed placing a "responsible" individual in Nowy Sącz, who would take on the duties of cooperative and educational instructor. He also referred to Muszyna as the center of activity, arguing in favor of this proposal by the existence of Society institutions there *Silskyi Hospodar* and *Vzaimna Pomich* (Mutual Aid). He pronounced Krynica to be the most appropriate place in the greater Nowy Sącz area, but warned that it was the "headquarters of the Moscophiles." He anticipated founding a center in Gorlice as well, where there was a school dormitory. The reinforcement of centers in Gorlice and Nowy Sącz was to be activated by Grybów as well.[7]

In the plan announced by Halushchynsky the city of Kraków, where *Prosvita* had branch headquarters, was treated as a separate issue. Attention was focused on Kraków in proportion to the rising numbers of Ukrainian young persons studying at Kraków institutions of higher learning. Halushchynsky even remarked that Kraków should become the headquarters of the Ukrainian movement for the Kraków province, and Lviv – headquarters for the entire Polish Republic.[8]

On 24 May 1926 the board of the *Prosvita* branch met in Nowy Sącz. Working on the basis of Halushchynsky's plan, they passed a resolution to create a post for educational instructor at the Nowy Sącz branch, with the task of directing the farming education in the counties of Grybów and Nowy Sącz. Money to pay the instructor's salary would come from self-taxation of the intelligentsia in said counties. The rate of monthly payments was fixed at the limit of 1–5 zloty, but there were occasionally higher payments, e.g. R. Kyshakevych of Gorlice put himself in for 10 zloty.[9] They also decided to send a letter to Metropolitan Sheptytsky asking for his support for the plan. The letter, whose final version was worked out in Lviv, signed by Halushchynsky and *Prosvita* Executive Board secretary Vasyl Mudry, was sent in June.

In reply to the Nowy Sącz branch's appeal, many positive declarations were addressed to *Prosvita* in Lviv in June and July. Refusals to apply self-taxation were rare and usually due to material hardship. More often, however, there were remarks made about candidates for the post of instructor. Taxpayers underscored the necessity of choosing the most suitable individual, so that their money "wouldn't get wasted," since the sum of the payments for social aims amounted for many to 15% of their income.[10]

---

[7]   Ibid., p. 9.
[8]   Ibid., p. 11.
[9]   Ibid., case # 11, pp. 2, 4, 9, 17, 33, 34.
[10] Ibid., p. 36.

A broader plan of action was outlined by the branch in Sanok, under the leadership of Fr. Omelan Konstantynovych, Mykhailo Tsar and Ivan Holeiko. Acting in agreement with the Sanok branch of the *Silskyi Hospodar* Society, on 5 August 1926 they sent a separate letter to Metropolitan Andrei Sheptytsky with a request for "help for the Lemko region, a land almost forgotten, threatened with the loss of national values."[11] The letter simultaneously contained a list of specific enterprises and proposed: 1) that the city of Sanok be recognized as the headquarters of the Lemko Region's development; 2) participation in the construction of premises in Sanok for the headquarters of Ukrainian institutions, 3) training of professionals in various fields for the needs of educational and economic work in the Lemko region, 4) the establishment of a farming school, 5) the establishment of reading rooms and trade cooperatives in every village. This letter was sent in the hopes of obtaining sizeable financial aid.

The spring and summer of 1926 were a time of discussion about the shape and methods of development of the Ukrainian national movement in the Lemko region. The general premises stated by Halushchynsky on 27 April and the local decisions taken by the Nowy Sącz and Sanok branches, prepared the foundations for a conference on Lemko regional issues specially organized by the *Prosvita* Executive Board.

The conference took place on 29 September 1926 in Lviv. 16 delegates representing the *Prosvita* Executive Board took part, both branches, Sanok and Nowy Sącz, as well as the pan-Ukrainian cultural and educational, economic, and financial institutions: *Tsentrobank* – the Central Co-operative Bank, the *Dnister* Insurance Company, *Ridna Shkola*, *Silskyi Hospodar*, and *Soiuz Ukrainok* (the League of Ukrainian Women).[12] Preparations for the conference had started at the beginning of September. The boards of both branches, after consultations with local activists, sent a list of proposed delegates to Lviv – six persons from each branch. In the end the branch delegations were reduced to three people. The Nowy Sącz branch was represented by Mykola Chekh (Gorlice), Oleksandr Dzerovych (Nowy Sącz) and Fr. Ivan Kachmar (Złockie), the Sanok branch by Fr. Mykola Holovach (Besko), Volodymyr Mosora (Sanok) and Ostap Zhuk (Bukowsko).[13] Pan-Ukrainian Lviv institutions were represented by Ivan Bryk (*Prosvita*), Volodymyr Bachynsky (*Dnister*), Lev Yasinchuk (*Ridna Shkola*), Kost Levytsky (*Tsentrobank*), Ostap Lutsky and Yuliian Pavlykovsky (*Revizyinyi Soiuz Ukrainskykh Kooperatyv* – RSUK), Mykola Tvorydlo (*Silskyi Hospodar*) and Iryna Pavlykovska, Mariia Strutynska and Olena Sheparovycheva (*Soiuz Ukrainok*). O. Lutsky was appointed chairman of the conference, and M. Brylynsky and P. Poluga as secretaries.[14]

---

[11]   CDIAL, f. 348, op. 1, case # 5, p. 25.
[12]   Ibid., case # 12, *Obizhnyk, protokoly, zaproshennia ta inshi dokumenty pro stvorennia tak zvanoho "Komitetu pratsi na zakhidnykh Zemlach"*, 1926, pp. 2, 3, 4, 7, 9.
[13]   Ibid., *Protokol konferentsii w spravi Lemkivshchyny 29 veresnia 1926 r.*, p. 55.
[14]   Ibid.

The conference was opened by the representative of the *Prosvita* Executive Board and chairman of the *Silskyi Hospodar* Society, Mykola Tvorydlo. He stressed the fact that the initiative of convoking the conference had come from social activists living in the Lemko region. Leading into the discussion was a broad program paper delivered by Sanok branch representative Ostap Zhuk. After a multifaceted description of the Lemko region, Zhuk presented a plan for economic and cultural-educational development of the Lemko region, based on a few basic guiding points. First of all he proposed creating an organizational center for all of the Lemko region in Sanok, which would fulfill the role of bridging the gap between the central boards of Ukrainian institutions in Lviv and their local branches. The choice of Sanok was supported by its proximity to Lviv and good transport connections. Further, the newly created center could engage in training instructors in the field of farming culture and education – "nation builders," "leaders of enlightenment," capable of conducting specialized courses to prepare others to perform in various professions. Zhuk calculated that the Lemko region and the ethnic Ukrainian areas belonging to it would need over 1300 instructors, who assuming they completed four courses yearly would be able to meet the needs of every village for a period of 11 years. In the future, the courses were to be transformed into popular schools or universities.[15]

Zhuk named the creation of farming schools for pupils from the Lemko region as a priority issue. He argued for this project in terms of the new economic situation in the region, which differed from the prewar situation due to the limits placed after 1918 on worker emigration to North America and Western Europe. The school was to give rise to improved levels of agricultural production through the development of specializations such as: raising livestock, dairying, orcharding, apiculture, raising poultry and fish, forestry and small farming industry.[16]

Next – as Halushchynsky had done – Zhuk discussed the tasks of the popular reading rooms. Illiteracy, common in the countryside, was to be overcome by itinerant teachers. The author closed his speech with a statement of the necessity for close cooperation between the Sanok center and the following organizations: *Tsentrobank*, *Tsentrosoiuz*, the central office for agro-industrial cooperatives for general purchasing and supply; *Maslosoiuz* (the central office for dairy cooperatives), *Narodna Torhovla* (the urban central office for consumer cooperatives), *Ridna Shkola*, RSUK (the Auditing Union of Ukrainian Cooperatives) and *Silskyi Hospodar* (Farmers' Society). With the help of these institutions the Lemko region would receive long-term investment credits, agronomist-instructors, warehouses of goods, etc.[17]

---

[15]   Ibid., *Referat O. Zhuka pro Lemkivshchynu (1926)*, p. 18. According to the statistics provided by Zhuk, up to 440 villages (250 in the Lemko region, 150 in Lesko County, 40 in the Strzyżów enclave) had to be divided between three instructors.

[16]   CDIAL, f. 348, op. 1, case # 5, p. 19.

[17]   In 1926 there were warehouses only in Besko, Lesko, Rzepedź, Sanok and Ustrzyki Dolne, i.e. in the eastern area of the Lemko region.

The representatives of said institutions who took part in the discussion signed a declaration offering manifold help to the Lemko region. Yuliian Pavlykovsky on behalf of the RSUK declared a 1% commission and presented a motion to create a Fund for the Defense of the Western Ukrainian Territories.[18] Volodymyr Bachynsky on behalf of *Dnister* promised aid in the form of organizing cooperative courses, and Lev Yasinchuk – help in developing education. Mykola Tvorydlo made an important comment, stating that the Lviv headquarters would be unable to complete its tasks without a coordinating organ, and put forth a petition to create a Lemko Committee under the auspices of the *Prosvita* Society which would include representatives of the central Ukrainian institutions in Lviv.[19]

It is worth noting the speech made by Oleksandr Dzerovych, a doctor from Nowy Sącz. He called the conference participants' attention to the psychological underpinnings of cultural and educational work among Lemkos. He stressed their pragmatism in everyday life. He recognized the satisfaction of daily needs as the basis for social work on national soil. The first matter of business, in his view, should be giving Lemkos e.g. dairying cooperatives. Dzerovych said: "The Lemko must first see that something is there [...] and only then will he join in organizational work [...]. Without initial credit, it is impossible to get started."[20] He spoke against the centralization of all organizational matters in Sanok. He stated that some of the work should be done by specially created organs in cities belonging to the western Lemko region, i.e. in Nowy Sącz, Grybów, and Muszyna, crammed between Lemko villages.[21]

At the end of the conference the master of ceremonies put the petitions of Pavlykovsky and Tvorydlo to a vote. The conference participants unanimously voted to create the Lemko Committee under the broad title of Committee for the Defense of the Western Territories, composed of representatives of nine Ukrainian cultural and educational, economic and financial institutions.[22] A Fund for the Defense of the Western Ukrainian Territories was also created.[23]

The Lviv conference resulted in a revival of both branches. On 11 November RSUK named Severyn Kozak instructor for the development of the cooperative movement.[24] I. Havranek, who was responsible for the organization of reading rooms and cooperatives, was assigned to the Nowy Sącz branch.[25] In the same month the

---

[18] CDIAL, f. 348, op. 1, case # 11, p. 56.

[19] Ibid., p. 55.

[20] Ibid., p. 56.

[21] Ibid.

[22] The members of the Committee, approved on 26 November 1926, were: V. Bachynsky (*Dnister*), S. Kozak (RSUK), Fr. L. Kunytsky (*Ridna Shkola*), M. Lazorko (*Narodna Torhovla*), K. Levytsky (*Tsentrobank*), V. Medvetsky (*Tsentrosoiuz*), M. Strutynska (*Soiuz Ukrainok*), M. Tvorydlo (*Silskyi Hospodar*) and a representative of *Maslosoiuz*.

[23] CDIAL, f. 348, op. 1, case # 11, p. 56.

[24] Ibid., p. 64.

[25] Ibid., case # 5, p. 46; *Zemlia i Volia* 1930, no. 28, p. 1.

Ukrainian intelligentsia made an attempt to break the Old Rusyn and Moscophile domination in Krynica, with the intention of creating a County Cooperative Union there. To that end, Y. Kachmarchyk, a lawyer in Muszyna who a few years earlier had been active in the Moscophile and Czechophile movements, worked together with Fr. Kachmar, V. Popadiuk of Słotwiny and a delegate from Lviv whose surname could not be determined.[26] A similar campaign intended to create a cooperative union was launched in Smerekowiec on 30 November 1926. In the presence of the local intelligentsia, approximately 100 residents of the surrounding countryside, and Lviv delegate Mykola Cherkavsky, Fr. Volodymyr Ardan put forward a petition to create an institution which would unite the cooperatives under the name Ukrainian Lemko Association in Gorlice County.[27]

The Sanok branch took concrete action, organizing a two-month cooperative-education course in October and November. The program included the theory and history of cooperatives, bookkeeping and calculating taxes, product research, and Ukrainian language and geography, and even ethics.[28]

In the spring of 1927 the Committee for the Construction of the Ukrainian People's Home was created in Sanok. The committee developed the charter for an institution called the Lemko Association Ukrainian People's Home, approved at the district level in November of that year. Fr. Omelan Konstantynovych chaired the organization's first board. The sphere of the Association's activities was designated as the counties of Brzozów, Krosno, Lesko and Sanok.[29] The site for the building's construction was bought in June 1928. The building was planned to house an industrial school with a dormitory and workshops, a theatrical concert hall, and office spaces for Ukrainian educational and economic associations.[30] A loan in the amount of $1,000 was taken out for the purchase of the site and the building's construction, and an appeal was made to the Ukrainian-Lemko emigre community for financial support. Among those who visited America for this purpose in late 1926 and early 1927 was Volodymyr Konstantynovych (a Sanok lawyer), who directed the committee for national school affairs. He popularized the idea of the Sanok Lemko Association in America, collecting financial resources to meet the needs of the construction committee.[31]

A practical result of the September conference was an increase in the number of *Prosvita* reading rooms established. Where up to 1924 eight reading rooms had

[26] CDIAL, f. 348, op. 1, case # 5, p. 43.

[27] AAN, MWRiOP, ref. # 928, p. 319.

[28] CDIAL, f. 348, op. 1, case # 11, p. 65.

[29] *Svoboda*, 26 September 1928, p. 2.

[30] S. Vanchytsky, "Lemkivshchyna – Samotsvit Ukrainy. Ohlad ukrainskoho suspilnoho zhyttia na Lemkivshchyni 1918–1944," *Lemkivskyi Kalendar na Bozhyi 1969 rik* Toronto-Passaic, NJ, p. 55.

[31] *Svoboda*, 26 January 1928, p. 2.

been revived, and in 1925 – five,[32] in 1926 there were 11,[33] in 1927 – 12,[34] and in 1929 – 13 reading rooms.[35] The years 1930–1931 saw a dramatic fall in the number of such institutions which opened, a fact no doubt linked to the general crisis of the Ukrainian movement in the pacification period.[36] The revival took place in 1932,[37] but beginning the following year, due to the state authorities' favoritism toward the Old Rusyns, the number of reading rooms established began to fall.[38] The era of administrative restriction of *Prosvita*'s development in the Lemko region began at that point. Still, some reading rooms withered away without interference from state actors, and it happened – as in the case of the Kachkovsky reading rooms – that repeat openings were organized, e.g. in Tyrawa Wołoska (1928 and 1929), Wisłok Wielki (1927 and 1931), Dudyńce (1926 and 1932), and Komańcza (1932 and 1936).[39] The pattern of the rise of *Prosvita* reading rooms in the interwar period is illustrated in Figure 3.

The crisis of the years 1930–1931, manifested in a sudden decrease in the number of *Prosvita* reading rooms founded, was overcome with relative ease. The Society's Executive Board, in concert with local activists, engaged in another initiative to activate the social and cultural life of the Lemko region. Tentative preparations involving the collection of reports on the state of Ukrainian national consciousness made in various regions by inspectors since 1932[40] led to the convocation of another all-Lemko conference, whose task was to develop and approve programmatic directives for educational work among Lemkos.

---

[32] Dąbrówka Ruska, Gładyszów, Milik, Nowy Sącz, Wujskie.

[33] Czerteż, Dudyńce, Leszczowate, Łosie (Nowy Sącz County), Pielnia, Piwniczna, Rudenka, Sieniawa, Wierchomla Wielka, Zagórz, Złockie.

[34] Hańczowa, Jastrzebik, Nowa Wieś, Pętna, Polany (Grybów County), Roztoka Wielka, Szczawnik, Turzańsk, Uhryń, Wisłok Niżny, Wisłok Wyżny, Wysowa.

[35] All reading rooms in the area of the Sanok branch. See CDIAL, f. 348, op. 1, case # 6350, 6351.

[36] Seven reading rooms in all were established in the Sanok branch's jurisdiction.

[37] In 1932 alone, 15 reading rooms were established in Daljowa, Dudyńce, Grab, Hłomcza, Karlików, Komańcza, Krempna, Łodzina, Międzybrodzie, Rzepedź, Stróże Wielkie, Tokarnia, Wisłoczek, Wola Sękowa, Zahutyń.

[38] In 1933, 10 reading rooms were established: Barwinek, Czeremcha, Jabłonica Ruska, Końskie, Kostarowce, Surowica, Szklary, Świerzowa Ruska, Wisłok Niżny, Zawadka Rymanowska (Barwinek, Kostarowce and Wisłok re-opening); in 1934 – four: Hyrowa, Maciejowa, Szlachtowa, Wola Niżna. In 1935, in Hroszówka, in 1936 – four: Komańcza, Puławy, Siemuszowa and Wysoczany, in 1937 in Radoszyce, in 1938 in Oparówka and Pawłokoma.

[39] CDIAL, f. 344, op. 1t, case # 259, *Zvit, protokol, lystuvannia ta inshi dokumenty pro diialnist povitovoho komitetu w Sianoku*, 1936, k. 13; CDIAL, f. 348, op. 1, case # 6350, 6351.

[40] A report on the state of Ukrainian national consciousness in the area of the Nowy Sącz branch prepared by inspector Fr. I. Kachmar on 10 October 1932 has been preserved. Kachmar names a series of areas in Nowy Sącz County, stating that the Ukrainian movement was better developed there throughout the branch's orbit. In Gorlice County he cited as important centers Gładyszów, Małastów, Pętna and Ropica Ruska, while in Grybów County he identified Berest, Brunary Niżne and Polany. See ibid., case # 5. p. 50.

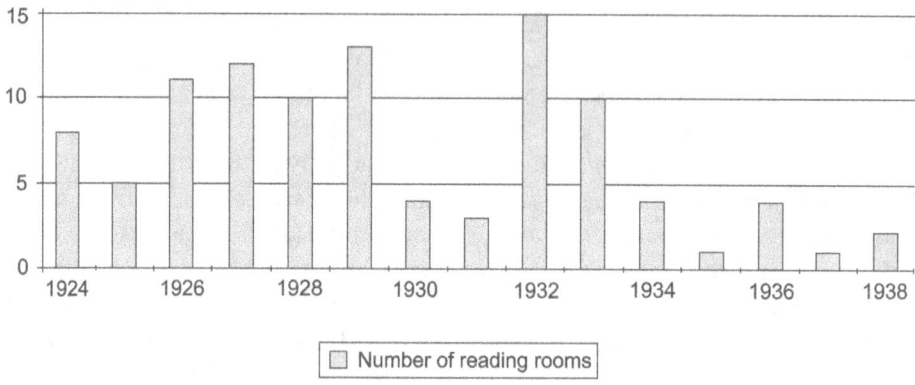

Figure 3. The number of *Prosvita* reading rooms established in the years 1924–1938

Source: CDIAL, f. 348, op. 1, various page numbers.

The conference took place on 13 December 1932 at the *Prosvita* branch in Lviv. Ostap Zhuk delivered the program paper. The speech contained harsh criticisms directed at the institution created at the 1926 conference, i.e. the Committee for the Defense of the Western Territories and the Fund for the Defense of the Western Territories. The speaker presented the state of religious attitudes: for each church there were 670 parishioners. Schooling was shown in a less favorable light: 820 students per school. Trade cooperatives and reading rooms, in spite of their preferential treatment in the resolutions of the previous conference, found themselves in the worst situation of all. There were 7,000 individuals per trade cooperative, and in reading rooms – 8,500.[41] Illiteracy tabled at an average of 50%, and in some mountain regions reached up to 100%.[42]

The author of the paper put forward a plan for educational work in the Lemko region. He drew the audience's attention to the necessity of maintaining two educational instructors through the *Prosvita* branch, one of whom would complete office tasks, while the other would conduct inspections in the area. Branch boards were to be looked after with particular care, which would consist in monthly financial support from the Executive Board of the *Prosvita* Society.[43]

It is striking how the Lemko region – similarly as in 1926 – was treated as part of the more broadly understood "Western territories." At the conference, Lemko problems were discussed in close connection with the Pogórze region (north-east of the Lemko region), inhabited partly by a Ukrainian population, but not a Lemko one.

---

[41]   Ibid., case # 5, p. 46.

[42]   Ibid.

[43]   Ibid., p. 48. 150 zloty were allotted monthly for the Sanok branch and 50 zloty for the Nowy Sącz branch.

In addition to the expansion of branches in Nowy Sącz and Sanok, it was resolved to establish branches in Jarosław, Leżajsk, and Bircza.[44]

The resolutions passed at the conference of 13 December 1932 differed from the conference of 1926 in that, along with the educational and economic issues covered, they allotted broader political meaning to the Lemko question, officially delegating it to the Ukrainian Parliamentary Representation.[45] Perceiving the enormous role of the church in Lemko life, a request was made to the Greek Catholic ordinariate in Przemyśl that it relay appropriate suggestions for pastoral work to the clergy there. Finally, it was resolved to create a special publication for the Lemko region and run a program of material aid for candidates from that region in need of education in the high schools of Lviv or Przemyśl. An interesting statement was made to the effect that the ties between the Lemko region (or, more broadly, the "Western territories") and Lviv should be more active than they had theretofore been, even at the cost of letting Lviv's ties to the Eastern territories go unattended.[46]

As a result of the conference of 13 December, the activities of the Committee for the Defense of the Western Territories, adjacent to which the Lemko Commission had been created became more energetic. The inclusion of the modifier "Lemko" in the name of the institution had doubtless been decided by its common use in the Old Rusyn press, disseminated in the Kachkovky reading rooms. An institution with the word "Lemko" in its name must have been considerably stronger power of persuasion in the Lemko consciousness than the earlier name approved in 1926.

The chief purpose, broadly understood, of the Lemko Commission, was "to defend the Lemko region from denationalization and lead the Lemkos toward full [Ukrainian] national consciousness."[47] Its plan of action embraced economic, cultural and school issues. Personnel issues were dealt with in detail, focusing above all on the intelligentsia. Markian Dzerovych, a doctor and well-known activist in Catholic Action in Lviv, was chosen as chairman of the Commission. The Commission also included Ivan Bryk, Ivan Gyzha and Lubomyr Makarushka[48].

In December 1932 a workers' meeting on the issue of educating Lemko youth was organized, and in 1933 at a junior high school in Przemyśl fourteen poor but gifted students from the Lemko region were receiving instruction at *Prosvita*'s expense. A considerably greater number of young Lemkos were educated – also at *Prosvita*'s expense – by craftsmen in several cities, mainly in Przemyśl and Lviv.[49] In 1933 the Commission remained in close contact with the twenty "private agents,"

---

[44] Ibid.

[45] Ibid., p. 49.

[46] Ibid.

[47] Y. Tarnovych, *20 rokiv nevoli. Lemkivshchyna pid polskym iarmom*, Krakiv 1940, p. 136.

[48] CDIAL, f. 326 t.ch., op. 1, case # 2, *Dohovir Lemkivskoi Komisii pry Holovnii Upravi Tov. Prosvita u Lvovi z red. Tarnovychem Yuliianom pro peredachu iomu prava na vedennia redaktsii i administratsii vydavnytstva dvokhtyzhnevyka "Nash Lemko"*, p. 1.

[49] Y. Tarnovych, *20 rokiv nevoli*, p. 137.

mostly Greek Catholic clergy, who provided information on the state of education in the Lemko region.[50]

Funds for the needs of the Commission were allocated from the Society's budget and a raffle was organized, the proceeds from which reached approximately 1,000 zloty in 1933. This money was used mostly on school stipends. In order to procure savings, the Commission entered into an agreement with schools whose directors were inclined to give a discount on tuition and dormitory fees. So-called open places, free of charge, diligently sought out and offered to young Lemkos by M. Dzerovych and Y. Tarnovych, were widely used. Furthermore, the Commission obtained help from private individuals interested in the development of education in the Lemko region. The Commission presumed that those young Lemkos educated outside of their native regions would return to their permanent places of residence.

Beginning in January 1933, the Lemko Commission, together with the Executive Board of *Prosvita*, conducted a campaign called "Book to the West," appealing to the Ukrainian population to send books to be distributed throughout the Lemko region. In answer to the appeal, packages with books and brochures in Ukrainian arrived at *Prosvita*'s address in Lviv from institutions and private individuals. These books, as well as brochures, calendars and other publications, were sent out through the agency of the local intelligentsia to local *Prosvita* reading rooms, and even to Kachkovsky reading rooms, their rival for influence among Lemkos located in the area penetrated by Moscophiles. Ivan Bryk chairman of the *Prosvita* Executive Board, supervised to ensure the campaign followed its proper course.[51]

In 1933 preparations for launching a press organ for Lemkos continued. Two young *Prosvita* activists, Petro Smerekanych and Yuliian Tarnovych – both from the Lemko region – dealt with the issue, together with Lviv publisher Ivan Tyktor. At Tarnovych's directive, the publication was initially to be called *Ukrainian Lemko*, but the Lviv voivodeship authorities reacted to that title with reservations, and accepted a second version: *Nash Lemko* (Our Lemko).[52] The publication was allotted legal status as an informative business biweekly. Its pronounced Ukrainian character caused frequent censoring of individual articles and sometimes whole issues. The first issue was confiscated in entirety. In 1934 *Nash Lemko* was subject to 19 instances of state censorship confiscations.[53]

The first chief editor of *Nash Lemko* was P. Smerekanych, born in Świerzowa Ruska. In the initial period of its existence, the magazine's editors were also Y. Tar-

---

[50]   CDIAL, f. 344 t., op. 1 t., case # 288, Spysok kerivnoho skladu UNDO na Lemkivshchyni z perelikom adres, pp. 1, 2. In the list, the following priests are given particular mention: Kachmar, Pleshkevych, Zlupko, Kornova, Stupak; as well as four secular activists: V. Blavatsky (Sanok), M. Cheliak (Zawadka Rymanowska), L. Kobani (Łosie), A. Varkhol (Barwinek).

[51]   AP K, UWKr, ref. # 279. p. 161; CDIAL, f. 348, op. 1, case # 2078, p. 5.

[52]   Y. Tarnovych *20 rokiv nevoli*, p. 331.

[53]   DALO, f. 1, op. 51, case # 1500, *Donesennie Lvovskogo gorodskogo starostva o konfiskatsii ukrainskykh zhurnaliv "Nash Lemko"*, passim.

novych and M. Dudra. In 1935 Smerekanych, having received a stipend from the Ukrainian Scholarly Institute in Berlin, left to study in Germany, and editorial duties were taken over by Tarnovych.[54] Formal transfer of the editorship of *Nash Lemko* to Tarnovych took place in November 1936. The Commission reserved the right to decide the content of every article.[55] The magazine was maintained partly with prepayments and voluntary contributions from private individuals. The *Dilo* publishing company provided significant financial help, often offering extensions of payment deadlines when other obligations necessitated such a request. The magazine attained considerable popularity in the region, working together with many freelance correspondents, including farmers as well, such as Mykhailo Khovanets (Doliny near Szymbark), Prokii Ksenych (Konieczna) and Mykhailo Semchyshak (Andrzejówka).[56]

The appearance of *Nash Lemko* inspired the Old Rusyns to found a magazine similar in nature. The enterprise was endorsed by the state authorities, who had an interest in the existence of a magazine to balance out the development of the Ukrainian movement among Lemkos. After the release of the fourth issue of *Nash Lemko*, the Lemko Association (*Lemko Soiuz*) came out with the first issue of its press organ, called simply *Lemko*, in Krynica.

The Commission launched a series of publications entitled "the Lemko Region Library." Up to the end of 1939 over 20 titles were published, including the works of Ivan Bugera, Vsevolod Yaroslavych, Frants Kokovsky, Yuliian Tarnovych, and others. At the same time, the number of Ukrainian publications sent to the Lemko region increased. In addition to *Nash Lemko*, some which achieved popularity included *Narodna Sprava*, *Narodna Trybuna*, *Novyi Chas*, *Pravda*, and *Ukrainskyi Beskyd*. Literature for children was not neglected either: it included *Svit Dytyny*, *Dzvinochok*, and others. These publications arrived in the Lemko region in combined numbers of about 100 copies per municipality.[57]

In spring of 1934 the interest of the Commission grew focused on centrally located areas in the West of the region. The revival of the Ukrainian movement was especially relevant in the environs of Dukla, Gorlice and Rymanów. In May, Committees for the Defense of National Rights and Educational Development formed in Rymanów and Wróblik Królewski, extending their activity to the surrounding localities. The main activists in said Committees were Stepan Varkholiak, a farmer

---

[54] *Holos Lemkivshchyny* 1965, no. 2, p. 3. Smerekanych states that *Nash Lemko* was a financial burden for Tyktor, who aimed to set it apart with a different publisher. He entrusted Tarnovych with this task, which led to the dismissal of Smerekanych in the spring of 1935. See P. Smerekanych, "Do 60-littia «Nashoho Lemka»," *Nashe Slovo* 1994, no. 34, p. 4.

[55] CDIAL, f. 326, op. 1, case # 2, p. 1.

[56] Ibid., case # 6, *Lysty ukrainskykh orhanizatsii ta pryvatnykh osib pro pomishchennia stattei i oholoshen, nadsylannia zhurnalu peredplatnykam, obmin vydanniamy, vidhuky chytachiv na statti ta in. 1934–1938*, pp. 84, 85, 86, 87, 91.

[57] AP K, UWKr, ref. # 352, p.n.n.

from Wróblik Królewski, and Kostiantyn Teply, a doctor residing in Rymanów.[58] These committees worked by means of self-taxation by Greek Catholic clergy from the Rymanów decanate and the affluent intelligentsia. Their main purpose was to create a strong Ukrainian base of operations for the central Lemko region – on a par with the headquarters in Nowy Sącz and Sanok. The funding from those sources proved insufficient, however, and at the meeting in Rymanów on 10 May 1934, at the request of S. Varkholiak, it was officially resolved to turn to the emigrant community in North America for financial aid.[59]

Until the mid-1930s aid reached emigrants exclusively through private channels. If funds were transferred for social goals, it was usually aid for a town or city, where the emigrants themselves had been born. In the USA and Canada there were various local Aid Committees. That situation changed with the moment of Myhhaiło Dudra's arrival in New York as special emissary of the Lemko Commission.[60]

In January 1934 in Ukrainian Lemko circles in New York the idea of creating a central aid committee for the Lemko Region took shape. As a result of an agreement between the New York committee and Dudra, a general congress of Lemkos was convoked in New York on 4 August 1935. At the congress the OOL (*Orhanizatsiia Oborony Lemkivshchyny*) [The Organization for the Defense of Lemkivshchyna] was created, with the task of supporting the Ukrainian movement in the Lemko region.[61] A new organization uniting Lemkos from the USA published a proclamation in which it called for contributions on behalf of the "Old Country": "Let us all stand to battle the enemy, and we shall surely be victorious. Let us give in this battle what we are able to give: material aid, […], a book, newspapers – an educational weapon to hand. Let us gather funds for the development of our press, for aid to poor students, for economic institutions […]."[62] In order to organize financial aid, the Fund for the Defense of the Lemko Region was established.[63]

Lemko emigrants joined in the new initiative with great energy. At the first USA Lemko Congress, convoked by the OOL on 6 June 1936 in Philadelphia, the charter of an organization whose full name was the Organization for the Defense of Lemko Western Ukraine (OOLZU, *Orhanizatsiia Oborony Lemkivshchyny Zakhidnoi Ukrainy*) was approved. Vasyl Levchyk was named chairman. Dudra also became a member of the Executive Board, taking over the function of chief organizer.[64] His duties included field work in areas where Lemkos lived, in big cities of the Eastern shore and the environs. He simultaneously was confirmed to continue in his post as

---

58   ULM, *Arkhiv Komitetu Dopomohy Lemkivshchyni, 1933–1936*, Stamford. Conn.–Scranton, Pa., p.n.n.
59   Ibid.
60   Y. Padokh, "Emihratsiia," in: *Lemkivshchyna. Zemlia–Liudy–Istoriia–Kultura*, vol. 2, New York–Paryż–Sydney–Toronto 1988, p. 473.
61   *Svoboda* 1935, no. 257, p. 3.
62   Quoted from ibid.
63   Ibid., 1937, no. 284, p. 3.
64   Ibid., 1936, no. 133, p. 1.

official emissary of the Lemko Commission. Three months later, on 10–11 September, a congress of Lemkos of North America met in Glen Spey, NY, at which a resolution to broaden the sphere of activity to include Canada was approved.[65]

The emigrant community's aid to the Lemko region flowed in via two streams: one to the Commission's budget and another directly to the communities involved. In the first case the Commission used funds obtained to pay for annual subscriptions to Ukrainian periodicals for *Prosvita* reading rooms in the Lemko region, in the second – aid reached youth studying in secondary school and was used to finance community construction enterprises such as building reading room locations.[66] The OOLZU's aid reached beyond simply *Prosvita* and the Lemko Commission. It also reached other Ukrainian institutions which were active in the sphere of the Lemko region, such as *Silskyi Hospodar* and *Ridna Shkola*.

The Lemko Commission's activity in the area depended on the local intelligentsia, which consisted mainly of clergy and teachers. The Greek Catholic Church possessed a dense network of parishes there and, in connection with it, enormous opportunities to influence the shape of the Lemko sociocultural and economic life through supporting appropriate initiatives. The Commission's establishment of closer relations with the clergy was merely the institutionalization of the previously existing state of affairs – since the late 19th century the priests had been spreading modern Ukrainian national consciousness among peasants.

Tough battles were waged against Moscophilism and Old Rusyns. This current of activity became especially strong after 1933, i.e. after the emergence of the Lemko Association and the introduction of Trokhanovsky's primer into schools. The Commission led a campaign to gather signatures to petitions to the MWRiOP in the matter of removing the primer intended for the teaching of the Lemko dialect. In Gorlice County the campaign was directed by Asafat Hryvna of Pętna, working together with Stepan Batiuk of Wysowa and Fr. Roman Horchytsky of Leszczyny.[67]

The effects of the Commission's activities were perceived by the Old Rusyns, who in their organ *Holos Naroda* stressed the theme of domination by "Ukrainian separatists." One of the correspondents of that weekly wrote: "Throughout our Russian villages, cooperatives are everywhere in the hands of Ukrainian agitators. In brief, another farmer is reaping the fruits in our field."[68]

In 1935 the administrative authorities ordered the dissolution of the Lemko Commission, and the Board of *Prosvita* was advised to abandon its interests in the Lemko region. The Commission, however, continued to exist, under the name "Commission for the Western Territories."

[65] Y. Padokh, op.cit., p. 473.
[66] ULM, *Arkhiv Miuzeiu, korespondentsiia*, 1936–1940, p.n.n.
[67] AP K, UWKr, ref. # 282, *Sprawozdania sytuacyjne miesięczne Wojewody Krakowskiego, I–XII, 1934*, p. 295 and ref. # 279, p. 406. A. Hryvna brought 18 caps of the type called "mazepynka" (a symbol of Ukrainian culture) which he distributed among the youth of the Lemko region.
[68] *Holos Naroda* 1928, no. 38, p. 1.

2. The local intelligentsia and other community organizations

The burden of educational field work rested on the shoulders of the local clerical and secular intelligentsia. The secular intelligentsia consisted of teachers, lawyers (attorneys, legal advisers, notaries) and doctors. Both groups worked together within Ukrainian institutions – besides *Prosvita*, mainly the Ukrainian Pedagogical Society *Ridna Shkola* and the agrarian institution *Silskyi Hospodar*.

The active involvement of the clerical intelligentsia raised the number of conversions to Eastern Orthodoxy among Greek Catholics which took place in the late 1920s and early 1930s. Church Ordinary in Przemyśl Fr. Bishop Yosafat Kotsylovsky set about taking action with the aim of putting a check on conversions. One of his first decrees bound individual deanery priests to make reports on the religious and moral state of their parish flock. Deacon priests were happy to tell of their parishes, but certain reports contained negative opinions and stressed the need for a mission. To coordinate missionary action, Kotsylovsky appointed an inspector for the Lemko region in the person of Fr. Ivan Kachmar, dean of Muszyna.[69]

Greek Catholic missions were begun in the summer of 1929 in parishes adjacent to Orthodox centers. On 4 June 1929 Grybów deacon Fr. Mykhailo Artemovych organized a deanery council in Binczarowa with eight Greek Catholic priests participating, at which methods for counteracting the development of Eastern Orthodoxy while simultaneously strengthening the Ukrainian movement were discussed.[70] In 1931 Bishop Kotsylovsky himself visited the Lemko region. The Greek Catholic population greeted him with the respect fitting for a Church dignitary, yet Old Rusyn and Moscophile reports refer to hostile attitude among the faithful in over a dozen places, where the bishop was even insulted.[71]

The activities of the priests in particular deaneries were coordinated by deanery congresses. The congress proceedings stressed not only the confessional aspect of the priests' engagement, but also the national side. At a congress in Łabowa on 15 June 1933, Fr. Kachmar spoke of the necessity to defend "our nationality and our language."[72] Similar slogans were advanced during the congress of Greek Catholic priests in Świątkowa Wielka on 24 October 1933, at which 16 priests from the counties of Jasło, Gorlice and Krosno were present.[73]

---

[69] AP P, ABGK, ref. # 4748, *Sprawy obrzędowe. Sprawozdania o stanie religijno-moralnym parafii, 1929*, p.n.n.

[70] AP K, UWKr, ref. # 327, *Sprawozdania informacyjne, miesięczne i tygodniowe Starostwa Powiatowego w Grybowie 1923, 1928–1932*, p. 39.

[71] In Wysowa, where the Orthodox population was relatively small, the bishop was pelted with stones by children. See I. Teodorovich, "Lemkovskaia Rus," *Nauchno-Literaturnyi Sbornik Halytsko-Ruskoi Matitsy*, Lvov 1934, vol. 8, p. 19.

[72] Ibid., ref. # 352, p. 121.

[73] Ibid., ref. # 279, p. 366.

The Greek Catholic clergy most actively engaged in the Ukrainian movement included, in Nowy Sącz County: Stepan Dmytryshyn (Maciejowa), Stepan Kornova (Łabowa), and Ivan Kachmar (Złockie); in Grybów County: Ihnatii Halushka (Brunary) and Myhhailo Zhuk (Śnietnica); in Gorlice County: Volodyrnyr Ardan (Zdynia), Yuliian Pleshkevych (Małastów), and Teodor Zeleny (Doliny); in Jasło County: Vasyl Ben (Ciachania), Panteleimon Saluk (Krempna), and Dmytro Stupak (Świątkowa Wielka); in Krosno County: Ivan Kliufas (Bonarówka); and a considerable number of priests in Sanok County. Frequently these were the first people to propose an initiative for establishing a reading room, to organize various kinds of professional improvement courses, to lead church choirs and theater groups.[74]

Information regarding the activities of the most energetically involved priests appeared not only in the Ukrainian press, but also in the Moscophile press. In the latter, the information was sometimes given an ironic context, but many actual enterprises of the pro-Ukrainian clergy were mentioned. *Zemlia i Volia*, the RSO organ targeted at the masses, excelled in this. Very often Frs. Kachmar, Kliufas and Stupak,[75] who were involved in the distribution of Ukrainian periodicals, books, brochures, and other publications, including *Narodna Sprava* (The National Question), *Nash Lemko* (Our Lemko), and the *Lemko Region Library* cycle, were mocked and scorned.

The majority of the Greek Catholic clergy represented the Ukrainian movement, but a certain group among them worked in support of the Kachkovsky reading rooms, organizing Thalerhof congresses at which the Ukrainian movement was publicly condemned. This attitude among the clergy brought forth a reaction from the Przemyśl ordinariate. On 19 September 1929 Bishop Kotsylovsky issued a ban on priests' participating in Thalerhof solemnities under penalty of suspension *ab ordine ipso facto*.[76]

A second socially engaged group among the intelligentsia consisted of teachers, white-collar workers, lawyers, and doctors. Teachers created their own organization under the name Ukrainian Teachers' Mutual Aid Society (*Tovarystvo Vzaimnoi Pomochi Ukrainskykh Uchyteliv*), which had branches in several counties.[77] Fairly soon, the Greek Catholic clergy had begun working in cooperation with teachers. At first their cooperation was spontaneous, but through *Prosvita* branches and reading rooms it quickly took on organizational forms. A sign of its organized character was the active involvement of said groups of intelligentsia in the activities of the *Prosvita* Executive Board in Lviv in 1926 and in the work of the Lemko Commission.

---

[74] CDIAL, f. 344, op. 1t, case # 552, *Zvity, skarhy ta inshi dokumenty pro stan shkil i navchannia na zakhidnoukrainskykh zemlakh*, p. 10.

[75] Numerous articles in annual issues from the 1930s.

[76] AP P, ABGK, ref. # 3757, Deacons' affairs. Reports on religious and moral conditions, p. 226.

[77] AP K, UWKr, ref. # 277, p. 28 and ref. # 352. p.n.n. The board of the Grybów branch consisted of: V. Merena (Bogusza) – president, A. Nishchota (Śnietnica) – deputy chairman, Y. Vonsovych (Królowa Ruska) – secretary, E. Svedyk (Brunary Wyżne) – librarian, S. Hutsulanka (Binczarowa) – inspector.

A noteworthy event was the creation in late 1929 and early 1930 of a secret organization called Constructing Ukraine, organized by the rector of Małastów, Fr. Yuliian Pleshkevych. Teachers from several areas came to work in the organization: Gładyszów, Krzywa, Pętna, Rychwałd, Smerekowiec and Zdynia, as well as peasants, members of the boards of several municipalities.[78] The organization had a far-reaching political program, expressed in the aspiration to the attainment of independence for Ukraine. In reality the sphere of its activity was significantly simpler, limited to funding stipends for Lemko youth going to school in Ukrainian intermediate schools. Fr. Pleshkevych's closest associates included Tymofii Pereima (Smerekowiec), Omelan Hryvna (Gładyszów), Yatsko Muzyka (Pętna), and the rector's brother, who took charge of organizing transport for youth to Ukrainian boarding schools.[79]

Another result of collaboration between both intelligentsia groups was the consolidation of the Ukrainian movement in Sanok region. Thanks to the efforts of Sanok high school professors Lev Gets and Ivan Fliunt, as well as Fr. Stepan Venhrynovych, I. Dobrianska, F. Kokovsky and others, a Ukrainian regional museum called the Museum of the Lemko Region (*Miuzei Lemkivshchyna*) was founded in Sanok in 1930. The museum took on the task of gathering valuable artifacts of the Lemko region's past: icons, manuscripts, etc. At first it was located in a room made accessible by Fr. O. Konstantynovych. In subsequent years the museum collections included objects from the 15th to the 17th centuries: icons, books, medals, coins, etc.[80]

The cultural, educational and political work carried out by the intelligentsia was supported by the lowest social stratum, i.e. the peasant population. *Prosvita* above all stirred pro-Ukrainian feelings, as its ranks swelled with supporters of that current, e.g. Mykola Trokhanovsky – chairman of the reading rooms in Polany, Yosyf Kovalsky (Polany), Pylyp Dutka, Sydoria Monchak, Andrii Skvirtniansky, Klymentii Varkholiak (Berest), Stepan Valyka (Świątkowa Wielka),[81] Ivan Pototsky (deacon in Brunary Wyżne). A significant group of farmers and field hands clustered around the Greek Catholic clergy, e.g. Yosyf Hornik of Maciejowa worked together with Fr. Dmytryshyn, Adam Barna, Semen Barna and Ivan Shost of Złockie worked together with Fr. Kachmar, Stepan Varshava (a student from Lviv) worked together with Fr. Kornova, P. Smerekanych of Świerzowa – with Fr. Stupak. A considerable fraction of the citizens of Krempna engaged in national-Ukrainian activity in the

[78] UWKr, ref. # 51, *Tygodniowe sprawozdania informacyjne starosty w Gorlicach do wojewody krakowskiego*, p.n.n. See AP P, Starostwo Powiatowe w Gorlicach 1918–1939, ref. # 3, *Sprawozdania sytuacyjne za czas od X 1923 do XII 1933*.

[79] AP K, SP G II, ref. # 7, *Sprawozdania tygodniowe wojewody krakowskiego 1929–1930*, p. IV/l.

[80] The Board of the Museum also included: M. Bazhaluk, V. Brovar, L. Bukatovych, V. Karanovych. See *Dilo* 1936, no. 104, p. 4; Y. Konstantynovych, "Muzei Lemkivshchyna v Sianotsi," *Nova Zoria* 1934, no. 52, Scholarly supplement; Y. Tarnovych, *Verhamy Lemkivskoho Beskydu. Mandrivnyi providnyk po Lemkivshchyni*, Lviv 1938, p. 61.

[81] AP K, UWKr, ref. #279, pp. 121–122, 337; *Beskyd* 1932, no. 30, p. 2.

local *Prosvita* reading room founded by Fr. P. Saluk. Farmers such as Vasyl Demia-novych, Ivan Dychko, and Hryhorii Sardyka were influential actors in the move-ment.[82] Some made rooms in their houses accessible for the needs of specialized courses organized by Ukrainian institutions.[83]

The local social groups mentioned earlier, the clerical and secular intelligentsia and peasant activists, worked mainly through the *Prosvita* Society, which constitut-ed a nationwide, supraparty organization. Still, alongside *Prosvita* more specialized organizations were active. Issues of schooling and extracurricular education were dealt with by the *Ridna Shkola* Ukrainian Pedagogical Society, while the economic development of the Lemko countryside was the province chiefly of the *Silskyi Hospo-dar* Society.

2.1. The Ukrainian Pedagogical Society (*Ridna Shkola*)

The initiative for developing *Ridna Shkola* throughout the Lemko region was proposed by the Executive Board of the Sanok branch of *Prosvita*, which on 12 Oc-tober 1924 sent a letter to the Ukrainian Pedagogical Society in Lviv asking that an "itinerant teacher" be assigned for the purpose of teaching courses in reading and writing for illiterates. On 2 October 1925 a circle was established in Sanok, chaired by Volodymyr Konstantynovych. The circle soon was transformed into a branch, and the first chairman of the board was Volodymyr Chaikivsky – a high school profes-sor; beginning in 1930 the branch was directed by Stepan Vanchytsky, whose deputy until the end of the interwar period was Fr. Stepan Mentsinsky. The organization's main purpose was to develop Ukrainian schooling "in the Western territories, those most exposed to Polonization."[84]

In the first period of the formation of the Society's structure, i.e. until the end of the 1920s, both the Sanok center and the Executive Board in Lviv oversaw the cam-paign to raise funds for the development of Ukrainian schooling. The campaign was conducted through the intermediacy of trusted associates, including lawyers, teach-ers, clergy and students from the Lemko region.[85] The *Ridna Shkola* branch in Sanok had a network which comprised cities and towns in the Krosno and Sanok coun-ties. The branch included eight members permanently residing in Krosno, centered

---

[82] AP K, KOS K, ref. # 49, *Protokół z konferencji oświatowej nauczycielstwa [...] rejonu łemkowskiego powiatu jasielskiego w Żmigrodzie 6 kwietnia 1933 r.*, p.n.n.

[83] E.g. in the house of P. Hahlovsky in Świątkowa Wielka, in January and February 1930, an agrono-mic-veterinarian course was held. See *Holos Naroda* 1930, no. 7, p. 2.

[84] CDIAL, f. 206, op. 1, case # 2426, *Zvity, protokoly, lystuvannia ta inshi materialy pro diialnist hurtka w misti Sianik, 1922–1939*, pp. 4, 8.

[85] In the monthly collections, sums even exceeding 100 zloty were obtained, e.g. in October 1928, 118 zloty in five cities or towns (Sanok – 100 zl, Wujskie – 5 zl, Rzepedź – 5 zl, Sanoczek – 5 zl, Czysto-horb – 3,5 zl); in November – 74 zl in seven (Besko – 25 zl, Szczawne – 12 zl, Wola Niżna – 10 zl, Komańcza – 9 zl, Płonna – 8,5 zl, Wisłok Wyżny – 6 zl, Czystohorb – 3,5 zl).

around Yuliian Nalysnyk, a local lawyer. Some archival sources mention a branch in Nowy Sącz with regard to the years 1926–1927, but it was not possible to establish more precise details as to its activities.[86]

A significant achievement of the late 1920s was the establishment in 1928 of a well-organized circle in Zawadka Rymanowska, which was looked after by Krosno activists. The main organizer was Volodymyr Kobii – a teacher in Zawadka.[87] Almost simultaneously a private Ukrainian school built at the expense of the citizens of Zawadka became active. The first teacher named to a position by the Executive Board in Lviv was Petro Ikalovych, followed by: Petro Sterpak and Olha Chaban. The success of the school mobilized the establishment of similar institutions in other localities. The state of elementary schools at that time was reported on by Sanok branch chairman Volodymyr Chaikivsky at the Society's congress in February.[88]

A successive stage in the development of *Ridna Shkola* in the Lemko region is marked by the activity of the Lemko Commission formed in 1932. In the spring of 1933 the board of the Sanok branch of *Ridna Shkola* submitted official authorization papers for its "private agents" residing in the cities in the Nowy Sącz and Gorlice counties (Grybów County no longer existed), for the purpose of conducting fund-raising among the local population. The preserved archival documents kept in the Central State Historical Archive in Lviv extensively illustrate the development of the Society's structures in Gorlice County, where the function of "private agent" was executed by Stepan Shmigelsky – a doctor in Gorlice. From March 1933 to June 1934 he raised funds, approaching mainly Greek Catholic clergy and teachers. In that period he collected approximately 150 zloty and transferred this sum to the Sanok branch and Lviv headquarters.[89]

Shmigelsky's activities, in cooperation with Roman Borysevych (a lawyer in Gorlice) and Roman Kyshakevych (a Gorlice confectioner), had the effect of bringing *Ridna Shkola* circles into being. The first circle to form was the one in Wysowa, whose organizer was Fr. Mykola Duda. It was named after Prince Volodymyr the Great and initially numbered 16 members. The circle in Ropica Ruska, named for Taras Shevchenko, was founded in June 1934 at the initiative of Ivan Zhelem, from Ropica, at the time a student in the Law School of Lviv University; it gathered 20 members initially. The founder of the Pętna circle in September 1934, which was named after Ivan Franko, was Asafat Hryvna.[90]

---

[86] CDIAL, f. 206, op. 1, case # 169, *Spysok povitovykh hurtkiv tovarystva zasnovanykh na terytorii Halychyny 1927, 1938*, p. 5.

[87] *Dilo* 1928, no. 171, p. 2; *Svoboda* 1928, no. 210, p. 2.

[88] A new board was then elected, which consisted of: V. Chaikivsky – chairman; six branch members: M. Kybalsky, Fr. S. Mentsinsky, B. Shulakevych, S. Vanchytsky, V. Vavryk, S. Venhrynovych; deputy branch members: Fr. M. Bentysh, S. Tsar, P. Yanishyn, V. Mykula; controlling commission: F. Kokovsky, Fr. O. Konstantynovych, Fr.V. Kunkevych. See CDIAL, f. 206, op. 1, case # 2426, p. 29.

[89] CDIAL, f. 206, op. 1, case # 745, *Lystuvannia, 1934*, p. 6.

[90] Ibid., case # 599, *Prokhannia meshkantsiv sela Vysova, Horlytskoho povitu do Holovnoi Upravy pro nadannia dozvolu na zasnuvannia hurtka ta spysok chleniv, 1934*, p. 1; case # 2192, *Prokhannia*

The activities of Shmigelsky, Borysevych, and others in the Gorlice County area induced the Executive Board of *Ridna Shkola* in Lviv to produce a plan for creating a county circle in Gorlice, which the planners intended to ease the burden of the Sanok center's work. Implementing the plan revealed itself to be impossible due to formal factors – they were unable to find 15 Ukrainians in Gorlice.

In December 1936, at the plenary congress of the Society, a resolution creating a Commission for Hutsul and Lemko Regional Matters was passed. This interest in the provincial areas was argued to be justified by the threat of "foreign national influences."[91] As a result of this heightened community activism, further *Ridna Shkola* circles were established in Jabłonica Polska, Szklary, Turzańsk and Wierchomla Wielka. A resident of Bodaki, Ivan Yatsiuka, even made an attempt in 1937 to found a *Ridna Shkola* for youth, which could not be effectuated, however, due to the liquidation by the state authorities of all youth circles existing under Society auspices.[92]

In the latter part of the 1930s, when the development of *Ridna Shkola* organizational structure in the Lemko region was hindered by the administrative authorities, attention was focused on the youngest, with nursery schools founded in time for intensified field labor in the harvest period. The first planned, organized nursery schools were started in July 1936 – at that time 20 nursery schools were established to serve about 500 children.[93] Another campaign on a wide scale was launched in 1938. In view of the negative experiences of the previous year, in which numerous districts had refused to allow branches of *Ridna Shkola* to be founded, requests to register seasonal nursery schools had been pouring into the county offices in Sanok and Brzozów since February 1938. Of the seven nursery schools proposed in Brzozów County (Hłudno, Izdebki, Jabłonica Ruska, Łubno, Siedliska, Ulucz and Wołodź), the district denied approval for starting one in Jabłonica Ruska. In Sanok County eight nursery schools were proposed,[94] and in Krosno – three.[95] While the nursery schools were being launched, the Province Office in Lviv sent a letter on 2 July 1938 to the board of the *Ridna Shkola* branch in Sanok, prohibiting the expansion of Society structure in the border zone.[96] In this period the state authorities' attitude toward *Ridna Shkola* did not deviate from its relationships with other Ukrainian institutions active in the sphere of the counties comprised by the Lemko region.

---

meshkantsiv sela Ropytsia Ruska, Horlytskoho povitu pro zasnuvannia hurtka im. T. Shevchenka, 1934, p. 4; case # 1942, *Zaiava meshkantsiv sela Pantna*, 1934, pp. 1–11.

[91] *SN* 1936, no. 6, p. 629.

[92] Toward the end of 1936 the state authorities ordered *Ridna Shkola* to dissolve the youth groups for youth aged 14–18. See CDIAL, f. 206, op. 1, case # 483, *Lyst vidpovid hromadskomu diiachu Ivanu Yatsiuku s. Bodaky pro zaboronu "ridnoshkolnyh hurtkiv dorostu," polskymy vlastiamy*, 1937, p. 2.

[93] S. Vanchytsky, op.cit., p. 51.

[94] Kostarowce, Lalin, Nowosielce Gniewosz, Pielnia, Sanok, Zahutyń, Zawadka Rymanowska, Zawadka Rymanowska–Abramów.

[95] Bonarówka, Krasna, Wróblik Królewski.

[96] CDIAL, f. 206, op. 1, case # 2439, p. 3.

The distribution of *Ridna Shkola* circles throughout the entire region was notably uneven. The relative saturation of the eastern Lemko region with them is striking, as well as their under-representation in the western part. This disproportion fostered stronger development of the Ukrainian idea in the counties of Brzozów, Krosno and Sanok than in the counties which belonged to the Kraków province. The *Ridna Shkola* circles scattered about the Lemko region developed a sense of connection to Ukrainian tradition among Lemko youth. They influenced the formation of the young pupils' personalities, and thus the contribution they made to the dissemination of the Ukrainian idea, despite their relatively weak organizational structure, must have been significant, though it began to pay dividends only in the era of WWII and afterward.

2.2. The Farmers' Society (*Silskyi Hospodar*)

The *Silskyi Hospodar* Society branches were placed much more evenly throughout the area of the Lemko region. This no doubt resulted from the nature of the organization, which worked on issues of rural economic development, so that *Silskyi Hospodar* was able to attract both Old Rusyns and Moscophiles.

The *Silskyi Hospodar* Society renewed its activity in 1924 through the creation of the Committee of Cooperative Organizations. In Sanok the Association of Lemko Cooperatives was active. *Silskyi Hospodar* published its own specialized periodicals in Lviv: *Silskyi Hospodar, Sad i Horod, Ukrainskyi Pasichnyk, Khliborobska Molod, Ukrainskyi Agronomichnyi Vistnyk* and a calendar book.

The organization had strong traditions in the Lemko region dating from the Austro-Hungarian era. In 1914 the greatest number of circles was located in Sanok County (22 circles),[97] while there were six circles in the counties of Grybów[98] and Nowy Sącz[99] and four in Gorlice County.[100] After the end of the First World War local Ukrainian activists set about rebuilding the previously existing organizational structure. Particularly energetic were the efforts of the Greek Catholic clergy who revived the circles in Bednarka (P. Shuflat), Czyrna and Piorunka (Fr. Kuzyk), Śnietnica (M. Zhuk), and Wujskie (P. Andreichuk). During this first period of rebuilding the Society's structure, secular activists included: V. Brenkach, I. Tsidylo, K. Fedorchak, I. Hryshko, V. Kachmarsky, V. Makukh, D. Olesnevych, P. Poshchak, A. Prytsik, and M. Rapach[101].

---

[97] Dąbrówka Polska, Doliny, Dobra Szlachecka, Komańcza, Lalin, Nowosielce Gniewosz, Odrzechowa, Pakoszówka, Polany Surowiczne, Posada Sanocka, Prusiek, Rzepedź, Sanoczek, Stróże Wielkie, Srogów Górny, Trepcza, Wisłok Niżny, Wisłok Wyżny, Wola Sękowa, Wolica, Zahutyń, see CDIAL, f. 348, op. 1, case # 5. p. 56.

[98] Berest, Czyrna, Florynka, Piorunka, Polany, Śnietnica.

[99] Jastrzębik, Maciejowa, Milik, Roztoka Wielka, Składziste, Złockie.

[100] Bednarka, Pętna, Ropica Ruska, Wysowa.

[101] CDIAL, f. 348, op. 1, case # 5, *Vykaz, kruzhkiv Kraievoho Hospodarskoho Tovarystva "Silskyi Hospodar" na Lemkivshchyni*, p. 56.

An exact reckoning of the number of *Silskyi Hospodar* Society circles in the Lemko Region is difficult to perform due to contradictory source information. Nonetheless, a statistical configuration for the 1930s allows a general grasp of its organizational structure. The entire area of the Lemko region was subsumed into two branches. The Sanok branch comprised the counties of Brzozów, Krosno and Sanok, while the circles in the area of the Kraków province were subordinated to the branch in Lutsk, in Volhynia. The Volhynia branch comprised five circles: three in Nowy Sącz County, and one each in the counties of Gorlice and Jasło, with a total of ninety-six members.[102] In 1936 the number of members fell to sixty and one circle in Nowy Sącz County was dissolved.[103] This state of affairs, i.e. four circles with 60 members, was recorded in the statistical configuration for 1938.[104] Statistics for the eastern Lemko region are only marginally more useful. Configurations for the 1930s invariably cite five circles for the Sanok branch, with 145 members.[105]

These circles were mainly involved in establishing trade cooperatives in the surrounding towns. The cooperatives worked at harvesting and selling farm produce, with eggs harvested most often. Well-organized circles had departments such as beekeeping, gardening, etc. The beekeeping department of the circle in Wróblik Królewski, run by Stepan Varkholiak, which produced honeycomb structures, achieved renown.[106] A significant part of the circles' activities dealt with cultural and educational issues, and in this sphere they supplemented the activity of *Prosvita* reading rooms, sometimes competing with them. Some circles had their own amateur theatrical troupes, e.g. in Wróblik Królewski.

The second half of the 1930s brought setbacks for the development of the Ukrainian movement in the Lemko region. The national assimilation policy implemented toward Lemkos represented administrative supplantation of Ukrainian institutions from the Lemko region. As a result of the campaign the Ukrainian movement in the area was reduced to its initial state, i.e. to the numerous national clusters grouped among the local intelligentsia. It should be noted here that the sport/firefighting organizations *Luh*, *Zaporozhets*, and *Strilets* had secondary importance in the process of the development of Ukrainian national consciousness. Towns where branches of these organizations operated were few.[107]

---

[102] CDIAL, f. 302, op. 1, case # 315, *Statystychni vidomosti pro organizatsiinyi stan filiialiv na 31 hrudnia 1933 r.*, p. 3.

[103] Ibid., case # 347, *Statystychne zvedennia pro stan organizatsiinoi roboty filiialiv na terytorii Volynskoho, Krakivskoho […] voievodstv, 1937*, pp. 17, 18.

[104] Ibid., case # 370, *Statystychni zvedennia pro orhanizatsiinyi stan filiialiv […] Krakivskoho […] voievodstv, 1937*, p. 21.

[105] Ibid., case # 334, *Statystychni vidomosti, zvedennia za terytoiialnoiu oznakoiu […], 1935*, p. 5.

[106] *Nash Lemko* 1936, no. 2, p. 1. Fr. R. Vynnytsky was the founder of a *Silskyi Hospodar* circle in Wróblik Królewski.

[107] Firefighting-athletic organizations were most highly developed in the Sanok region, in Sanok, Wujskie, and Załuż. *Luh* had branchs in Bonarówka (Fr. I. Kliufas, P. Soltysyk) and Barwinek

3. The Ukrainian National Democratic Alliance and Ukrainian Parliamentary Representation in view of government policy in the Lemko region

Covering UNDO (the Ukrainian National Democratic Alliance) and the URP (Ukrainian Parliamentary Representation) in a single subchapter results from the close cooperation between these two organizations. UNDO played a leading role among Ukrainian political parties and most members of the Ukrainian parliamentary representation created each time as a result of successive rounds of elections were recruited from this party. The Ukrainian Club, constituted in 1922 and formed by deputies chosen from the districts of the former Russian partition, dealt with the question of the Lemko region in the context of the peripherally situated ethnically Ukrainian territories. After the decision of the Council of Ambassadors in the matter of Galicia, Ukrainian deputies published an official protest, in which they referred to Volhynia, the Chełm region, the Polisia region, Pidlashia, Eastern Galicia, Bukovina (Bukovyna), and Subcarpathia as Ukrainian territories.[108] In later years as well, up until the collapse of the Second Polish Republic, Ukrainian Parliamentary Representation maintained the necessity of holding onto all Ukrainian lands in Poland, defended the Lemko region as an integral part of those lands, and opposed every attempt to push Lemkos out of the Ukrainian national movement.

In the mid-1920s, when the government authorities took numerous steps to weaken the position of Ukrainians in the Polish Republic, (the issue of the Ukrainian university, Władysław Grabski's laws in the borderlands, agrarian reform), the process culminated in the consolidation of Ukrainian centrist forces. Another threat to the Ukrainian center was the rise of nationalist and Communist forces in the Ukrainian milieu. At the end of 1924 conversations among representatives of the Ukrainian National Workers' Party (*Ukrainska Partiia Natsionalnoi Roboty*), the Ukrainian People's Labor Party (*Ukrainska Narodno-Trudova Partiia*) and Ukrainian deputies and senators with connections to these parties began. After a period of negotiations lasting several months, on 11 July 1925 a new centrist organization was created – UNDO.

UNDO's social program aimed to win peasants and workers. The main area of party activity was the region of the former Eastern Galicia, but UNDO gradually gained influence in Volhynia and the Lemko region. The more important Ukrainian culture and education organizations, such as *Prosvita*, *Ridna Shkola*, social, credit, and economic institutions including *Tsentrobank*, *Tsentrosoiuz*, *Narodna Torhovla*, *Silskyi Hospodar*, and the *Dnister* Insurance and Credit Association, and firefighting

---

(Fr. T. Kabarovsky, P. Litynsky), *Zaporozhets* in Łabowa, *Strilets* in Małastów, see AP K, UWKr, ref. # 277.

[108] "Komunikat Klubu posłów ukraińskich do Sejmu i Senatu," *Republika* 1923, no. 74; M. Papierzyńska-Turek, *Sprawa ukraińska w Drugiej Rzeczypospolitej 1922–1926*, Kraków 1979, p. 182.

and sport associations, e.g. *Luh* and *Sokil*, were under the party's sway. From the beginning of its existence, UNDO played a leading role in Ukrainian political life in the Second Polish Republic.

The founding congress, on 11 July 1925, was simultaneously the first party congress, at which a political platform was developed as the basis for a program to be elucidated in detail at a later date. With regard to the Poles, the platform proclaimed that UNDO would lead a struggle in the western Ukrainian territories to reject the "validation of the legal nature of Polish rule in that region." According to the premises contained therein, the struggle was to be conducted by means of foreign, mandated representation for the western Ukrainian lands. These premises changed after UNDO's Second Congress, which took place on 19–20 November 1926; the point about foreign representation was deleted from the program. The second congress approved the program and the party charter.[109]

UNDO was not a party in the traditional sense of the word. It constituted a kind of national front. Aside from Lviv and a few larger cities, there was no registration of members, and member dues were collected only sporadically. Different counties were led by permanent National County Committees elected by local congresses. The party structure in the Lemko region was precisely something in the nature of a national front, bringing together mainly different segments of the intelligentsia. UNDO's penetration of the Lemko region began shortly after the second party congress. During the period between the second and third congresses, i.e., between November 1926 and December 1928, five counties in the Kraków province had UNDO National Committees organized: Gorlice, Grybów, Jasło, Nowy Sącz and Nowy Targ, which were led by "private agents."[110]

The structure of the party in the areas of the Lemko region which belonged to the Lviv province was in somewhat better shape; the main political center there was Sanok, with support from smaller centers in Krosno–Rymanów, Lesko, and Ustrzyki Dolne. Correspondence maintained between the board in Sanok and party authorities in Lviv reveals that the UNDO committee in Sanok was hampered in its work by the vibrant Moscophile traditions left over from the prewar era. UNDO's main activists in the area included the lawyers V. Blavatsky, Y. Nalysnyk, and S. Vanchytsky; the physicians V. Karanovych and K. Teply; high school teachers such as V. Chaikivsky; and representatives of various services, e.g. agronomist P. Litynsky and the clergymen P. Andreichuk, M. Dorotsky, A. Kot, P. Maziar, M. Sukhy, and I. Tym-

---

[109] *III Narodnyi Zizd Ukrainskoho Natsionalno-Demokratychnoho Obiednannia v dniakh 24 i 25 hrudnia 1928 r. (Zvit zlozhenyi na pidstavi stenohrafichnoho protokolu)*, Lviv 1929, pp. 3–4.

[110] In the counties which belonged to the Kraków province, the "private agents" were priests (I. Kachmar, S. Kornova, Y. Pleshkevych, D. Stupak, V. Shevchuk, A. Zlupko), doctors (O. Dzerovych, S. Shmigelsky), lawyers (R. Borysevych), farmers (D. Khomiak, D. Mykhaliak, P. Vakhlovsky) and one student, M. Dudra. See CDIAL, f. 344, op. 11, case # 288, *Spysok kerivnoho skladu UNDO na Lemkivshchyni z perelikom adres*, pp. 1, 2.

chak, as well as the peasants M. Tsar (Zahutyń), M. Cherepianka (Siemuszowa), I. Lypka (Dudyńce) and V. Kachmarsky (Bonarówka)[111].

The Third UNDO Congress, held 24 and 25 December 1928,[112] had considerable importance for the development of organizing party activity in the provinces. A significant part of the deliberations was devoted to organizing county structures. This issue was broadly discussed by deputy Ostap Lutsky, who underscored that UNDO constituted "a front for all Ukrainians that goes beyond class" and should pay close attention to work in the regions: "every County Committee should be organized in such a way that it can identify and satisfy as quickly as possible the pressing needs of the population in each area of national life in the county."[113] Lutsky sharply criticized the theretofore existing practice in Committees of neglecting particular issues in their organizational work, leaving culture and education to *Prosvita*, school matters to *Ridna Shkola*, and economic issues to *Silskyi Hospodar*. Lutsky concluded with a call for appointing officials at each National County Committee of UNDO responsible for culture and education issues, farm production, youth instruction, women's organizational work, etc., which was faithfully reflected in the congress's resolutions.[114]

Pressure placed on organizational issues in the counties remained linked to the idea of spreading UNDO's activities to counties populated only partly by Ukrainians. In keeping with the idea of a national front, Committees were to become headquarters for social work in the regions. They were assigned the task of taking full control over all organizations in the area and coordinating their development in close agreement with the Executive Board in Lviv. From this perspective, the congress resolutions of December 1928 constituted a breakthrough for party organization in the provinces. Furthermore, despite the fact that the congress – when addressing the problem of the regions – referred mainly to Volhynia, the Chełm region and Polisia, nonetheless the resolutions on issues of county organization related in equal measure to the Lemko region. The 1928 congress instituted relationships between social organizations active in the region (*Prosvita*, *Ridna Shkola*, *Silskyi Hospodar*), making them politically subordinate to UNDO County Committees. Until that point each organization had exchanged information on statutory work with its own structural network. Only at the level of the Executive Boards of the disparate institutions had communication with UNDO headquarters in Lviv occurred. An example of this was the occasional lack of coordination between Ukrainian institutions, which had often

---

[111] AAN, MSW, ref. # 1042, *Referat naczelnika Wydziału Społeczno-Politycznego Urzędu Wojewódzkiego Lwowskiego pt. "Sprawy Ukraińskie,"* 1935, p. 18; CDIAL, f. 344, op. 1t, case # 301, *Spysky chleniv UNDO na terytorii Halychyny, 1938,* p. 51.

[112] *III Narodnyi Zizd,* pp. 5, 107. The congress brought together participants from 82 districts, including representatives of the Lemko region from five districts (Baligród, Jasło, Krosno–Rymanów, Lesko, Sanok).

[113] O. Lutsky, "Orhanichna pratsia na mistsiakh," in: *III Narodnyi Zizd,* p. 113.

[114] *III Narodnyi Zizd,* pp. 115–120, 144–154.

duplicated the same forms of activity in the same towns (e.g. two theatrical circles in Wróblik Królewski).

The resolutions of the UNDO congress of 1928 heralded a change in this practice and though their implementation in many counties would require a long wait, still, at the dawn of the 1930s UNDO through the intermediacy of its county structures managed to take control over social life in most counties of the former Eastern Galicia. In the case of the Lemko region success was less striking, but the resolutions taking force improved organizational work there, buttressing the Ukrainian national movement, and, more importantly – they gave the Lemko region a direct political connection to the UNDO Executive Board and Ukrainian Parliamentary Representation.

3.1. Against "regionalization" – with hope for "normalization"

The manoeuvres of RP (Polish Republic) governments intended to weaken the Ukrainian movement in the western borderlands of the Ukrainian ethnic sphere were perceived by Ukrainians as a denationalization campaign. There were protests against the attempts to support the regional autonomy of Ukrainian ethnographic groups: the Boikos, Hutsuls and Lemkos. That campaign capitalized on cultural, religious and historical differences between Ukrainian regions. It was based on using one set of tactics on Ukrainians living in the Białystok, Lublin and Kraków voivodeships, and another on the population in the entire zone of the eastern voivodeships. The lands furthest west, Pidlashia, the Chełm region and the Lemko region, were the subject of political and legal manoeuvres in the 1920s which intended to isolate these regions from the other Ukrainian territories. The Ukrainian press defined this policy as "regionalization."

The principle of "regionalization" was introduced and implemented in a manner painful for Ukrainians, through the intermediacy of the Grabski borderland laws, which set the Ukrainian population apart in laws. Deputy Serhii Khrutsky spoke out in the parliamentary forum against the principle of regionalization embodied in the laws. During his discussion of the laws he stated that they were striving toward the "Polonization of the Ukrainian population" through Utraquism and "unequal treatment of the totality of lands peopled by the Ukrainian population – the exclusion of the Chełm region, Pidlashia, and the Lemko region."[115] Khrutsky protested against the ban on founding private Ukrainian schools in the area.[116]

The political changes which took place in the RP after the May Coup (1926) did not fundamentally change Polish-Ukrainian relations. Legislation which had taken force in the pre-May era continued to be binding. Thus UNDO and URP

---

[115] *Sejm Rzeczypospolitej Polskiej, Sprawozdania stenograficzne* (hereinafter – Sejm RP), 146th meeting of the Sejm of the RP, 9 July, column 9; M. Papierzyńska-Turek, op.cit., p. 231.

[116] R. Torzecki, *Kwestia ukraińska w polityce III Rzeszy (1933–1945)*, Warszawa 1972, p. 74. Statistical configuration showing the decrease in the number of schools with Ukrainian as language of instruction after 1924, see J. Tomaszewski, *Rzeczpospolita wielu narodów*, Warszawa 1985, p. 95.

came to the defense of the national rights of the Ukrainian population of Pidlashia and the Chełm and Lemko regions. The problem was broadly discussed at the Third Congress of UNDO, which was critical of the state's nationality policies, accusing the government of working to split the Ukrainian population into separate territorial groups and supporting separatist movements among Ukrainians. The congress resolution on this issue expressed a protest against "the Polonizing, exterminationist policy of Poland toward the Ukrainian nation."[117]

Regionalization was put into action continuously until the outbreak of the Second World War. The determination of successive governments to do so may have been driven by increasingly inflamed Polish-Ukrainian relations (including terrorist acts organized by the OUN, Organization of Ukrainian Nationalists, pacification campaigns organized by the authorities, etc.). Minimalizing the sphere controlled by the Ukrainian movement was supposed to bring closer ties between borderlands and central areas. The Lemko region, heavily overrun with Polish settlements, became the object of particular attention from government circles. At the beginning of the 1930s it was subjected to national assimilation, a policy given broad support by Old Rusyns. With regional policy becoming increasingly obvious in the Lemko region, the Lemko issue began making frequent appearances in deputies' interpellations and UNDO congress resolutions. It must be added, however, that it was always mentioned in relation to the entirety of the Ukrainian problem in the RP.

In the first half of the 1930s, government circles took advantage of internal interdenominational conflicts among Lemkos and supported a plan for establishing an Apostolic Administration of the Lemko Region – as a Greek Catholic church province of Old Rusyn orientation, formally subordinate directly to the Holy See. The Apostolic Administration of the Lemko Region was created on the strength of the decree *Quo optius consuleret* published by the Vatican on 10 February 1934. It included nine decanates separated from the Przemyśl diocese: in Bukowsko, Dukla, Dynów, Gorlice, Grybów, Krosno, Muszyna, Rymanów and Sanok. Only rudimentary source information remains, rendering detailed knowledge of the circumstances of this church province's development. One finds statements in the literature on the intention of holding back the development of Eastern Orthodoxy by this means, but the emergence of the Apostolic Administration was used as part of RP nationality policy for isolating the Lemko region from Ukrainian Greek Catholic church influence, which flowed from Lviv and Przemyśl.[118]

Fertile ground for the creation of the Apostolic Administration was prepared by Old Rusyns of Greek Catholic persuasion who were ill-disposed toward the Przemyśl

---

[117] *III Narodnyi Zizd*, pp. 109–110.

[118] See J. Giertych, "Po utworzeniu biskupstwa unickiego na Łemkowszczyźnie," *Myśl Narodowa* 1934, no. 14; "Administrator Apostolski Łemkowszczyzny," *Oriens* 1935, no. 1, pp. 11–13; T. Śliwa, "Kościół greckokatolicki w Polsce w latach 1918–1939," in: *Kościół w II Rzeczypospolitej*, ed. Z. Zieliński, Lublin 1980, pp. 149–164; B. Prach, "Apostolska Administracja Łemkowszczyzny," in: *Łemkowie w historii i kulturze Karpat*, vol. 1, ed. J. Czajkowski, Rzeszów 1992, pp. 229–311.

Greek Catholic ordinariate. In the summer of 1933, during papal nuncio Francesco Marmaggi's visit to Krynica, a delegation of Old Rusyns handed him a memorial in which they proposed creating a separate bishopric for the Lemko region. This initiative had full support from the administrative authorities, as expressed in a secret letter from the starost of Nowy Sącz to the Kraków governor on 20 October 1933, in which the starost, Maciej Łach, stressed the advantages to the nation which would result from the creation of a bishopric.[119] The matter was discussed much earlier during the deliberations of the Committee for Lemko Affairs and one can only judge that the campaign undertaken there was a joint effort between Old Rusyns and government circles, though with a different intention for each partner. When the idea of moving on to the stage of Lemkos' national assimilation began to ripen in government circles, Old Rusyns were feeding on illusions of receiving concessions for the development of their own national existence. Those most faithful to the government even came forward with a project for joining an unspecified number of Greek Catholic parishes to the Roman Catholic diocese in Tarnów.[120]

The conservative fraction of Lemko society, tied to the *Lemko Soiuz* and the RSO, accepted the Apostolic Administration. The Lemkos tied to UNDO, on the other hand, were opposed to the AAL. The Ukrainian press was opposed to it and wrote about the anti-Ukrainian foundations of the AAL's creation. *Dilo* protested against the "division" and "experiments conducted on the Ukrainian population," with other criticisms directed at the Polish government and the Vatican.[121] Questions linked with the AAL were discussed at the meeting of the UNDO Executive Board on 10 March 1934. The board released a communiqué in which it expressed the view that the Vatican's creation of the AAL coincided with "the guiding principles of Polish so-called regional policy" and was directed against "the national and religious feelings of Ukrainians in the western Ukrainian territories."[122] The communiqué stated that the formation of the AAL, in spite of the Vatican's declaration of its motives to be exclusively religious (facing the threat from Eastern Orthodoxy), in the eyes of the Ukrainian community took on political significance and was directed against the "ecclesiastical and national unity of the Halychyna province."[123] The communiqué expressed anxiety that the establishment of a seminary for the needs of the AAL far from Ukrainian centers would "be used by Polish actors for their regional policy toward Ukrainians."[124] The highest UNDO party authorities tasked the URP with raising this issue in parliament and submitting relevant testimony to the Holy See.

---

[119] *Lemkivskyi Kalendar*, 1966, pp. 124–125.

[120] *Lemkivska problema. Napysav Lemko*, Lviv 1933, p. 14.

[121] Calling into question the Vatican's solicitude for Lemkos' Catholicism, *Dilo* pointed to the issue of the Roman Catholic Ukrainian population in the area of the southeastern voivodeships, ironically stating that an Apostolic Administration ought to be created for them too. See *Dilo* 1934, no. 54.

[122] *SN* 1934, nos. 2–3, p. 249.

[123] Quoted from *SN* 1934, nos. 2–3, p. 249.

[124] *Dilo* 1934, no. 70, p. 1.

In autumn of the same year (1934), the government in its decree of 1 October dissolved the District Court in Sanok, which was responsible for 10 municipal districts: Baligród, Bircza, Brzozów, Bukowsko, Dynów, Lesko, Lutowiska, Rymanów, Sanok, and Ustrzyki Dolne. The municipal courts in Brzozów and Dynów were joined to the District Court in Rzeszów, and the others (except Bircza) to the District Court in Jasło. The subordination of the entire area of the Lemko region situated in the Lviv province to the district court in Jasło, with the appeals court in Kraków, made using Ukrainian language in lodging appeals impossible, since in the Kraków province, in accordance with the Grabski laws, only the state language, i.e. Polish, could be used.[125] This issue would return repeatedly in later years during deliberations in the Sejm, mainly in discussions of the budget for the Ministry of Justice. For example, it was extensively described by deputy Volodymyr Tselevych on 12 January 1937 in a speech in which he criticized the liquidation of the District Court in Sanok. Similarly, Stepan Biliak, while discussing the rights of Ukrainian language in government offices, demanded that the Sanok District Court be reactivated.[126] In spite of protests, the decision remained firm.

The school system was also used in the process of isolating the Lemko region. The introduction of Trokhanovsky's primer into school curricula had echoes which resonated widely. Ukrainian circles unambiguously read this move as an element of the policy of "regionalization." In the Sejm this issue returned in budget debates. The intensity of the discussions is shown by the speeches of Dmytro Velykanovych, who called the introduction of textbooks with the Lemko dialect into school programs "the pedagogical error of the twentieth century."[127]

Administrative limits on the development of *Prosvita*, *Ridna Shkola* and other Ukrainian institutions in the Lemko region, the creation of the AAL, the dissolution of the District Court in Sanok, and the elimination of Ukrainian language from schools all served to heighten the reaction from the URP and UNDO. The unity of the Lemko region "with the rest of the Ukrainian nation" was defended in the Sejm by S. Biliak, S. Baran, V. Tselevych, D. Velykanovych, and A. Hryvnak, and in the senate by O. Kysilovska, I. Makukh, and A. Horbachevsky. These members of parliament accused the government of "implementing one policy in Polisia, another in Volhynia, and still another in the Lemko region," of creating a separate nation – an Old Rusyn one (Makukh),[128] of experimenting by creating a category of "people from here" in Polisia (Horbachevsky),[129] of supporting Moscophilism (Hryvnak), of

[125] See S. Baran, "Sianik i Yaslo," *Dilo* 1934, no. 208, pp. 1–2; *Dziennik Ustaw Rzeczypospolitej Polskiej* 1924, no. 78, item 757, *Ustawa z dnia 31 lipca 1924 r. o języku urzędowania sądów, urzędów prokuratorskich i notariatu.*

[126] Sejm RP, *40 posiedzenie z dnia 16 lutego 1937 r.*, columns 70–71; *Dilo* 1937, no. 8, p. 5.

[127] Sejm RP, *14 posiedzenie z dnia 21 lutego 1936 r.*, column 56.

[128] *Dilo* 1935, no. 60, p. 5.

[129] *Senat Rzeczypospolitej Polskiej. Sprawozdania Stenograficzne* (hereinafter – Senat RP), *71 posiedzenie z dnia 27 lutego 1935 r.*, column 82; *Dilo* 1935, no. 54, pp. 1–2.

engaging in a provocation against the Ukrainian nation, introducing Trokhanovsky's primer into school programs (Tselevych),[130] etc. Numerous Ukrainian voices in parliament stressed the need to maintain unity throughout the ethnically Ukrainian sphere, and demanded a free hand for the activities of Ukrainian institutions in all regions populated by Ukrainians. These issues returned every time department budgets were discussed: for the ministries of internal affairs, justice, education, and religious denominations, and even those of agriculture and public works.

After the outcry in parliament the matter returned to the provinces. The main venue for official appearances was Sanok. The Sanok congress of the UNDO County Committee of 7 December 1935, which gathered 40 delegates from 16 towns, was critical of government policy.[131] The resolutions there approved expressed a protest against the limitations placed on the development of Ukrainian institutions in the Lemko region. On 14 May 1936, at the initiative of the UNDO County Committee in Sanok, the first all-Lemko political conference was held, assembling 184 representatives from the counties of Sanok, Krosno, Brzozów, Jasło, Gorlice, Lesko and even Rzeszów. The conference also featured the participation of invited representatives of the URP, V. Tselevych and S. Vytvytsky.[132] The proceedings were opened by the chairman of the Sanok UNDO Committee, Vasyl Blavatsky, after which speeches were made by Ukrainian deputies. Their speeches dealt with RP policy toward the Lemko region, referring to the political context of the AAL's creation, the liquidation of the District Court in Sanok, etc. After the speeches a discussion developed, in which the speakers demanded more frequent contact with deputies from the "Lemko neighborhood" and expressed indignation at the obstacles placed before Ukrainian institutions in the Lemko region.

During the discussion, in addition to voices from the intelligentsia, peasants took the floor. Longer orations were made by V. Kachmarsky of Bonarówka, O. Serednytsky of Ulucz, Y. Shchitka of Jabłonica Ruska, and I. Vilha of Regetów.[133] Craftsmen and tradesmen also spoke, e.g. A. Gots of Dąbrówka Ruska and Y. Pachovsky of Komańcza.[134] As a result of the discussion, resolutions condemning the existing government policy toward the Lemko region were unanimously passed. The Sanok congress took the firm position that "the Lemko region is considered an inseparable part of one Ukrainian nation, and no man's attempts to tear the region from the Ukrainian trunk shall succeed."[135] Ukrainian Parliamentary Representation was declared the Lemko region's representative in parliament, and the assembly's full

[130] *Dilo* 1937, no. 17, p. 7.
[131] CDIAL, f. 344, op. 1t, case # 259, *Zvit, protokol, lystuvannia ta inshi dokumenty pro diialnist povitovoho komitetu v Sianoku*, p. 13.
[132] *SN* 1936, no. 3, p. 251.
[133] Ibid. Short statements were made by P. Dembinsky (Kulaszne), I. Laikosh (Hołuczków), I. Malyniak (Kostarowce), F. Sehin (Rzepedź), see *Dilo* 1936, no. 111, p. 4.
[134] CDIAL, f. 344, op. 1t, case # 259, pp. 16, 17, 18.
[135] *SN* 1936, no. 3, p. 251.

confidence in it expressed. The congress was dominated by secular delegates, which fact however did not deter the delegates from recognizing the Bishop of Przemyśl Yosafat Kotsylovsky and his priesthood for their contribution to the national and religious revival of the Lemko region.

The congress made a series of resolutions of a protest nature. Above all it demanded the liquidation of the AAL or at least the appointment of a Greek Catholic clergyman of Ukrainian nationality to a responsible post. A demand was issued for Ukrainian language to be newly introduced "into Lemko schools with Ukrainian children." The right of Lemkos to purchase land through the parcelling-out of great estates was stressed, and the hiring of Ukrainian workers in workplaces of the Lemko region was demanded.[136]

A separate resolution demanded the reactivation of the District Court in Sanok and the expansion of its jurisdiction to include the counties of Brzozów and Krosno, as well as its reattachment to the District Appeals Court in Lviv. The eighth and last resolution took the form of a call to "struggle for our rights and existence as a nation" under the leadership of UNDO together with URP. Following the Sanok political conference, similar meetings were organized in smaller centers. The scope of topics discussed at them did not extend beyond the resolutions of the Sanok congress, however.[137]

Despite the protests from the Ukrainian side, the government authorities continued in their previous course of nationality policy. It was based on the decidedly polar opposition between the Polish government and the UNDO–URP coalition. No compromise was worked out on this issue until the end of the Second Polish Republic. Because UNDO nonetheless felt equally responsible for the fate of Ukrainians outside of Poland, Ukrainian politicians were inclined to compromise on the Polish segment, keeping their sights on Ukrainian issues at the international level.

In the mid-1930s events occurred which forced UNDO to revise its existing policies. Chief among these was the fiasco endured by the Ukrainians in the forum of the League of Nations, where the tendency to uphold the *status quo* in border disputes prevailed, in contradiction of the forward-looking UNDO program for building a Ukrainian nation from the ethnically Ukrainian territories situated in Poland, the USSR, Rumania and Czechoslovakia. A more immediate perspective forced them to take realistic steps. Events in Soviet Ukraine (the Great Famine and the extermination of Ukrainian elites) disposed them toward cooperation with the RP. For their part, government circles were weakened by the existence of a strong internal opposition and counted on the support of the Ukrainian minority in elections. In their complex internal and external political situation, the politicians in UNDO were willing to undertake attempts to come to an agreement with the government,

---

[136]   CDIAL, f. 344, op. 1t, case # 259, p. 18.
[137]   Similar conferences were held in Lesko, Przemyśl, and Ustrzyki Dolne. See *Dilo* 1936, no. 83, p. 5.

the more so since the existing policies of the party in the years 1928–1935 had not brought the expected results.[138]

In February 1935 the president of UNDO, deputy Dmytro Levytsky, gave a speech in the Sejm which some commentators interpreted as an offer of conciliation. Levytsky pointed to the Polish government, letting it be understood that a compromise in Polish-Ukrainian relations would depend on the position taken by the Polish side, and posited the thesis of normalizing relations on the basis of a shared anti-Soviet political platform and territorial autonomy for the Ukrainians in Poland.[139] The offer was initially dismissed by minister of the interior Kościałkowski, who in ministry budget discussions on 14 February 1935 accused Ukrainian parliamentarians of being "two-faced," i.e. presenting one interpretation to the government and another in public speeches.[140] The affair soon appeared in the press. *Dilo* published Levytsky's reaction, in which he demanded that Minister Kościałkowski provide facts to substantiate his accusation.[141] At a meeting on 27 February, Senator Horbachevsky also spoke against Kościałkowski's statement, referring in his remarks to various aspects of the policy of "regionalization" implemented by the government toward Pidlashia and the Chełm, Hutsul and Lemko regions.[142]

Nonetheless, in late May and early June of 1935 preliminary talks began between Kościałkowski and the politicians of UNDO. The government was interested in normalizing relations with Ukrainians largely because of the approaching elections. The agreement gave a guarantee of participation by Ukrainian parties in the elections, which the government was counting on, knowing the position of Polish opposition parties. The issue of an agreement with the government at first gave rise to dissonance within UNDO, since some party members took a firm position in favor of boycotting the elections. But finally the idea won out, though a group of party members led by I. Kedryn, D. Levytsky and M. Rudnytska, mistrustful of the ruling government cabinet, were opposed. Mudry and Tselevych, on the other hand, who represented UNDO in close talks with the government, were fervent supporters of the agreement. Both also led a propaganda campaign in favor of "normalization" in the Ukrainian milieu, stressing the benefits that were intended to be gained. URP submitted a list of 18 points or postulates to the government, which the government viewed favorably. The government consented to, among other things, the introduction of exclusive official use of the term "Ukrainian,"[143] bilingual signs on govern-

---

[138] *Dilo* 1937, no. 152, p. 3.

[139] Ibid., no. 150, p. 3.

[140] A. Chojnowski, *Koncepcje polityki narodowościowej rządów polskich w latach 1921–1939*, Wrocław 1979, p. 203.

[141] See *Dilo* 1935, no. 43, p. 1.

[142] Senat RP, *71 posiedzenie z dnia 27 lutego 1935 r.*, column 82; *Dilo* 1935, no. 54, pp. 1–2.

[143] Moscophile and Old Rusyn circles protested against this. See *Oświadczenie protestacyjne towarzystw i organizacji ruskich przeciw urzędowemu wprowadzeniu terminu "ukraiński" zamiast "ruski"*, Lwów 1936.

ment office and city council buildings, and curtailment of the "regionalization" campaign in the Lemko region.[144] Persuading the Ukrainian community to support the idea of an agreement, at the UNDO rally of 5 November 1935 Mudry assured the gathering that this was realpolitik conducted in full awareness of the mutual dangers for the state and for the Ukrainian nationality.[145] The agreement did not signify resignation from the ultimate goal toward which the campaign was working within the Polish nation – "territorial autonomy for all Ukrainian lands in Poland, i.e. [...] the creation of a separate autonomous entity in all Ukrainian ethnographic territories within the borders of the Polish nation."[146]

The new electoral law, which rejected the principle of representation of whole communities by political parties and redirected voting to individuals, was also a source of division. Because candidates for deputy posts called district assemblies, the change meant that in mixed districts Poles had an advantage. In discussing the planned electoral law at the constitutional commission in the Sejm on 13 June 1935, S. Khrutsky stated that the procedure outlined in the plan would make it impossible to elect Ukrainian candidates from the Chełm and Lemko regions to the Sejm.[147] A similar position was taken by S. Biliak, who opposed the plan on behalf of URP, during another debate on the subject on 25 June.[148] An electoral compromise concluded at the last moment was based on both sides committing to voting without deletions.

For the government's purposes "normalization" was a tactical move tied to the 1935 elections. UNDO (in treating Ukrainian independence as a prospective program) was aiming for an agreement at the cost of inner frictions (the *Dilo* group remained in the opposition). The government did not in fact change the guidelines of its existing nationality policy, but made modifications aiming to implement Kościałkowski's 1936 program, i.e. it started on the path of Polonization of the western boundary of the sphere of Ukrainian settlement. Thus the "regionalization" policy was not only not curtailed, but was expanded through support of the so-called *szlachta zagrodowa* (petty nobility) and greater military involvement. A separate issue is the pressure from the national-democratic milieux (but not only them) on the native Polish population in the borderlands, whose judgment later governments would have to heed.[149]

In such conditions "normalization" did not meet the expectations of UNDO politicians. In the Ukrainian press, and also in the parliamentary forum, doubts arose regarding the advisability of continuing this political tack. A critical evaluation of the course of the normalization process was presented in the Sejm by one of its proponents, V. Tselevych. In the discussion of the interior ministry's budget, he

---

[144] *Dilo* 1937, no. 150, p. 3; A. Chojnowski, op.cit., p. 205.

[145] *SN* 1935, no. 6, p. 620.

[146] Sejm RP, *4 posiedzenie z dnia 5 i 6 grudnia 1935 r.*, column 99.

[147] *Dilo* 1935, no. 162, p. 3.

[148] Sejm RP, *145 posiedzenie z dnia 25 czerwca 1935 r.*, columns 60–64; *Dilo* 1935, no. 167, pp. 1–2.

[149] J. Tomaszewski, op.cit., pp. 99–100.

reminded those present of the point in the agreement which bound the government to conducting a uniform policy toward all Ukrainian lands. He then said:

> If the normalization of Polish-Ukrainian relations is to be lasting and achieve a [lasting] foundation in Ukrainian society, all attempts to break up the Ukrainian nation within Polish borders into separate regional groups must be dispensed with [...] the government's policy toward Ukrainians must be one and the same, both in the region of the former Galicia together with the Lemko region, and in Volhynia, Polisia, Chełm region, and Pidlashia.[150]

Tselevych devoted a significant part of his oration to issues facing the Lemko region, accusing the government of creating there a "reservation, in which only Russophile associations can exist." Tselevych finished his speech with the demands familiar from earlier years.

Doubts as to the future of "normalization" were further expressed by Mudry in an article entitled "Experiences and observations" published in *Dilo* on 12 April 1936, in which he drew attention to the attitude of Polish public opinion in the "East Lesser Poland" area toward the idea of an agreement with Ukrainians, accusing the Polish population there of paralyzing all action toward satisfying the Ukrainians' needs as a nation.[151] He was especially critical of the local state administration. The agreement had not been based on mutual understanding and it is difficult to judge, whether such a thing was possible at all. The intentions of UNDO and the government fell wide each of the other, and Mudry at the budget session in the Sejm accused the government side of lacking the will "to sincere fulfillment of [the agreement]."[152]

The opposition group took a critical stance – understandably – toward the idea of an agreement with the government. In July 1937 *Dilo* published a questionnaire on the subject of "normalization," and the editors then printed the most interesting responses to it. Among others, the opinions of deputies D. Levytsky, V. Kuzmovych, H. Tershakovets, and Fr. S. Onyshkevych – former deputy to the Viennese Imperial Council were printed there. All pointed to the negative consequences of "normalization" – to the facts of the government's failure to keep its word regarding the 18 points of the agreement. The respondents accordingly took up the question of the "regionalization" policy and protested "against the breaking up of Ukrainians into the ethnic groups of the Lemkos, Hutsuls, and Volhynians."[153] Tershakovets in his questionnaire stated that Ukrainian life had been driven back from the political platform to the level of ethnic groups, giving the Lemko and Hutsul regions as examples.[154]

---

[150] Quoted from *Dilo* 1936, no. 17, p. 3.
[151] V. Mudry, "Dosvidy i sposterezhennia," *Dilo* 1936, no. 81, p. 2. See *SN* 1936, no. 3, pp. 248–249.
[152] *Dilo* 1935, no. 328, pp. 1–2.
[153] Ibid., 1937, no. 203, p. 3.
[154] *SN* 1937, nos. 4–5, p. 424.

The increasing dissatisfaction within the ranks of UNDO due to the failure of "normalization" found an outlet in a change to the organization's previous policies. Issues raised many times in parliament concerning the regions populated by Ukrainians, not only in terms of maintaining and developing Ukrainian national culture, but also in the area of economic development, were not being responded to by state administration activity. Increasingly UNDO returned to the demand for territorial autonomy, which it raised at the Fifth UNDO Congress on 4–5 January 1938. With reference to the evaluation of the 1935 agreement the relevant congress resolution spoke of the necessity for raising the demand for the conferment of territorial autonomy on Ukrainian ethnographic lands with their own parliament, government, and army.[155]

The Lemko issue was contained in the broad outline of government policy toward Ukrainians, demanding "unified nationality policy toward the whole Ukrainian community, as one uniform, organic whole in political and legal terms."[156] Starting from the assumption that the government side had not kept the terms of the agreement, the Congress passed a resolution in which it stated that:

> since 1935 an intensified Polonization campaign has begun in the Lemko region, the Hutsul region, Polisia and Pidlashia [...]. A campaign to denationalize the Ukrainian petty nobility and to Latinize the Greek Catholics has begun [...]. Polish actors use procedures to create some Rusyn political group which is supposed to be the negation of the political currents in the Ukrainian community.[157]

The Fifth UNDO Congress criticized the period of "normalization," and thereby deepened the conviction among Ukrainians that a change from the previous political tack was needed.

The transformations which took place in Europe in 1938, in particular the Third Reich's tactical advancement of the Ukrainian question, which fed hopes for building a Greater Ukraine with German assistance, accelerated the URP's decision to make an interpellation regarding autonomy.[158] The draft defined in detail the area of the proposed territorial entity, comprising the whole of the Lemko region. The act was hastened by the declaration of the UNDO Central Committee on the issue of the Ukrainian people's place in the Second Polish Republic, passed 7 May 1938, which expressed a protest against: "breaking up the national unity and cohesion of the Ukrainian nation [...] and creating a fiction about the existence of distinct [...] ethnic groups in the form of Rusyns, Lemkos, Hutsuls, Volynians and Poleszuks."[159]

---

[155] *Dilo* 1938, no. 7, p. 7.

[156] Quoted from *Dilo* 1938, no. 7, p. 7.

[157] Quoted from ibid.; *SN* 1938, nos. 1–2, p. 103.

[158] CDIAL, f. 344, op. 1t, case # 22, *Proiekt statutu "Halytsko-Volynska Zemlia" skladenyi deputatamy ukrainskymy dla rozhladu v soimi*, pp. 1–8. The government recognized this plan for autonomy as an attempt to change the political system of the RP.

[159] "Deklaracja Centralnego Komitetu UNDO w sprawie położenia narodu ukraińskiego w państwie polskim, przyjęta na posiedzeniu dnia 7 maja 1938 r.," in: Z. Pełeński Poray, *Polityka UNDO*

The hopes of Ukrainians reached their apogee after the creation of the autonomous region of Carpathian Ukraine in November 1938. Criticism toward the period of "normalization" became increasingly harsh. Mudry spoke in the Sejm of "aggressive Polish nationalist elements, which official circles have followed."[160] Tselevych, criticizing the stance of the government side, stated that "in relations between the minority and the majority, between the state-holding nation and the minority-nation, the key to normalization is held by the state-holding nation, and the choice of means which the state employs in dealing with it does not depend on the Ukrainian population."[161] The demand for autonomy was not accepted before the speaker's staff, a decision whose justification was argued by the demand's "ostentatious" character, i.e. its method was seen as "an unjustified defense by an unjustified attack."[162]

The idea of autonomy returned repeatedly after the decision of the Council of Ambassadors in March 1923. The lack of autonomy resulted in the gradual dwindling of Ukrainian cultural potential in the Second Republic (by comparison with its condition in the Galician period). UNDO and URP made a concerted effort to open possibilities for the development of Ukrainian culture in all areas populated by Ukrainians, with equal determination in Lviv, the Chełm region or the Lemko region. The 1935 agreement theoretically created opportunities for both nationalities, but it is difficult to judge whether this was truly possible. P. Dunin-Borkowski wrote on the doubts facing such an arrangement in the article cited below:

> An agreement can bring benefits only when a state concludes it with another state. Between a state and a people an agreement is actually inconceivable, since the people which concludes the agreement would see it as one stage in its progress, while the state would obviously want to see in the agreement a solution and the pacification of a certain segment.[163]

The failure of the attempt to reach an agreement in 1935 pushed both parties back toward distant positions. It meant a policy defeat for UNDO, by which it rendered possible the growing significance of nationalist forces in the Ukrainian milieu and had a negative influence on the defensive capability of prewar Poland and the shape of Polish-Ukrainian relations during the war.

---

w świetle autonomicznej deklaracji Centralnego Komitetu UNDO z dnia 7 maja 1938 r., Lwów 1938, p. 12.

[160] Sejm RP, *3 posiedzenie z dnia 3 grudnia 1938 r.*, column 48.
[161] Sejm RP, *11 posiedzenie z dnia 16 lutego 1939 r.*, column 134.
[162] Ibid., column 9.
[163] P. Dunin-Borkowski, "Punkt wyjścia w sprawie ukraińskiej w Małopolsce Wschodniej," *Droga* 1929, no. 6, p. 567.

Chapter IV: The Lemko region in the nationality policy of the Second Polish Republic

1. The immediate postwar period

The fall of the Lemko republics put an end to the Lemko postwar searchings for a national identity other than Polish. Despite the fact that changes occurred in the general consciousness of the community and its elites, it was the rebirth of the Polish state, absorbing the Lemko region throughout the northern slope of the Carpathian mountains, which marked out the prospect of Polish citizenship for Lemkos and the necessity that all issues of sociopolitical life be dealt with in terms of Polish statehood.

The immediate afterwar years proved to be a test of Lemkos' loyalty to the state, which process was highlighted in the context of military matters: registration for conscription and conscription itself.[1] In early 1921, based on the reports of State Police Posts (PPP), districts sent lists to the government in Lviv of persons who were shirking military service. In each case of disloyalty an investigation, intended to force the conscript to be brought before the registration commission, was decreed. This task belonged to the police, but its execution was made difficult by the mountainous and wooded terrain of the municipalities in which draft-dodgers found convenient hiding places. The administrative authorities, following orders from a higher court, conducted searches (not only for Lemkos) and raised the share in operational costs for those municipalities which did not provide conscription registration lists at the appointed time.[2]

The many instances of desertion constituted a separate problem for the military and civil authorities. The Second Bureau of the General Staff determined that deserters were mostly going to Czechoslovakia through illegal border crossings along

---

[1]   AP K, SP G II, ref. # 45, *Sprawy wojskowe: wypełnianie obowiązku wojskowego przez Rusinów z terenu powiatu, 1921, 1923*, p.n.n.; AP K, SP NS, ref. # 85, *Akta prezydialne Starostwa Powiatowego w Nowym Sączu, 1919–1939*, p.n.n.

[2]   AAN, MWRiOP, ref. # 474, *Parafie greckokatolickie – obsada: Nominacje, prezenty, instytucje kanoniczne przedkonkordatowe*, vol. 1, 1920–1923, p.n.n.; AP K, SP G II, ref. # 43, *Sprawy wojskowe, pobór do wojska, nadzór nad rejestracją poborowych, 1922*, p.n.n.

the entire length of the frontier. This phenomenon became so widespread that the Presidium Department in Kraków sent specific orders in a letter of 13 November 1923 to all districts close to the border, demanding the use of heightened measures for protecting the national border.[3] Said directives were conveyed through official channels to all County Government Police Headquarters (PKPP) and local state police posts. In each case of desertion the police conducted an investigation. There were incidental deaths of deserters during police pursuits.[4]

The lack of acceptance of Polish statehood in many Lemko regions was connected with the strong feelings of ties to Russia, e.g. during the 1921 census in Żegiestów some village residents declared that "Rusyns [...] are not subject to the Polish census" and in the corresponding rubric checked "Russian subject." The concept of "Polish citizenship" was identified with the Roman Catholic Church.[5]

Beginning in 1918 the administrative authorities conducted surveillance of the Lemko milieu, more than once relying on the help of local informers (also Lemkos).[6] At the recommendation of court authorities, districts prepared lists of clerks of non-Polish nationality. The first to be evaluated were police functionaries, the border service and the treasury guards. Beginning in the spring of 1919 the districts and County Military Police Commands exchanged confidential written correspondence with the province authorities in preparation for a campaign to transfer all questionable employees to centrally located counties. The lack of trust in clerks of Ukrainian nationality frequently stirred the emotions of those making evaluations, which was reflected in the contents of their professional correspondence.[7] A result of this was the hiring on the police force and in other uniformed services of ethnically Polish functionaries. Similar action was taken when manning positions in the post office due to a fear that they might be transformed into "Rusyn institutions and places of Russophile propaganda."[8]

Testing the mood of the populace also involved investigating the level of influence of the Greek Catholic Church and its impact on the political consciousness of Lem-

---

[3] AP K, SP G II, ref. # 44, *Sprawy wojskowe, nadzór nad rejestracja poborowych*, p.n.n.

[4] Such an incident occurred in Florynka on 30 May 1921. During pursuit by PPP sentries in Kąclowa, J. Ozga and J. Morański, deserter T. Maksymchak, staying overnight in his parents' house, died from a rifle bullet. See AP K, SP G II, ref. # 43, *Sprawy wojskowe 1919–1921*, p.n.n.

[5] AP K, SP NS, ref. # 85, p.n.n.

[6] AP P, *Starostwo Powiatowe w Jaśle, 1918–1939*, ref. # 20, *Działalność antypaństwowa (wykaz osób aresztowanych: podejrzanych o szpiegostwo), 1919–1925*; Ibid., ref. # 21, *Inwigilacje osób podejrzanych, 1920–1927*; AP K, SP NS, ref. # 85, p.n.n.

[7] For example, the director of the Treasury Circle in Nowy Sącz in a letter of 14 May 1919 sent to county government offices wrote: "The Byzantine hypocrisy which consists in taking an oath with a view to the government salary and acting through deeds or through omission to secretly harm the nation, should always, but particularly in the present period of transition be condemned with all the means at our disposal." See AP K, SP G II, ref. # 3, *Referat organizacyjny, sprawy osobowe urzędników*, p.n.n.

[8] AP K, SP NS, ref. # 85, p.n.n.

kos. The authorities' intention was to isolate Lemko parishes from Greek Catholic clergy with connections to the Ukrainian movement. After the release of a pastoral letter from Greek Catholic bishops in 1919 devoted to the situation of the Ukrainian people, the Lviv government in a letter of 14 October instructed the districts of Gorlice, Grybów, Jasło, Krosno, Nowy Sącz and Sanok to investigate whether it had been read out in churches and what its effects on the population were. The involvement of some local police posts went considerably further and there were incidents where packages addressed to parish offices were confiscated through the intermediacy of clerks who had been persuaded to cooperate.[9]

Beginning in 1919 on the orders of voivodeship authorities, districts investigated the political mood among Greek Catholic priests. As a result of dispatches from police and local informers, the most politically active parish centers were identified and the clergy was divided into adherents of the Old Rusyn orientation, the Moscophile one or the Ukrainian.

This line of action continued up to the end of the 1920s. Local administrative authorities intensified their surveillance as a result of secret reports from the Ministry of the Interior on the enhanced activity of the Ukrainian national movement in Czechoslovakia and the former Eastern Galicia which reached county government offices through the intermediacy of the Presidium Department of the Kraków province.[10] County authorities affirmed the aversion of the Lemko population to Polish statehood on the basis of Lemkos' attitude toward service in the Polish army and feared any kind of internal or external campaign which could energize political feeling left over from the era of the Lemko Republics.

In the western part of the region there was considerably greater fear of a revival of the Moscophile or Czechophile movement than the Ukrainian one, while in the eastern part the reverse situation applied. This divergence in fears resulted from the different tendencies in political activity among Lemkos in the years 1917–1920, which in the eastern Lemko region were oriented toward ZUNR, and in the western toward Russia and Czechoslovakia. This was fostering Ukrainian settlement in the western areas of the Lemko region, streaming in from the lands of the former Eastern Galicia. It should be emphasized that the administrative authorities in the Gorlice, Grybów, Jasło, and Nowy Sącz counties made no attempt at that time to curb this migration.

In the western region the Moscophile and Old Rusyn milieux were particularly subject to surveillance.[11] The districts gave emphatic support to Ukrainian candidates for Greek Catholic presbyteries. This attitude among the authorities was reflected in the contents of official correspondence, in which we read: "filling parish posts [...] with Ukrainian priests would be advisable for political reasons [...], since

[9]   Ibid.
[10] AP K, SP G II, ref. # 10, *Sprawy dotyczące agitacji na rzecz oderwania się Łemkowszczyzny od Polski*, p.n.n.
[11] AP K, SP NS, ref. # 85, p.n.n.

powerful Moscophile influence in this part of our nation in the Lemko region, which are opposed to its activities, would thereby be checked."[12] Thus the political orientations which had developed within the Lemko community were turned against each other. The key difference amounted to which side one chose to support. If in the first half of the 1920s there had been support for Ukrainians against Moscophiles and Old Rusyns, the efforts of authorities beginning in the later part of the decade were directed towards weakening the Ukrainian movement.[13]

In the period preceding the Sejm and Senate elections in 1922 in some areas of the western Lemko region the shared feelings of hostility to the Polish nation-state rose to the level of a rapprochement between Old Rusyn and Ukrainian activists. Ukrainian political circles declared a boycott of elections, thereby demonstrating their non-acceptance of the Polish state. On 27 May 1922, Ivan Ohiienko, Minister of Education and Religious Denominations in the council of the Ukrainian National Republic, language specialist, professor at the secret Ukrainian university and later professor at the University of Warsaw, came to the municipality of Powroźnik together with his family. According to letters from the PPP in Muszyna to the District of Nowy Sącz of 3 September 1922, since the time of his residence in Powroźnik the local peasants had begun to show hostility toward the Polish state, a proof of which was claimed to be the absence of municipality leaders H. Klymkovsky of Wojkowa and I. Shchavynsky of Powroźnik and the secretaries of their respective municipality offices, O. Pyroh and D. Lohaza, from the pre-election session in Nowy Sącz on 29 August.[14] The leaders and secretaries of all other municipalities in Nowy Sącz County took part in the session; they received detailed instructions concerning action to be taken prior to the election. Similar instructional meetings for municipal authorities were held in the other counties.

In the case of I. Ohiienko's anti-election agitation, the police headquarters in Nowy Sącz delegated a special emissary to Muszyna, senior leader W. Pilch, who established that agitation was being conducted by Ohiienko in league with the Greek Catholic rector from Żegiestów, Fr. R. Pryslopsky, until recently active in the Moscophile movement. In a report to headquarters of the State Police in Nowy Sącz, the functionary quoted a fragment of Fr. Pryslopsky's speech, which he alleged stated that "[...] the Rusyns here are not planning to vote, since they do not have a Rusyn deputy or a candidate of Rusyn nationality who would run for the Sejm from that district."[15]

An investigation of Ohiienko showed that he had maintained contact with local clergy and teachers of Ukrainian orientation, making numerous trips to their places of residence. The anti-election agitation strengthened the antipathy of the Lemko population toward elections, since – as agitators proclaimed – "the Rusyn question

---

[12]   Ibid.
[13]   AP K, SP G II, ref. # 20, *Sprawy graniczne*, p.n.n.
[14]   AP K, SP NS, ref. # 85, p.n.n.
[15]   Ibid.

has not been satisfactorily resolved in the League of Nations, and Poland has been entrusted only with provisory oversight over the population." The police, however, did not obtain a legal basis for arresting agitators, who were careful in their operations not to act openly against the state authorities.[16]

The activities of Ohienko and Pryslopsky led to the convocation in Krynica Zdrój of an all-Lemko gathering for the purpose of discussing the position of "Rusyns of the Lemko Lands" toward the approaching parliamentary elections. The assembly, which took place on 18 October 1922 in the "Wiktoria" hotel, was attended by representatives of the Gorlice, Grybów, and Nowy Sącz counties as well as delegates from Lviv. Yaroslav Kachmarchyk opened the assembly, after which congress authorities were chosen.[17] The main speakers were Anton Gensiorsky and Kosma Pelekhaty, both from Lviv. In their speeches they discussed the Lemko question in the context of general Ukrainian affairs in Poland and called for a boycott of elections, stating that participating in the elections would mean acceptance of Polish statehood. The Lemko speakers were Fr. Y. Khylak, Fr R. Pryslopsky, Fr. A. Sembratovych, M. Trokhanovsky and the farmers M. Rusyniak of Wierchomla Wielka and M. Gromosiak of Krynica Wieś. They did not speak against the Polish state, but all talked of the "Rusyn injury." At the end of the congress a resolution declaring a boycott of Senate and Sejm elections in November 1922 was unanimously approved. A similar assembly for the eastern Lemko region took place slightly earlier in Sanok, where a boycott of elections was also called.[18]

In accordance with the resolutions of the assemblies in Sanok and Krynica the Lemko population, except for some sporadic incidents, did not generally participate in the elections. The small number of votes in Rusyn municipalities came from Poles and Jews and less frequently from Czechs and Germans.[19]

The boycott by the Ukrainians throughout the former Galicia caused a serious decrease in voter turnout; in some counties only 18% of those legally eligible voted.[20] In the Lemko region, e.g. in Grybów County, voter turnout wavered between 0% (Berest, Bogusza, Czarna, Czertyżne, Jaszkowa, Kamianna, Polany, Wawrzka) and 8% (Brunary Wyżne) where in Polish municipalities the average was 70–80%.[21]

The elections signaled the non-acceptance of the Polish state by the Lemko population. A change in this position occurred after the decision by the Council of Ambassadors on 14 March 1923 granting Poland rule over Eastern Galicia. The decision brought the Ukrainian question in Poland from the international arena into

---

[16]   Ibid.
[17]   K. Bulanda of Krynica became Chairman, with A. Gogots of Polany as deputy chairman and D. Lohaza of Krynica as secretary.
[18]   AP K, SP NS, ref. # 85, p.n.n.
[19]   APK, SP G II, ref. # 11, p.n.n.
[20]   A. Próchnik, *Pierwsze piętnastolecie Polski niepodległej. Zarys dziejów politycznych*, Warszawa 1983, p. 109.
[21]   AP K, SP G II, ref. # 11, p.n.n.

the realm of Polish internal policy. Poland was not, however, entirely freed from its international obligations, which arose from the Minority Treaties, so that the state authorities faced the necessity of regulating the state's relationships with minorities.

2. Assimilation: state or national

On the strength of the Treaty of Versailles and the Treaty of Saint-Germain-en-Laye, the Council of Ambassadors took the decision to recognize the eastern borders of Poland delimited in the Treaty of Rome.[22] This decision met with satisfaction from the Polish government, but simultaneously stirred fears, since the Republic of Poland had to consider the contingency of a Ukrainian interpellation in the League of Nations. The pre-1926, pre-reform government had established legal regulations which influenced the shape of Polish-Ukrainian relations up until 1939. The general program boiled down to strengthening Polish possessions, which was intended to be achieved through military colonization and development of Polish schools and the Catholic Church.[23]

The political program toward the Ukrainians was formulated by Prime Minister Władysław Sikorski in late March and early April 1923 in two documents: a proclamation to the citizens of the eastern borderlands and a secret paper on government policy directives in the borderlands. This program was the first official demand for Ukrainians to be "assimilated into the state."[24] It put forward the concept of regionalism, and recommended using the existing religious, cultural and social differences in the Ukrainian community. It proposed seeking out those milieux which were loyal and creating from them a Ukrainian conciliatory party.[25] Sikorski correctly deduced that in light of the Council of Ambassadors' decision, the position of Ukrainian circles would be subject to revaluation; that they, like the Polish government, would seek a path of mutual understanding. Based on these guiding principles, contacts were made with Moscophiles, who already during Sikorski's premiership had received certain economic concessions.[26]

The direction for nationality policy indicated by Sikorski lost its importance as the right gained an increasingly strong position in the nation. The minister of the department of internal affairs in Grabski's government, Władysław Sołtan, at a meeting of the Council of Ministers on 25 January 1924, appeared with a paper

---

[22] See R. Torzecki, *Kwestia ukraińska w polityce III Rzeszy (1933–1945)*, Warszawa 1972, pp. 20–31.

[23] J. Lewandowski, "Konflikt polsko-ukraiński na tle konfliktów narodowych w Europie środkowo-wschodniej w XIX i XX w.," *Warszawskie Zeszyty Ukrainoznawcze*, vol. 2, Warszawa 1994, p. 84. O kolonizacji wojskowej, see T. Böhm, "Osadnictwo wojskowe na Kresach Wschodnich w II Rzeczypospolitej," *Dzieje Najnowsze* 1992, nos. 1–2, pp. 3–12.

[24] R. Torzecki, *Kwestia ukraińska w polityce III Rzeszy*, p. 21.

[25] Ibid., p. 25.

[26] Ibid., p. 81.

containing a series of plans for the Ukrainian question. These proposals aimed to ensure the nation's influence on matters relating to the Greek Catholic Church in a future concordat with the Vatican, to introduce a greater number of subjects taught in Polish in schools, to colonize the border areas along the Zbruch River and build a railway line from Jarosław to Lviv and the oil basin, in addition to which they repeated the demand for creating a Ukrainian conciliatory faction and offering its members profitable concessions.[27]

Grabski's government took important steps toward regulating the legal status of the southeastern voivoideships, in the form of what were called the borderland plans: on the state language and the official language for national and local administrative authorities, the official language for courts, prosecutorial offices and notaries, and on the organization of the school system. Preparatory work began in April 1924 and was led by the Commission of Four.[28] The commission's deliberations were held in secret, which caused tensions in the Ukrainian community, expressed in a large number of protest meetings, also on the Boiko-Lemko border, in Sanok and Lesko.

The legislative plan presented to the Sejm was based on the following premises: it gave supremacy to the official state language, i.e. Polish, and the mother language of a given minority residing in the borderland would fulfill a supplementary function; it introduced and legally sanctioned the term "Rusyn" in place of "Ukrainian" despite the use of the latter by the population and the existence of a parliamentary faction with that name. The Sejm passed the laws on 31 July 1924.

It is important to emphasize the treatment of the Ukrainian population in these laws, which refused them the name they had established over decades. The legislators' intentions were to eliminate the "Ukrainian issue" by reducing it to the "Rusyn" issue. The success of this procedure would mean the regression of the historical process to at least the late 19th century, i.e. to a time, when the premise *Gente Ruthenus natione Polonus* was a valid current in Polish political thought, and some Polish milieux were inclined to see Rusyns as Poles, and Rusyn language as a regional dialect of Polish.[29] One can here second M. Papierzyńska-Turek's assertion that the laws in question aimed at the Polonization of the Byelorussian, Lithuanian, and Ukrainian populations.[30]

Right-wing circles enunciated a program for national assimilation of Ukrainians. The main premises of this concept were contained in the articles written by

---

[27] See M. Papierzyńska-Turek, *Sprawa ukraińska w Drugiej Rzeczypospolitej 1922–1926*, Kraków 1979, pp. 216–217.

[28] S. Grabski, E. Starczewski, H. Löwenherz, S. Thugutt.

[29] J. Moklak, *Relacje między ukraińskim ruchem narodowym a moskalofilstwem w Galicji Wschodniej w latach 1866–1890*, MA thesis (typescript), Jagiellonian University, Kraków 1985, p. 24.

[30] M. Papierzyńska-Turek, op.cit., p. 233; P. Stawecki, *Następcy Komendanta. Wojsko a polityka wewnętrzna II Rzeczypospolitej w latach 1935–1939*, Warszawa 1969, p. 171. In October 1923 the government made the decision that for "legal, historical and ethnographical" reasons the use of the term "Rusyn" was mandatory. See AAN, PRM, *Protokoły posiedzeń Rady Ministrów, Protokół 71 z dnia 31 października 1923*.

Stanisław Grabski, theoretician of the ND (National Democrats) and practically concerned with nationality issues, who published a series of articles collectively entitled "Borderlands and nationalities" in the *Lviv Morning Courier* in July 1930. He advocated the numerical expansion of the Polish population along a broad strip of the Przemyśl–Ternopil line using colonial methods. By this means the Ukrainian ethnic sphere was expected to split into two parts.[31] An analogous position was taken by Jędrzej Giertych, who stated that the Ukrainian question in Poland's borders did not amount to a nationality, but rather a political doctrine. Similarly to Sikorski, but from a different perspective, he judged that from the point of view of the RP's interests the Old Rusyn movement should be supported, as a counterweight to the Ukrainian national movement.[32]

At the meeting of the Council of Ministers on 18 August 1926 Józef Piłsudski, at that point minister of military affairs, underscored the necessity of re-orienting the government's program in regard to nationality issues and proposed a "careful" transition from national assimilation to state assimilation. This concept was discussed in an article by former Lviv governor Piotr Dunin-Borkowski entitled "Starting point for the Ukrainian question in East Lesser Poland." Borkowski launched the slogan: "the more loyal citizens, the stronger the state."[33] As an example to be followed he cited Austria-Hungary, which by giving its Polish subjects cultural autonomy had managed to strengthen their ties with state institutions considerably. In his formulation, the basis for civic assimilation was keeping the non-Polish population satisfied with the conditions offered them by the nation-state.[34]

The goal which he presented should, he suggested, be fulfilled by institutional solutions; he stipulated the establishment of a separate territorial unit composed of the areas of the southeastern voivodeships and part of the Lublin province. Ukrainians residing in that area would be able to obtain broad cultural autonomy, and political cooperation on the Ukrainian side would be based on ties with the conciliatory group involved with UNDO and some Old Rusyn groups.[35] He did not touch on the Lemko question, however, no doubt for reasons relating to the fact that it had not yet been raised in political circles, although as governor he must have been acquainted with the problem, since he had made numerous decisions relating to Krosno and Sanok counties. With regard to the Moscophiles, he did not plan on political cooperation with them, based on the premise that they amounted to an insignificant percentage of the Ukrainian community and were not politically important.

---

[31] T. Piotrkiewicz, *Kwestia ukraińska w Polsce w koncepcjach Piłsudczyzny 1926–1930*, Warszawa 1981, p. 128. See S. Grabski, "Kresy i narodowości," *Lwowski Kurier Poranny* 1930.

[32] J. Giertych, *O program polityki kresowej*, Warszawa 1932, p. 31.

[33] AAN, MSZ, ref. # 5320, *Polityka narodowościowa na ziemi czerwińskiej*, p. 5.

[34] P. Dunin-Borkowski, "Punkt wyjścia w sprawie ukraińskiej w Małopolsce Wschodniej," *Droga* 1929, no. 6, p. 569; T. Piotrkiewicz, op.cit., p. 130.

[35] T. Piotrkiewicz, op.cit., p. 123.

The Lemko question as a separate issue in the nationality policy of the ruling camp became apparent as an offshoot of a border policy toward the Ukrainian population and resulted from the desire to strengthen the conciliatory parties. In 1931 in the Nationality Section of the Ministry of the Interior, the main principles for the process of civic assimilation of the non-Polish population were approved, postulating "cooperation with loyal elements which take a position for national unity and the nation-building efforts of the state."[36]

The development of the nationality policy program for the Lemko region was preceded by multifarious investigations of social, psychological and political issues connected with the Lemko population, conducted by Władysław Wielhorski, official in charge of special missions at the Presidium of the Council of Ministers of Poland. Wielhorski's assignment was to gather information on the social life of Lemkos, to describe the typical traits of their mentality, their attitude to religion, toward political campaigns developed in the Lemko region, etc. The results of the investigations were contained in a typed manuscript entitled "the Lemko region" prepared in November 1933. This work contains a broad description of Lemko social life and became the basis for forming the RP's nationality policy toward the Lemko region.

First Wielhorski performed an analysis of the social structure in the region under investigation. Distinguishing between the sparse intelligentsia residing in cities and towns (Bukowsko, Dukla, Gorlice, Jasło, Krosno, Krynica, Lesko, Muszyna, Sanok) – representatives of the so-called "free occupations" and the teachers and priests scattered about the Lemko region – Wielhorski formulated conclusions about the one-layer Lemko community, consisting almost exclusively of peasants, simultaneously defining the psychic nature of this collective. He wrote:

> Lemkos as an ethno-cultural entity are marked by great solidarity and strong allegiance to their home life and ways. They are less good at actively fighting for their collective existence, or [...] attacking an opponent – but they have considerable powers of resistance in defending threatened components of their distinct group. For these reasons, they collectively possess many features which are firmly rooted and change over time only with difficulty. They form a sociological constant on the primitive level of a one-layer peasant community. The traits of sociological invariability are in this case based on a group of definite biological features which guarantee the durability of the collective instinct. Thus a sociological constant has underneath it a biological constant. Hence its durability.[37]

Defining the hierarchy of values in the social life of Lemkos, he put concern for protecting living conditions in the top place, and in the area of cultural life indicated religious matters, to which he attributed their "extreme conservatism and love for tradition."[38]

---

[36] AAN, MSW, ref. # 935, p. 4.
[37] AAN, MSZ, ref. # 5219, W. Wielhorski, *Łemkowszczyzna* (typescript, 1933), p. 6.
[38] Ibid.

Based on the lack of an existing ethnically mixed Polish-Lemko sphere, Wielhorski defined the attitude of the Lemko population toward Poles, indicating the existence of a powerful heterogeneous element among Lemkos, which made mutual ties difficult. In his investigation of the attitude toward the Polish state, he posed the thesis that it was neither hostile, nor friendly, but rather "a-Polish, i.e. indifferent, other" and added that Lemkos "have a tendency to loyalty, to the extent that Ukrainian propaganda has not persuaded them to change their position."[39]

Wielhorski also defined the attitude of the Lemko population toward the cultural sphere of eastern Europe, writing that "a [Lemko] feels that he belongs to the East and regards the cultural inheritance of Eastern Slavdom as its own. It clings to him rather through instinct than reason, considering the level of his culture, but it clings to him very forcefully."[40] He underscored the conservatism of Lemkos in terms of cultural traditions developed since the times of Kyivan Rus, drawing attention simultaneously to the ease with which they submitted to the influences of Moscophilism and the Old Rusyn movement.[41]

Pointing to the conservatism in many areas of community life, Wielhorski attempted to outline the main direction in the development of Lemko political thought. The point of departure for his evaluation was an analysis of the intelligentsia's behavior. He stated that the leaders of the Lemko separatist movement demonstrated "noteworthy sobriety" in their evaluation of the political situation in their region and that in their view the fulfillment even of the boldest expectations of supporters of the Ukrainian movement, i.e. the establishment of a Ukrainian nation along the San River, would still leave the Lemko region within Poland's borders. He expressed this thought in the following words: "Lemkos due to their geographical position are doomed to perpetual co-existence with the Polish nation-state." According to Wielhorski's report, those words were the contents of a resolution passed at a meeting of Old Rusyn circles in Krynica in 1933.[42]

The material he had gathered allowed Wielhorski to formulate tentative premises for a nationality policy program in the Lemko region which was divided into several problem areas: the school system, cultural and educational issues, and economic issues.

In the area of schooling he drew particular attention to the necessity of selecting teacher cadres, who in his opinion should be found in the Polish or Lemko community. He definitely ruled out the Ukrainian intelligentsia from the lands of the former Eastern Galicia, stating that "Ukrainian nationalists ought to be completely eliminated from the mass of elementary school teachers [in the Lemko region]."[43] In order to gain the sought-after cadres he proposed forming a separate Lemko peda-

---

[39] Ibid., p. 10.
[40] Ibid.
[41] Ibid., p. 11.
[42] Ibid., p. 12.
[43] Ibid., p. 16.

gogical college or creating a parallel course at the teachers' college in Nowy Sącz taught in the Lemko dialect, specially for candidates for teaching posts in the Lemko region. The chief purpose of this campaign was to inhibit the trend toward Lemko youth studying in Ukrainian intermediate schools in the former Eastern Galicia. In matters of extracurricular education, he proposed support for the Old Rusyn reading room movement and suggested the establishment of a popular weekly publication with a section directed at farmers (advice), and literary and political section which would mold thought among Lemkos in the desired directions.[44]

In the domain of economic issues he postulated the necessity for lifting the Lemko region out of the generally rampant destitution of everyday life. He proposed the construction of paved roads and development of the forestry industry, crafts, decorative arts, etc. On the question of agrarian relations he came out in favor of reparceling farm land and surrounding Lemko villages with professional care, which would indirectly lead to stronger feelings of loyalty to the RP among Lemkos. The first task at hand was, he claimed, to limit the influence of Ukrainian credit unions and trade cooperatives in the economic life of the Lemko region.

For the purpose of coordinating operations aimed at assimilating Lemkos into the Polish state Wielhorski proposed making changes to the administrative division of the country by joining the counties of Krosno and Sanok to the Kraków province. He further proposed a change in the internal borders of Sanok County by joining the part of Lesko County inhabited by Lemkos to its territory, and detaching the northern areas inhabited by a non-Lemko Ukrainian population. These changes were intended to concentrate proactive state policy on the Lemko region in one administrative center.[45]

A few months after Wielhorski's development of tentative premises for policy toward the Lemko region, the first organizational structures designed for its implementation were created. Beginning in March 1934 there was an active Committee for Nationality Affairs in the Polish government, of which Wielhorski became the first director.[46] At the inaugural meeting of the Committee, on 2 March, the general directives for nationality policy were discussed and a Commission for Scientific Study of the Eastern Territories was called into being. At the second meeting, on 8 March, the principles for government policy on the Lemko region were delineated. At meetings of the Committee on 1 and 7 March its activities were expanded. The Commission for Eastern Orthodox Affairs and the Committee for Polisia Affairs were then created.[47]

Important organizational changes to the Committee on Nationality Affairs were made at the meeting on 19 March 1935, which was chaired by Prime Minister Marian Zyndram-Kościałkowski. The resolution approved at the meeting precisely for-

---

[44]   Ibid., pp. 16–17.
[45]   Ibid., p. 17.
[46]   AAN, PRM, ref. # 148-1, *Uchwala o powołaniu Komitetu do Spraw Narodowościowych*, p. 1.
[47]   Ibid., pp. 1–2.

mulated the Committee's tasks and narrowly defined the makeup of its personnel. The Committee's tasks comprised four thematic areas: developing directives on nationality policy, gathering materials necessary for the development of premises for nationality policy, coordinating economic operations with the premises of nationality policy and inspiring community initiatives in support of government policy.[48]

The permanent members of the Committee were: the president of the Council of Ministers as chairman, minister of the interior as deputy chairman, and the ministers of foreign affairs, military affairs, religious denominations and public education, agriculture and public works or people appointed by them as representatives. The participation in committee activities of representatives of other departments in their areas of expertise was also anticipated. A separate point of the resolution allowed the participation in committee work of persons from outside the government, in particular experts in nationality issues, who were invited by the chairman to collaborate. At the same time, an Office of Nationality Policy was created in the RP government, as executive organ of the Committee on Nationality Affairs. The head of the Office was the state official designated by the Prime Minister.[49]

Within the Committee on Nationality Affairs a Committee on Lemko Regional Affairs was created, whose members included representatives of the departments of internal and military affairs and the school superintendents of the Kraków and Lviv districts. The executive organ of the Committee was the Subcommittee for Lemko Regional Affairs, whose members included the starosts of Nowy Sącz (the chairman), Gorlice, Jasło, Krosno, Sanok, and Lesko Counties and the inspectors of the Gorlice, Krosno, Nowy Sącz, and Sanok school districts. Other members were the superintendent of the Kraków School District, the vice-governor of Kraków, representatives of the Headquarters of District Corps no. V in Kraków and no. X in Przemyśl, representatives of the department of military affairs, the head of the Border Guard Inspectorate, and invited specialists from scholarly circles.[50]

Ludwik Ręgorowicz, ministerial inspector responsible for, among other things, schooling of national minorities, believed that the Committee and Subcommittee should include a representative of MWRiOP, a function which he himself ended up performing. Furthermore, Ręgorowicz stated that the area of the Committee and Subcommittee's activities should overlap with AAL and should include Brzozów County.[51]

Theoretical aspects played an important role in the preparation of different strains in nationality policy. This task rested on the shoulders of the Commission for the Scientific Study of the Eastern Territories, which assembled regional scien-

---

[48] Ibid., p. 5.
[49] Ibid., pp. 5–6.
[50] L. Ręgorowicz, *Materiały do dziejów wychowania. Zagadnienie łemkowskie w Polsce*, Jagiellonian Library, ref. # P. 64/64, p. 17.
[51] Ibid., pp. 17–18.

tific units. The Lemko unit created in 1934 was led by Professor Jerzy Smoleński.[52] It gathered many specialists from various fields in the social and natural sciences. The topics of research were set broadly, to cover many aspects, and included the following disciplines: physiography, geomorphology, sociology, ethnography as well as issues of demography and nationality, and the conditions of leisure and recreation in the Lemko region.[53] The work was carried out under the auspices of Jagiellonian University and the Polish Academy of Arts and Sciences (*Polska Akademia Umiejętności*). Thorough knowledge of the Lemko region allowed them to make piercing political judgments.

In the years 1934–1935 the process of building organizational structures for the needs of RP nationality policy was completed. The Lemko issue was tied to the Ukrainian question, though it was simultaneously treated as separate. Soon a compromise was reached between the two contradictory concepts of national assimilation and state assimilation, in the form of a synthesis contained in the program presented at the forum of the Committee on Nationality Affairs in January 1936 by Prime Minister M. Zyndram-Kościałkowski.

The idea of this program was to create a strong Ukrainian Polonophile movement in the eastern and southeastern voivodeships, but excluding ethnically mixed areas and those in ethnically Polish regions, i.e. the Bug River counties in the Lublin province, the nine counties with close access to Lviv (Horodok, Yavoriv, Lviv, Mostyska, Rava, Rudki, Sambir, Sokal, Zhovkva), a few counties on the San River (Dobromyl, Jarosław, Lubaczów, Przemyśl) and the counties of which the Lemko region was comprised. The Ukrainian population residing in said counties was to be assimilated into the nation.[54] However, in the other regions of southeastern Poland, Kościałkowski proposed implementation of the concept of state assimilation through the support of Ukrainian communities in places where there was a chance of forming loyalties to the RP among them. The basis for fulfilling these premises was to be the principle of full equality with the Polish population for Ukrainians. Kościałkowski designated a particular role for Polish institutions of culture and education, and for economic, youth and school institutions.[55]

It was probably during this period (the mid-1930s) that a brochure (no date or place of publication) in the form of a tour guide and handbook to the Lemko region was published, containing an additional chapter entitled "Hints for interaction with the population." A direct link could not be established between this publication and

---

[52] AAN, PRM, ref. # 8-54, *Sprawozdanie z prac naukowo-badawczych Komisji Naukowych Badań Ziem Wschodnich za czas 21 IX 1936 do 30 IX 1937*, p. 182; "Badania nad Łemkowszczyzną," *BP-U* 1936, no. 18, p. 179.

[53] AAN, PRM, ref. # 8-54, pp. 181, 185, 191; J. Smoleński, "Łemkowie i Łemkowszczyzna," *Wierchy* (Kraków) 1935, vol. 13, pp. 57–58.

[54] AAN, MSW, ref. # 808, *Tezy w dziedzinie narodowościowej, styczeń 1936*, p. 12; M. Siwicki, *Dzieje konfliktów polsko-ukraińskich*, vol. 1, Warszawa 1992, pp. 253–254, document no. 55.

[55] Ibid.

the architects of government policy toward the Lemko region, but its contents fit with the directives described above. The brochure's anonymous author propounds a clearly defined position to the reader, i.e. through "gaining the confidence of Lemkos" he prescribes "making way for the joining of their culture with ours."[56] In case of a conversation about national feelings he suggests accepting the designations "Rusnak," "Rusyn," or "Lemko," but objecting to the term "Ukrainian." Finally he puts forth a vision of Lemkos accepting Polish national consciousness, stating that "many [of them] can take pride in belonging to the rank of gentleman."[57]

The announcement of Kościałkowski's program occurred in the new political environment in which the RP found itself after the death of Józef Piłsudski. Internal differences soon appeared within the reform camp. Since the late 1920s Polish army officers had played an increasingly large role in successive government cabinets, and their influence on the course of internal policy in the nation had risen since the time of intensified rivalry between Prime Minister Walery Sławek, President Ignacy Mościcki, and General Inspector of the Armed Forces Edward Rydz-Śmigły. The importance of the army was rising with the rise in Rydz-Śmigły's position; as a result of an agreement with Mościcki, he was able to arrange for the formation of Felicjan Sławoj-Składkowski's government.[58]

An important factor in connection with the army's role in internal political affairs was the RP's geopolitical position. Crammed between two major powers, the country had to pursue the cultivation of an ability to defend itself from external threats. This ability, in the opinion of some officers (e.g. M. Tokarzewski-Karaszewicz, leader of the District Corps in Lviv, and W. Scaevola-Wieczorkiewicz, leader of the District Corps in Przemyśl), could guarantee a stable internal situation in border areas. It was understood that the loyalty of the borderland community was a guarantee of the country's ability to defend itself against the possible threat from the East. The nationality question was becoming a key factor in the process of gaining the desired loyalty of Ukrainians.[59]

After the speech by Prime Minister Kościałkowski, a retired lieutenant colonel, an important step which testified to the military's engagement in nationality affairs was represented by the speeches of Minister of Military Affairs Tadeusz Kasprzycki, one of the main architects of army policy, who also had control over that department in Składkowski's government. He linked political issues closely with denominational ones, e.g. at a briefing with district commanders on 2 July 1936 he said:

---

[56] "Wskazówki postępowania z ludnością," in: *Łemkowszczyzna*, n.p.p., n.d.p., p. 1. I used the copy kept in the Jagiellonian Library, ref. # B23422 II.

[57] Ibid., pp. 3–4.

[58] H. Jędruszczak, T. Jędruszczak, *Ostatnie lata Drugiej Rzeczypospolitej. 1935–1939*, Warszawa 1970, pp. 58–62.

[59] T. Prus-Faszczewski, *Małopolska Wschodnia a zagadnienie obronności państwa*, Warszawa 1939, pp. 27–28.

The state, and by the same token, the army [should] strive to [...] expose adherents of different confessions to the assimilating influence of Polish culture in a pro-state spirit, and where possible, as e.g. in particular with regard to Slavic minorities, the process of Polonization in the religious and ecclesiastical sphere be given clear and fixed attention.[60]

Kasprzycki developed this program at meetings of the Commission on Scientific Study of the Eastern territories, of which he was chairman.

Particular attention was devoted to the area of the former Eastern Galicia, to which key political and military significance was attributed in view of its rich raw materials (crude oil, potassic salt). Due to the fact that the area was inhabited by a Ukrainian population, the military circles feared potential mobilization problems. For the purpose of increasing the numbers of Poles there, the army had since 1930 been developing a Hutsul campaign and a campaign dependent on energizing the petty nobility.[61] The demand for Polish colonization in the southeastern voivodeships kept reappearing until the late 1930s, in the context of Poland's defensive capability.

At the beginning of 1939 the government set about developing a long-term and multifaceted plan for Polonization of the southeastern voivodeships, adapting a political line outlined by the military to the needs of civilian governments.[62] The zone in which the concept of national assimilation had been implemented was moved further east; it included not only the counties incorporated earlier, Bibrka, Drohobych and Turka, but also the western part of the Ternopil province and most of the counties in the Stanislaviv province. The pro-Polish campaign went forward in the Lublin region and Volhynia. Further restrictions were imposed on Old Rusyns in the Lemko region beginning in June 1938, with preparations made for closing the publication *Lemko*. In accordance with the decree of Nowy Sącz starost K. Adamski, Lemko issues were to be discussed in the Polish weekly *Głos Podhala* (the Voice of Podhale), issued in Nowy Sącz. The Lemko region lay outside the range of borderland affairs, but the nationality question had equal importance there, hence the bitter rivalry between government circles and Ukrainian organizations for influence among Lemkos and other ethnic groups which spoke dialects of the Ukrainian language. Historians underscore

---

[60] Quoted from P. Stawecki, op.cit., pp. 171–112; W. Paruch, "Mniejszości narodowe w myśli politycznej obozu piłsudczykowskiego (1935–1939)," in: *Polityka narodowościowa państw Europy środkowowschodniej*, eds. Jacek Z. Pietraś, Andrzej Czarnocki, Lublin 1993, p. 93.

[61] W. Paruch, op.cit., pp. 99–100. See S. Jastrzębski, *Kim jesteśmy? O szlachcie zagrodowej w Małopolsce Wschodniej*, Przemyśl 1939; R. Horoszkiewicz, *Szlachta zaściankowa na ziemiach wschodnich*, Warszawa 1937; W. Pulnarowicz, *Rycerstwo polskie Podkarpacia (Dawne dzieje i obecne obowiązki szlachty zagrodowej na Podkarpaciu)*, Przemyśl 1937.

[62] Colonel Z. Wenda, vice-marshal of the Sejm, in an interior ministry budget discussion on 16 February 1939 stipulated that "the Polish Nation is the only lord of its State, and no obstacles can stand on the path of its development and the fulfillment of its vital interests in areas with mixed populations." See Sejm RP, *11 posiedzenie z dnia 16 lutego 1939 r.*, p. 9 and *SN* 1939, nos. 1–2, p. 106.

the fact that the guiding purpose of the military's policy was its interest in defending the Republic, but this was nonetheless achieved using the methods of the camp which proclaimed the principles of a nationalist ideology.[63]

3. In the realm of educational and extracurricular issues

The implementation of national assimilation policy in the 1930s led to the removal from the Lemko region of the intelligentsia (clergy and teachers), first Ukrainian and then Old Rusyn.

The first round of repressions hit the teachers, which may have resulted from the fact that until the creation of the AAL the state authorities had little influence on arrangements in Greek Catholic dioceses. In matters concerning cadres they were limited to choosing candidates for rector from the *terno* (three candidates) presented by the ordinariate. A campaign against teachers of Ukrainian orientation began shortly after the 1930 elections and initially took the form of a post-election repression. Decisions on teacher transfers were made by district school authorities at the recommendation of district superintendents connected with the Committee on Lemko Affairs. Article 58 of the resolution of 14 July 1926 on the "transfer of teachers for the good of the school" served as the legal basis for such actions.[64]

Most often they were transferred to schools located in wholly Polish communities, and the vacant posts were filled with teachers of Old Rusyn orientation. This was the price the state authorities paid for the pro-government stance of the Old Rusyns. L.Ręgorowicz in one of his reports for the Committee on Nationality Affairs wrote: "Old Rusyns looked with indifference on the removal of Ukrainian teachers, and were even favorably disposed toward it."[65] Such behavior confirmed their conviction regarding the authorities' good intentions toward the Lemko region and had the effect of intensifying loyalties toward the state. This situation changed after a few years, when the authorities set about (in mid-1936) removing Old Rusyn teachers from schools and replacing them with teachers of Polish nationality.

Ręgorowicz raised the issue of education in the Lemko region more broadly in the forum of the Committee on Nationality Affairs. In a memorial prepared in January 1936 he came out in opposition to the idea of transferring Ukrainian teachers to ethnically Polish areas. Stipulating that in fact with regard to policy in the Lemko region the effect of the campaign was the intended one, he nevertheless pointed to

---

[63] A. Chojnowski, *Koncepcje polityki narodowościowej rządów polskich w latach 1921–1939*, Wrocław 1979, p. 239.

[64] AAN, MSW, ref. # 808, p. 9. It sometimes happened that as a result of such a transfer a married couple was separated, e.g. D. Mandziuk of Tylicz was transferred to Olkusz County, and his wife stayed on as a teacher in Tylicz, see *Dilo* 1934, no. 195, p. 1. Administrative transfers were also imposed on Polish teachers in ethnically Polish regions.

[65] L. Ręgorowicz, *Materiały do dziejów wychowania*, p. 7.

the negative aspect of this phenomenon, in terms of Polish schools. Ordinarily the transferred teacher either was politically active in the new Ukrainian milieu (to the extent that residents of Ukrainian origin allowed it) or joined the Polish political opposition movement. Indicating this state of affairs, Ręgorowicz proposed putting a restraint on the process of transferring Ukrainians to Polish schools and the initiation of efforts toward obtaining work for them in Polish cultural and educational organizations on the territory of the Lemko region or in local cities.[66] However he had to yield on this notion after Kościałkowski's program was brought into force. In a comprehensive summary of the Lemko region's school system in 1937, he stated that elementary schools in places with a large Polish percentage of the population "ought to be entirely Polonized." He referred thereby to schools in Brzezowa, Krynica Wieś, Tylicz and Wysowa.[67]

The state authorities' attitude toward the school system in the Lemko region can be divided into two phases. In the first, the authorities flirted openly with the Old Rusyn movement, granting it many concessions in the development of culture and education. Furthermore, the opposition of Old Rusyn instruction to the Ukrainian model caused even greater quarreling between the two political orientations, already rivals in so many other areas of community life. Protection from the state gave Old Rusyn organizations a decisive advantage, against which the spokesmen Ukrainian Parliamentary Representation protested in vain. At a meeting of the Committee on Nationality Affairs on 22 February 1936 it was resolved to leave the demands of Ukrainian parliamentarians, put forward by deputy Vasyl Mudry, in the matter of changing government policy in the Lemko region, unanswered.[68] In the 1930s, as a result of the removal of Ukrainian teachers from Lemko schools, their numbers progressively dwindled and in 1937 in the Kraków School District was reduced to seven: four in Nowy Sącz County, three in Gorlice County and one in Jasło County.[69]

Cooperation with the Old Rusyns reached its apogee when in 1933 the primer developed by Metody Trokhanovsky was put into use in schools[70] and Trokhanov-

---

[66] AAN, MSW, ref. # 953, L. Ręgorowicz, *Memoriał w sprawie stosunków narodowościowych i wyznaniowych w województwach wschodnich i południowo-wschodnich Państwa Polskiego* [Memorial in the matter of nationality and interdenominational relations in the eastern and southeastern voivodeships of the Polish State], January 1936, pp. 13–14.

[67] L. Ręgorowicz, *Materiały do dziejów wychowania*, p. 18.

[68] AAN, PRM, ref. # 148-3, *Uchwały Komitetu do Spraw Narodowościowych dot. Niemców, Ukraińców itp. – materiały statystyczne, 1936*, pp. 36, 57, 100.

[69] L. Ręgorowicz, *Materiały do dziejów wychowania*, p. 8.

[70] See *Bukvar. Persha knyzhechka dla vseludnykh shkol*, Lviv 1933. This primer raised deep loyalty to the RP in children's spirits, by means of e.g. the text "The Emblem," "3 May," "The Standard of the Polish State," "Mr. Marshal's Name-Day," "Mr. President." See Y. Tarnovych, *20 rokiv nevoli. Lemkivshchyna pid polskym iarmom*, Krakiv 1940, pp. 115–118; T. Duda, "Życie polityczne Łemków sądeckich i gorlickich w latach 1926–1939" [The political life of Lemkos of Sącz and Gorlice 1926–1939], *Rocznik Sądecki* (Nowy Sącz) 1992, vol. 20, pp. 77–89.

sky was offered a teaching position at the intermediate school in Stary Sącz, where it was hoped teachers would be molded for the Lemko region.[71]

Trokhanovsky's primer was in large part based on a Polish primer, even including reprints of some illustrations to the text. The degree of its acceptance in the Lemko community varied. Old Rusyn circles, i.e. the *Lemko Soiuz*, aimed to expand its importance in the teaching process, but on the other hand complaints were addressed to the Board of Education in Kraków and the School Inspectorate in Sanok from parents demanding the primer's removal from school *curricula*. Such a demand was made by e.g. the parents of children in four villages in Nowy Targ County (Biała Woda, Czarna Woda, Jaworki and Szlachtowa). In the summer of 1936 they sent a delegation to the Board in Kraków with a request for the introduction of a Ukrainian primer into the program of instruction.[72] The most frequent protests, however, were made in Sanok County. Because school authorities intended to popularize the primer throughout the area of the Lemko-Boiko borderland, there were also protests in Lesko County.[73]

Sometimes these protests came too late. An eloquent example was the village of Łopienka, where in the 1935–1936 academic year Trokhanovsky's primer had been introduced into the *curriculum*. Toward the end of the first half-year concerned parents came to the school inspector with a request that it be replaced by a Ukrainian primer. Inspector Szemielowski responded in a situation where a new conception in nationality policy already reigned, i.e. where it was recognized that "the preservation in elementary schools of the Lemko region of the Lemko dialect and the Cyrillic alphabet, a symbol of Byzantine culture, was counterproductive and illogical with regard to ultimate goals."[74] In a letter to the School Council in Łopienka of 6 March 1936, Szemielowski wrote: "[…] in that school in first and beginning classes Polish primers will be mandatory, and schoolchildren will receive instruction in Polish. In this regard, Rusyn primers or *bukvars* will not be introduced."[75] Thus the role of Trokhanovsky's primer in school policy in the Lemko region was finished after three years of its use.

The second phase in the government's education policy was signalled in the speech by Prime Minister Kościałkowski at the meeting of the Committee on Nationality Affairs on 19 October 1935. Individual directives were elaborated by Ręgorowicz. The previously existing method was applied again, with the difference that this time teachers of Old Rusyn orientation were removed from Lemko schools.

---

[71] *Lemkivska problema. Napysav Lemko*, Lviv 1933, p. 11.

[72] *Dilo* 1936, no. 160, p. 4.

[73] CDIAL, f. 344, op. 1t. case # 552, *Zwity, skarhy... Petycja rodziców dziatwy w wieku szkolnym do Pana Ministra Wyznań Religijnych i Oświecenia Publicznego w sprawie tzw. "Łemkiwśkoho Bukwaria"*, p. 25.

[74] L. Ręgorowicz, *Materiały do dziejów wychowania*, p. 18.

[75] Quoted from *Dilo* 1936, no. 63, p. 3.

Over the course of the year the number of Old Rusyn teachers fell to 19,[76] while the number of ethnically Polish teachers grew dramatically. In 1937 at 39 Lemko schools in Nowy Sącz County there were 43 teachers of Polish nationality, at 46 schools in Gorlice County there were 44, and at 12 schools in Jasło County there were 16 (Kraków School District). Courses in the Lemko dialect were organized specially for them in Nowy Sącz and Sanok.[77]

The new school policy for the Lemko region was a source of disappointment with state authorities in Old Rusyn circles. This feeling was manifested in protest campaigns against the removal of Old Rusyns from schools. The transfer of Mykola Yurkovsky, a teacher in Skwirtne, to Szczekociny in the Kielce province, became a widely echoed issue. The event caused serious anxieties in the community, which led to a schoolchildren's strike and a boycott of the teacher of Polish nationality assigned to them, Zydkowicz. Yurkowsky himself, declining to leave his area for a time, hid out in the local church. All Old Rusyn organizations in the Kraków province stood in his defense, and Lemkos of Ukrainian orientation joined them. He was supported by teachers and priests, both Greek Catholic and Eastern Orthodox. The board of the RSO Committee in Skwirtne sent three delegates to the MWRiOP in Warsaw, in order to force its agreement to allow Yurkovsky to remain in Skwirtne.[78] The local authorities made an effort to break the strong resistance from the community, presenting him as a border smuggler, a partner in Jewish financial intrigues, etc.[79]

Community anxieties in Skwirtne brought about an intervention by Ręgorowicz, who suggested postponing Yurkovsky's transfer and waiting out the stike. As a last resort he proposed sending "a loyal and calm Rusyn (a Lemko)" to replace the Pole in Skwirtne, all the more so since the Old Rusyns themselves were conducting talks on the subject with the Kraków vice-governor Piotr Małaszyński.[80]

In the 1937–1938 school year changes were entered to the program of instruction based on removing Lemko dialect as language of instruction and making it instead one of the subjects. Periodically conferences for Polish teachers were held with the participation of school inspectors, where they discussed "tactics for working in Lemko schools."[81] Schools in localities with neighboring Polish schools were gradually being dissolved. For the purpose of taking a uniform approach to issues relating

---

[76] L. Ręgorowicz, *Materiały do dziejów wychowania*, p. 8. In Nowy Sacz County – 9, Gorlice – 9, Jasło – 1.

[77] AAN, MSW, ref. # 1058, *Sprawozdanie z posiedzenia Podkomitetu do Spraw Łemkowszczyzny za okres V 1937–V 1938*, p. 58.

[78] CDIAL, f. 148, op. 1, case # 102, *Materiialy pro finansovo-hospodarsku orhanizatsiinu i publikator-sko-vydavnychu diialnist "Halytsko-ruskoi Matitsy" (powidomlennia, lysty, wypysky, zaiavy), 1937–1939*, pp. 14, 16.

[79] L. Ręgorowicz, *Materiały do dziejów wychowania*, p. 8. See CDIAL, f. 148, op. 1, case # 102, p. 14.

[80] L. Ręgorowicz, *Materiały do dziejów wychowania*, p. 8.

[81] AAN, MSW, ref. # 1058, *Report from the meeting of the Subcommittee on Lemko Regional Affairs*, p. 58; M. Siwicki, op.cit., vol. 1, pp. 251–252, document no. 54.

to the school system in the Lemko region, a plan took form in MWRiOP circles of detaching the counties of Brzozów, Krosno, Lesko and Sanok from the Lviv School District and joining them to the Kraków district. Protests against the rise in the number of teachers of Polish origin rose anew from parents opposed to the sending to the Lemko region of teachers not knowing the Ukrainian language.[82] Some Polish teachers also protested, whose work was made considerably harder because of their lack of knowledge of the local language.

Various Polish community organizations, such as *Strilets* (Sagittarius), the "Hunters' Fire Brigade," the Popular School Association (*Towarzystwo Szkoły Ludowej*, TSL), the Organization of Farming Associations, scout organizations and others took an interest in the Lemko region. Above all they supported the small agglomerations of the Polish population scattered about the Lemko region, e.g. in settlements remaining in the wake of former small industrial centers (Huta Polańska, Huta Wysowska, Oderne) or in areas of former bishops' estates (e.g. Muszyna, Jaśliska). In some cases, there were Roman Catholic chapels in such places, but due to the lack of a permanently residing priest worship services were not held regularly, so there were large temporal gaps between them. In these conditions the chances for keeping Polish culture alive were limited. The few Roman Catholic Poles in the area inevitably attended Greek Catholic churches, in time completely abandoning the Roman Catholic Church. This was an effect of assimilation, often occurring as a result of the majority's cultural domination over the minority.

The administrative authorities and community institutions tried to help the Polish population living in Lemko villages. The TSL Executive Board established a nationality-based land register and took a census of the Polish population, which revealed that Poles were a small and poor group. TSL reading rooms distributed school textbooks and prayer-books free of charge and carried out the construction of People's Homes in Brunary Niżne, Huta Wysowska and Tylicz. Branches of the Farmers' Associations organized courses in various areas of farming and though held in Polish, they were designed for all village residents.[83]

The Polish reading rooms established in Lemko villages, however, did have a national character. The tendency in this direction had begun in 1928 and was related to the impact of the BBWR. The TSL, the Roman Catholic clergy and the Polish teachers began working together on a local basis. One example of this was the opening of the Podhale Reading Room in Łabowa on 8 February 1930, as a result of the efforts of the local TSL circle, the Roman Catholic rector of Nawojowa, Fr. Walenty Wcisło,

---

[82] Worthy of note were the protests in Nowy Sącz County, e.g. a protest signed by P. Chulak, A. Dudiak, M. Hashchak and D. Revilak, from Leluchów, addressed to the school inspector in Nowy Sącz against appointing teachers not conversant in Ukrainian at schools in the Lemko region. See *Diło* 1937, no. 20, p. 1.

[83] AAN, MSW, ref. # 1058, pp. 62–64; CDIAL, f. 182, op. 1, case # 306, p. 38; *Ludowiec* 1927, no. 14, p. 4.

a few Polish teachers from Łabowa and the surrounding villages, and BBWR deputy Adam Stadnicki.[84]

Together with the implementation of the reform governments' program for the Lemko region, the activities of Polish community organizations became political in character. Moscophile sources mention occurrences of the use of coercion on Lemko youth, who signed up for *Strilets* circles under threat of punishment in the form of a fine.[85] This form of pressure brought opposing reactions not only from among Lemkos, but also from the Polish populace. In some Lemko villages members of *Strilets* circles were merely government workers enlisted by their superiors, e.g. in Śnietnica. Nevertheless in some areas of the Lemko region the campaign did bring the expected results. Only in Tylicz did the Catholic Young Men's Association, the Circle of Country Hostesses, the TSL and the Catholic Action circle become active.[86] Great importance was attached to the purchase of land from Lemko hands. In Krynica in the years 1920–1939 building plots were purchased for the sum of five million zl.[87] Ręgorowicz drew particular attention to the district of Krempna and Jaśliska, where a wedge was being driven into Polish settlement by Lemkos right up to the national border. The expansion of Polish centers in the region may have led to the division of Lemko settlement into two parts.[88]

The TSL bureau in Kraków was particularly active, with the help of centers in Gorlice, Jasło, and Nowy Sącz, wielding guardianship over the operating reading rooms in the environs of Lemko villages. The area of the Lemko region which fell within the Lviv voivodeship was subordinated to the Eastern Branch of the TSL. Well-organized reading rooms operated in Wysowa and Oderne. Oderne often served as the location for congresses of the Polish population of the Lemko region, in which representatives of county, school, military and police authorities took part.[89] Harvest festival ceremonies were organized there at which members of reading rooms appeared in traditional Krakovian attire. TSL circles and reading rooms also grew up in Gładyszów, Flasza, Florynka, and many places of the eastern Lemko region.[90]

---

[84] AP K, UWKr, ref. # 352, *Sprawozdania sytuacyjne tygodniowe, miesięczne Starostwa Powiatowego w Nowym Sączu 1930–1933*, p.n.n.

[85] E.g. in Jabłonica Polska the founders of the *Strilets* circle threatened the youth with a fine in the amount of 50 zl. According to a press notice, Lemko youth signed up "faster than the Poles." See *Zemlia i Volia* 1930, no. 28, p. 4.

[86] K. Pieradzka, *Na szlakach Łemkowszczyzny*, Kraków 1939, p. 200.

[87] CDIAL, f. 182, op. 1; case # 462, p. 52.

[88] L. Ręgorowicz, *Materiały do dziejów wychowania*, p. 19.

[89] AP K, TSL, ref. # 60, *Zestawienie nieruchomości będących własnością Towarzystwa Szkoły Ludowej z wyszczególnieniem celów, którym służą*, p. 2; *Nasha Sprava* 1936, no. 40, p. 556.

[90] AP K, TSL, ref. # 33, *Sprawozdanie Zarządu Głównego TSL z działalności Towarzystwa Szkoły Ludowej za rok 1936, Kraków 1937*, pp. 52, 56 and ref. # 34, *Sprawozdanie Zarządu Głównego TSL […] za rok 1937, Kraków 1938*, pp. 54, 76; AAN, MSW, ref. # 1058, *Materiały dotyczące Łemkowszczyzny*, pp. 63–64.

In the years 1937–1938 many schools managed in accord with education authorities were returned to use, e.g. in Huta Polańska. The collections of private libraries were expanded in Gorlice, Jasło and Nowy Sącz by a total of 831 volumes, worth over 1600 zl. To facilitate library services in villages farther out, the TSL launched a branch of the Jasło library in Krempna with appropriately selected literature (over 200 volumes). That library was used not only by the Polish population of Huta Krempska, but also by Lemkos from the surrounding villages.

In the years 1937–1939 the TSL Executive Board became engaged in work to strengthen the Roman Catholic Church's position in the Lemko region. At first the establishment of Roman Catholic parishes in Skalnik and Wysowa was anticipated along with the organization of religion classes for children of Roman Catholics.[91] At a meeting of the Subcommittee on Lemko Affairs in May 1938 religious affairs were broadly discussed and the amount of a grant for Roman Catholic institutions was decided. The report for 1937 shows that the Subcommittee was working to establish Roman Catholic parishes in Kąclowa, Komańcza, Skalnik and Żegiestów and rectories in Cisna, Huta Polańska, Izby, Łabowa, Męcina, Oderne, Śnietnica, Wierchomla Wielka and Wysowa.[92] Since 1936 TSL had made supplied funds for the construction of the church in Wysowa,[93] and in later years also in Huta Polańska and Łabowa, and the sum of 4,000 zl was allotted for the purchase of a plot of land and the construction of a church in Śnietnica.[94] There were also plans to build Roman Catholic churches in Uście Ruskie and Krempna.[95] With abundant help from the TSL construction began on many Roman Catholic chapels in areas in the counties of Brzozów, Krosno, Lesko and Sanok.[96] These campaigns on the one hand corresponded to RP nationality policy, and on the other, aimed at arresting the process of the Polish population's assimilation.

The strengthening of centers inhabited by the Polish population went in tandem with administrative limitations on the development of Ukrainian and Moscophile institutions, and in the second half of the 1930s Old Rusyn institutions as well. The first step taken was limiting the development of *Prosvita*, and beginning in 1936 restrictions were imposed on Kachkovsky reading rooms. One of the first of these, whose activities had been suspended on suspicion of "practicing politics," was the reading room in Powroźnik (1936). The legal basis for the authorities' action was generally Article 16 of the law on associations.[97] The boards of reading rooms were

[91]   L. Ręgorowicz, *Materiały do dziejów wychowania*, pp. 18–19.
[92]   AAN, MSW, ref. # 1058, p. 59.
[93]   AP K, TSL, ref. # 33, p. 53 and ref. # 34, p. 54; CDIAL, f. 326, op. 1t., case # 7t., *Zhurnalni ta hazetni statti pro borotbu katolytskoi tserkvy z pravoslavnoiu na Lemkivshchyni ta moskvofilstvom i insh. 1936–1938*, p. 1.
[94]   AAN, MSW, ref. # 1058, pp. 62–63.
[95]   *Dilo* 1938, no. 248, p. 5; *Nash Lemko* 1938, no. 22, p. 5.
[96]   AAN, MSW, ref. # 1058, pp. 37, 62.
[97]   *Dziennik Ustaw Rzeczypospolitej Polskiej* 1932, no. 94, item 808.

accused of not having their cashier books in order, not having member lists, etc.[98] The contents of libraries were monitored with regard to Ukrainian publishers. It sometimes happened, as in the case of the suspension of the Kachkovsky reading room in Węglówka's activities in July 1939, that a few volumes published by *Samoosvita* kept in the reading room's library served as the basis for the decision of the Krosno starost. On that basis the administrative authorities formed their accusation of Ukrainian national propaganda, without regard to the political orientation of the Kachkovsky Association, which was against the Ukrainian idea. This was one of a few examples of the local authorities' lack of knowledge of political relations in the Lemko region.[99] Reading room boards suspended in their statutory activities filed appeals to the Province Office in Kraków or Lviv and "private agents," usually lawyers, came to the defense of the reading rooms.

Starting in 1936 the state authorities developed their activities in several institutions which were united by the idea of expanding the centers of Polish culture in the Lemko region. Ręgorowicz in one of his reports prepared for the MWRiOP referred to cities and towns which should be developed "as the most important points for the propagation of Polish culture."[100] In Nowy Sącz County he indicated Krynica, Muszyna, Tylicz and Żegiestów, in Gorlice County – Wysowa, in Jasło County – Krempna and Skalnik, and in Sanok County – Jaśliska.[101]

4. Religious issues in nationality policy

Religious issues, involving both the Greek Catholic Church and Eastern Orthodoxy, occupied an important place in nationality policy for the Lemko region. In the 1920s the state authorities' relationship with the Greek Catholic clergy did not extend beyond surveillance of it. After the fall of the ZUNR, numerous arrests of clergy members showing explicit hostility toward the Polish nation-state were made. These arrests mostly were focused on the clergy in Sanok County, and to some extent in Krosno County.[102] The priests were assessed on the basis of their attitude toward state holidays, e.g. the 3 May holiday declared on 29 April 1919. The provisions of the concordat also placed an obligation on priests to pray for the president of the Polish Republic. Reports of starosts stated that a considerable number of Greek Catholic clergy were disposed "unkindly" toward the Polish state and were not ful-

---

[98]   CDIAL, f. 182, op. 1, case # 272, pp. 88, 89.

[99]   Ibid., pp. 91–94. In fact the books which were the basis for the suspension of the reading rooms dealt with natural sciences.

[100]   L. Ręgorowicz, *Materiały do dziejów wychowania*, p. 18.

[101]   Ibid., pp. 18–19.

[102]   AAN, MWRiOP, ref. # 928, *Sprawy osobowe księży. Antypaństwowa działalność kleru greckokatolickiego w Małopolsce 1919–1938*, p. 41.

filling their duties as specified in Article VIII of the concordat.[103] The escalation of this phenomenon could reach the level of a danger to the state, but was hindered by religious conflicts in the Lemko region in the late 1920s and early 1930s, i.e. the sudden growth of the Eastern Orthodox faith.

The state authorities unofficially used Eastern Orthodoxy to advance their own political goals. At the fifth meeting of the Committee on Nationality Affairs in Warsaw on 20 December 1935 a resolution was passed in which the Committee stated that "the Eastern Orthodox Church should become a tool enabling the introduction of Polish culture into Eastern territories."[104] During the period of the first interdenominational conflicts, Kraków governor Mikołaj Kwaśniewski in a letter to MWRiOP of 28 September 1929 expressed the view that the spread of Eastern Orthodoxy in the Lemko region

> is not [...] dangerous to the State, relatively harmful [...], Eastern Orthodox believers move to the Old Rusyn camp and by doing so become opposed to the campaigns of chauvinistic Ukrainian national parties, which without exception take a hostile stance toward the Polish Nation and State, while the Orthodox clergy for the most part firmly stress their loyalty to the State.[105]

Similarly Wielhorski in his work "The Lemko Region" produced a plan for providing support to Eastern Orthodoxy among Lemkos, noting that it would be possible to maintain this line of action in the long term only "when the Eastern Orthodox Church in Poland ceases to be an institution serving Russian cultural expansion."[106] Finally the authorities' support for Eastern Orthodoxy depended on the toleration of priests fulfilling pastoral functions illegally and the granting of permission to build chasovnias [sacral buildings of that era] or Orthodox churches even without the required documentation.

Despite the extensive growth of Eastern Orthodoxy in 1926 the Greek Catholic Church continued to comprise the greater part of the Lemko population and fostered the formation among Lemkos of a Ukrainian national identity. In government circles there were expectations that the situation would change as a result of the disengagement from the Greek Catholic Przemyśl diocese of nine deacons operating in the Lemko region and the creation of the Apostolic Administration for the Lemko

---

[103] Ibid., pp. 173, 249. Article VIII of the concordat referred to the duty to say a prayer "for the prosperity of the Republic and Mr. President." For example in 1927 the following Greek Catholic priests did not comply with Article VIII: M. Bubniak (Roztoka Wielka), Y. Khylak (Leluchów), I. Fenych (Wojkowa), S. Kornova (Łabowa), V. Mokhnatsky (Tylicz), O. Papp (Wierchomla Wielka), R. Pryslopsky (Żegiestów), M. Rybak (Maciejowa), V. Smolynsky (Nowa Wieś), and E. Venhrynovych (Mochnaczka Niżna). In Gorlice County: M. Khodachek (Doliny), A. Lomnytsky (Rozdziele), P. Shuflat (Bednarka), and M. Volychkevych (Rychwałd). In Krosno County: O. Malarchyk (Węgłówka), D. Pyroh (Ciechania). In Sanok County: Y. Hnatyszak (Lalin) and others.

[104] Quoted from AAN, PRM, ref. # 148-3, p. 76.

[105] AAN, MWRiOP, ref. # 1043, *Małopolska, delimitacje 1927–1929*, p. 230.

[106] W. Wielhorski, op.cit., p. 16.

Region (AAL), which initially had headquarters in Rymanów, and beginning at the end of 1937 in Sanok.[107]

Issues arising from the agreement to create the Apostolic Administration were discussed at the government summit on 16 April 1934. The conference was hosted by the head of the Nationality Department of the Ministry of the Interior, Henryk Suchenek-Suchecki, with the director of the Department of Religious Denominations of the MWRiOP, Franciszek Potocki, present. First they discussed personnel issues, in particular methods for assuring the candidate for the post of administrator "the furthest-reaching support and all possible assistance, not excluding financial."[108] They resolved to put the 20-room villa in Rymanów Zdrój at the administrator's disposal and submitted a proposal to allot an appropriate sum of money for the building of a diocesal church and a special residence for the administrator, who was also to receive "horses and a carriage or an automobile." Suchenek-Suchecki drew their attention to the need to fill the position quickly, since, as he told them, "a delay will do some harm and may be taken advantage of by Yosafat Kotsylovsky [the Greek Catholic bishop of the Przemyśl diocese]." The first to be considered for the candidacy were Fr. Bishop Hryhorii Lakota and Fr. Mykola Nahorniansky. The matter of appointments to curia member positions in the AAL was also brought up.[109]

In addition to personnel matters, the question of training seminarians for the needs of the AAL was also a subject of discussion. The first proposal, which involved assigning students to the Greek Catholic seminary in Stanyslaviv fell through when Bishop Hryhorii Khomyshyn opposed it. Next the idea of training seminarians in Kraków was put forward. The seminarians would be placed in a special dormitory and would attend the theology faculty of Jagiellonian University. Both the dormitory and its head would be paid by the Polish government.[110]

For the remainder of the conference Suchenek-Suchecki noticed that alongside the question of preparing new priests, an important issue was removing the rectors who were conducting pro-Ukrainian agitation from the Lemko region. Suchenek-Suchecki stressed that these matters should be discussed in detail with the administrator and notations to the concordat which anticipated transfers of priests to other parishes utilized. He proposed far-reaching personnel changes, even involving an intervention by the government at the Vatican in support of the campaign.[111]

---

[107] AAN, MWRiOP, ref. # 625, *Administracja Apostolska dla Łemkowszczyzny – pomieszczenia i dotacje dla alumnów* [Apostolic Administration for the Lemko Region – accommodations and grants for seminarians] *1934–1938*, pp. 74, 169. In this matter on 15 November 1937 the deputy chief of the Social and Political Department of the Province Office in Kraków, S. Wroński, visited Rymanów and Sanok. For the administrator's headquarters, the villa of Zofia Reichlowa, widow of the former mayor of Sanok, was chosen. The costs of adaptation were fixed at 5,000 zl, and the annual rent was 4,000 zl. The villa was rented for five years.

[108] AAN, MSZ, ref. # 5219, p. 37

[109] Ibid., pp. 37–39; *BP-U* 1933, no. 8, p. 10; *Zemlia i Volia* 1933, no. 19, p. 4.

[110] AAN, MSZ, ref. # 5219, pp. 37–39.

[111] Ibid., p. 39.

Many other issues were discussed at the conference. Suchenek-Suchecki, referring to the suggestions of ministers B. Pieracki and T. Schätzl, propounded a plan to expand the boundaries of the AAL to the east by joining three new deaneries to it, an idea viewed negatively by Minister Józef Beck.[112] At the end they discussed the growth of Eastern Orthodoxy within the bounds of the AAL and determined that the authorities would make all necessary efforts to protect Greek Catholic property in the event of attacks by Orthodox believers on churches, etc.[113]

The position to be taken toward Greek Catholic priests of Ukrainian orientation was discussed by government circles at the meeting of the Subcommittee on Lemko Regional Affairs on 10 April 1935 in Nowy Sącz. As a result of their deliberations, chaired by vice-governor P. Małaszyński, the expediency of exerting influence on the AAL administrator toward transferring politically active priests was underscored anew. According to *Dilo* out of 140 priests over 120 represented a Ukrainian orientation.[114] The phenomenon of transferring priests to different parishes continued until the end of the interwar period. Successive administrators, Vasyl Mastsiukh (1934–1936) and Yakov Medvetsky (from 7 October 1936) used this method to not only implement the government's guidelines in matters of nationality policy, but also, as Old Rusyns, to carry out their own program, arising from their aversion to the Ukrainian movement. The high rate of personnel changes in AAL parishes is shown by the announcements of rectorship vacancies posted each time in the AAL publication *Visti Apostolskoi Administratsii Lemkivshchyny*.[115]

Many remarks focused on the seminarians, ensuring that they would be trained at a good distance from Ukrainian influences. Preliminary discussion of this problem took place during the conference on 16 April 1934. Later, at the meeting of the Subcommittee on Lemko Regional Affairs on 16 April 1935, Małaszyński stated that the formation of clergy cadres for the Lemko region should remain concentrated in a purely Polish area.[116]

The government circles' proposition was accepted by Fr. Mastsiukh, who became the first administrator. His acceptance caused protests in the Ukrainian Greek Catholic community. Ukrainian groups publicly expressed the view that the AAL's training of seminarians in a Roman Catholic institution of learning under the circumstances of the nearby existence of Greek Catholic seminaries in Przemyśl, Lviv, and Stanyslaviv was aimed at "detaching the Lemko region from the Ukrainian trunk."[117]

---

[112] The campaign to join three deacons in Lesko County to the AAL began in March 1934. It was led by the village-mayors of the municipalities of Łupków and Smolnik, who collected signatures among peasants in the surrounding villages. According to *Dilo* county authorities had direct oversight over the campaign, see *Dilo* 1934, no. 93, p. 2.

[113] AAN, MSW, ref. # 5219, p. 40.

[114] *Dilo* 1937, no. 151, pp. 3–4.

[115] See AP P, AAL, ref. # 90, *Protokoły zmian na stanowisku proboszczów 1935–1943*, passim.

[116] Besides Kraków which had already been proposed earlier, Małaszyński proposed Częstochowa.

[117] *Nash Lemko* 1935, no. 23, p. 5.

Mastsiukh was further confronted with the ban he had placed on hanging cloths near icons in churches, which was interpreted as a step toward the destruction of Ukrainian traditions in the Greek Catholic Church. At the same time the MWRiOP set the number of seminarians and the monetary amount to be granted for supporting them. In the seminary's first academic year, i.e. 1935–1936, four seminarists finished their training but the number was to reach nine in 1938. Częstochowa Bishop Fr. Teodor Kubina agreed to accept seminarians to the diocesal seminary in Kraków, and the MWRiOP sent him information concerning financial affairs.[118]

The AAL conducted recruitment in Rymanów, but all candidates had to undergo verification by the Kraków Province Office as to their attitude toward the nation and its government.[119] The seminarians' staying in Kraków fostered the fulfillment of the educative aims agreed upon together by the government and the AAL authorities, but vacations spent at home with their families worked counter to these efforts. This problem became unmistakably apparent after the first year of instruction, and was observed by the seminary authorities. Fr. Stanisław Czajka, provost of the college (most certainly unaware of the government's policy), in a letter to Fr. Medvetsky of 13 January 1938 expressed doubts as to the advisability of training seminarians in Kraków by writing: "[…] the clerics feel generally aggrieved that they must live in a Latin seminary, that they must pray in a liturgical language not their own, that they cannot go to vespers in [a Greek Catholic] church each Sunday" and proposed to Medvetsky that they create their own seminary, since, as he put it, "only a superior in one's own rite and the feeling of one's own community give the right results."[120] In July 1938 the Częstochowa bishop refused to train further seminarians for the AAL, justifying his position on the grounds of their negative attitude toward the Latin rite.[121] Kraków governor Michał Gnoiński tried without success to solve the problem by organizing a dormitory in Rymanów, where seminarians would spend their vacation in an administrator's care.

In talks between the representatives of the Interior Ministry and the papal nuncio in Warsaw, after the signing of the agreement on creating the AAL (9 February 1934), the training of seminarians was reserved solely for seminaries approved by the government. Due to the impossibility of accepting more classes at the Częstochowa seminar (only those classes which had already started could continue their studies) – a change which took place after provost Czajka's declaration in a letter to Medvetsky of 22 September 1937 – the documents of candidates for first-year studies were

---

[118] AP P, AAL, ref. # 61, *Korespondencja z Min. Wyzn. Religij. i Ośw. Publ, w sprawie kształcenia duchownych, 1935–1942*, pp. 12, 30. Grants were to be paid in advance, in the amount of 53 zl 75 gr monthly for each seminarist.

[119] The first candidates (H. Buranych of Wawrzka, M. Durkot of Rychwałd, M. Kopystiansky of Puławy, A. Orshak of Weglówka) received positive evaluations from the Kraków Province Office.

[120] AP P, AAL, ref. # 61, p. 59.

[121] AAN, MWRiOP, ref. # 625, p. 112.

sent to Rymanów, and government circles began their search for a different Latin institution.[122]

Meanwhile Medvetsky, without consulting with the MWRiOP, began making efforts to place seminarians in the Papal Eastern Seminary in Dubno. He obtained permission from the authorities of that institution in writing on 30 September 1937, and in mid-October the seminarians began their course of study.[123] Medvetsky informed MWRiOP about this *post factum* stating that he considered the seminary in Dubno "a fitting educational center" for his seminarians in view of the possibility of teaching the Eastern liturgy, which the Kraków seminary did not provide at the right level and in the desired atmosphere.[124]

The attempt to place the seminarians in Dubno was one of a small number of decisions taken by Medvetsky independently in performing the offices of his post as AAL administrator. The attempt should be seen as the result of genuine concern for the proper preparation of the seminarians for work as priests of the Eastern rite. For government circles, however, political views were more important. The papal seminary in Dubno remained under government control, so once informed of Medvetsky's decision, the MWRiOP, through the intermediacy of the Kraków Province Office, began its efforts to persuade the administrator to change his decision.

Through a telephone message left by Stanisław Orsini-Rosenberg on 29 September, the ministry urged the Kraków province authorities to speed up their search for an appropriate location for training seminarians. The search was led by vice-governor Małaszyński, but all Kraków seminaries refused to accept additional candidates, justifying their decision by the lack of available openings. Małaszyński therefore resolved to address the ordinary of the neighboring Tarnów diocese, Bishop Franciszek Lisowski, who supported the authorities' policy on the Lemko region and proposed organizing a whole course of instruction for all Lemko clergy.[125] The Tarnów diocese's involvement may have been due to the fact that the southern area of the diocese was interspersed with numerous Greek Catholic parishes, while the nearest Roman Catholic parishes were located outside the Lemko region and only nominally were located at the country's border.

Under pressure from the authorities, Medvetsky recalled his seminarians from Dubno and agreed to have them be trained in Tarnów, informing the MWRiOP of his action in a letter of 22 November 1937. One of the fundamental reasons for this decision was the question of financing their studies. The ministry several times made it understood that funds for seminarians from the MWRiOP budget would be paid out "for seminaries responsible to the government."[126] In Tarnów the semi-

---

[122] Ibid., p. 45.

[123] See AP P, AAL, ref. # 63, *Papieskie Seminarium Duchowne w Dubnie, kształcenie alumnów, 1935–1939.*

[124] AAN, MWRiOP, ref. # 625, p. 65.

[125] Ibid., pp. 51–52.

[126] Ibid., p. 80.

narians were housed in the Missionaries' cloister, and Fr. Bronisław Szymański,[127] transferred to the cloister, was charged with their care.

On the eve of the new academic year, on 20 July 1938, there was a meeting in Bishop Lisowski's quarters in Tarnów, attended by Stanisław Wroński from the Socio-Political Division of the Province Office in Kraków. Fr. Szymański also took part in the meeting. They discussed Bishop Lisowski's proposition of the previous year, i.e. housing all AAL seminarians in Tarnów.[128]

Bishop Lisowski showed a great deal of interest in implementing the plan, searching Tarnów for a building fit to serve as a dormitory. In the conversation with Wroński he put forward the proposition that in view of the necessity for housing all seminarians in one center in the provost's care, the ministry had decided to rent a separate building or renovate the Missionary building, e.g. by building another floor. Bishop Lisowski stressed the fact that costs would have to be considerable, but added that the program of seminary studies had been expanded to six years, and that the "lack of Greek Catholic clergy in the Lemko region [was] increasingly felt, the number of seminarians [was] growing, and the parish should be staffed with loyal clergy, supporters of the Polish nation-state."[129] Lisowski furthermore named two candidates for the post of provost to supervise the AAL seminarians.[130]

Wroński informed Fr. Medvetsky of the decision to group the seminarians together in one seminary in Sanok on 18 August 1938.[131] Medvetsky at first opposed the idea, referring in their conversation to the plan to house all seminarians in the Papal Clergy Seminary in Dubno. He justified his position in terms of the fear that the charge could be repeated in the Ukrainian press that (as had been asserted in 1937, when he recalled the seminarians from Dubno), that he was "putting his hand to Latinization and Polonization in the Lemko region."[132] Under pressure from Wroński, however, who cited the possibility of ceasing funding from the MWRiOP budget, he agreed to all the demands from the government. Acceding to having the Roman Catholic seminary in Tarnów, he expressed the view that "that environment is the most appropriate [...] for education, both religious and civic, since it is far from Ukrainian influences which have reached seminarians even in Kraków."[133] He also agreed to the ordination of seminarist Apolinarii Dutkevych to the priesthood, which was a move against his own government office, since Bishop Lisowski had already put forth a plan for a change of administrator in conversation with voivode-

---

[127] AP P, AAL, ref. # 61, pp. 46, 47, 51.

[128] AAN, MWRiOP, ref. # 625, p. 115.

[129] Ibid., p. 124.

[130] A. Dutkevych – one of the older seminarians and O. Slyvynsky – rector in Tudiów (Kosiv County) known to have Polonophile tendencies.

[131] AAN, MSW, ref. # 1080, *Materiały w sprawie kształcenia alumnów dla Łemkowszczyzny* [Materials in the matter of training of seminarists for the Lemko Region], 1938–1939, pp. 13–16.

[132] AAN, MWRiOP, ref. # 625, p. 139.

[133] Ibid., pp. 148–149.

ship authorities.[134] Furthermore, filling the post of provost for AAL seminary students with a Greek Catholic priest took away from Medvetsky of his oft-repeated argument that in Tarnów the seminarians were "deprived of the Greek Catholic liturgy."[135]

On 29 August 1938 Fr. Szymański came to the Province Office in Kraków. In the presence of governor Małaszyński he made clear his readiness to accept all seminary students of the AAL, declaring that due to the cramped nature of the lodgings in Tarnów, it had been decided to transfer [his own] seminarians to Kraków and that "this decision was made by Missionary Ltd. in accordance with Polish reasons of state in the Lemko region."[136] Beginning on 1 October 1938 all AAL seminarians began their studies at the Roman Catholic seminary in Tarnów. In the academic year 1938–1939 there were 9 seminarists studying there.[137]

The conference in Sanok (18 August) was preceded by Wroński's meeting with Sanok starost Wojciech Bucior, who then took part in talks with Medvetsky and Siekierzhynsky – chancellor of AAL curia.[138] Once again the discussion dealt with the need for removing politically active Greek Catholic clergy from the Lemko region. It was jointly decided to transfer several priests and deliver warnings to "those manifesting aggressive nationalistic activity," and in a report from the conference Wroński wrote that "Medvecky and Siekierzhynsky revealed a lot of understanding for these issues from the point of view of Polish reasons of state."[139] A separate issue was the discussion of the plan for a magazine called *Verkhovyna*, the publication of which had been initiated by government circles. Starost Bucior and Wroński were working to convince Medvetsky of the need for its creation. Medvetsky, however reluctantly, turned editorial matters over to Fr. Vendzilovsky. The above decisions must have been difficult for him, if in his conversations with government representatives he sensed that his influence in the province's administrative activities was steadily waning; at the end of the Sanok conference he even expressed doubts as to the usefulness of the AAL's existence.[140]

From 1937 onward the government authorities' position tended distinctly toward transforming its administrative apparatus into a tool of nationality policy in the Lemko region. The first symptoms of this phenomenon appeared in the general letter of the District Command Corps No. V in Kraków to the governors of Kraków and Lviv, the commander of District Corps X and VI, and Nowy Sącz sta-

---

[134] Ibid., p. 141.

[135] Ibid., p. 73.

[136] Ibid., p. 153.

[137] M. Bilovsky (Sadkowice), P. Fetsitsa (Hańczowa), Y. Fedovych (Wyszatyce), V. Yesyp (Ustjanowa), V. Lesyk (Przedrzymichy), Y. Melnyk and V. Melnyk (Paprotno), V. Pastavetsky (Rumno), S. Vatral (Śnietnica). See AAN, MSW, ref. # 1080, p. 28.

[138] AAN, MWRiOP, ref. # 625, p. 147.

[139] Ibid., p. 149.

[140] Ibid.

rost M. Łach of 23 July 1937. Lieutenant Colonel Horak expressed the view that candidates for AAL seminarist positions should be accepted only from the ranks of "Uniate Poles and [...] and the so-called petty nobility."[141] Efforts toward making the AAL a Polish institution were also apparent during the establishment of new Greek Catholic parishes. For example in the case of the parish in Wisłoczek planned by Fr. Medvetsky, the MWRiOP confidentially informed the province authorities that the creation of new parishes in the Lemko region "could take place in the event that a guarantee were given that in the newly created parish Polish language would be allowed in sermons and in special services."[142]

After the decision on matters relating to the training of seminarians for the AAL, government circles took on the question of a change to the post of administrator. The reason appears to have been Medvetsky's independent decision in the matter of placing seminarians in Dubno. At a meeting of the Province Committee for Lemko Regional Affairs in Kraków on 27 May 1938 starost Bucior spoke out against Medvetsky, but the candidacy then put forward of Fr. Poliansky was nevertheless not accepted. The position which corresponded to the newest premises of nationality policy toward the Lemko region was taken by Kraków governor Józef Tymiński. He stated that posts in the AAL would be correctly staffed in a successful manner only when the office of administrator was filled by a priest of Polish nationality, who had changed to the Eastern rite.[143] On this occasion the head of the Socio-Political Division of the Kraków Province Office, Z. Muchniewski, declared that the matter had been discussed in Kraków with the director of the Department of Religious Denominations of the MWRiOP where it was agreed that the issue would be decided the following year, in 1939.[144]

5. The elections of 1928, 1930, 1935, and 1938

In the 1928 parliamentary elections, Ukrainians in the southeastern voivodeships abandoned their boycott tactic and participated. In contrast to the elections of 1922, when the then-government maintained relative neutrality, in the elections of 1928 it took one side in the electoral campaign. Minister of the Interior Felicjan Sławoj-Składkowski sent out a circular to starosts in which he recommended that the membership of District Electoral Commissions be packed with those who were "loyal to the policies of the current government."[145] The Polish-Rusyn Association

---

[141] This problem was raised vociferously in the Ukrainian magazines *Nash Lemko, Dilo, Ukrainskyi Beskyd*, and *Misionar*. See AAN, MWRiOP, ref. # 625, p. 42; Y. Tarnovych, *20 rokiv nevoli*, pp. 124–126.

[142] See AAN, MWRiOP, ref. # 471, *Cerkwie, majątki*, p. 656.

[143] AAN, MSW, ref. # 1058, *Materiały dotyczące Łemkowszczyzny*, p. 47.

[144] Ibid.

[145] A. Próchnik, op.cit., p. 223.

"Zgoda" (Agreement) also conducted a political campaign, as did the Kraków publication *Lemko*, printed in the Roman alphabet.

For the purpose of representing the government faction in elections, the BBWR was created using the organs of civic administration: the voivodeships, districts, municipality offices, and police.[146] The rationale for Minister Składkowski's decrees was that the districts would spring into action aimed at winning the populace for the BBWR, a duty which weighed first and foremost on the heads and secretaries of Municipality Offices, and next winning some teachers and Greek Catholic clergy. The second group (which were few in number) included the deacon of Grybów, rector of the parish in Czyrna, Fr. Mykhailo Artemovych.[147] Among the heads and secretaries of municipality offices there were more frequent instances of refusal to cooperate, so that e.g. in the municipalities of Grybów County near the border only Sylvester Mikhnevych, village mayor in Czertyżne, "exerted activity in this direction, in order that [Lemkos] would vote for the BBWR."[148] It should be noted that among the individuals approached by the districts, many came out against the government even before the elections. There were some cases of municipalities where the people approached "unanimously betrayed the trust placed in them and at the time of the vote the population [...] fought ticket no. 1 (the BBWR) with outright fanaticism."[149]

From January 1928 on, the Lemko region became the ground of agitation conducted by the RNO and RAP. The first group represented pro-Russian tendencies, and the second stood on a position of loyalty to the Polish state. The administrative authorities did not immediately perceive the differences in the programs of these parties and in the period preceding the 1928 elections did not make efforts toward gaining the votes of Old Rusyns. On the contrary, the governor of Lviv, P. Dunin-Borkowski, proposed to them that they create a joint electoral bloc with the RNO.[150]

The governor's intervention led to an agreement by both parties, who supported the Union of Russians in the elections and developed a campaign in favor of ticket no. 20. For the purpose of coordinating the pre-election campaign the Commission of Five was created, which made an appeal to voters. The appeal called them to defend the rights of the Church and to support the RZN "in the name of the shared

---

146 Ibid.

147 AP K, SP G II, ref. # 12, *Wybory 1928 r.*, p.n.n.

148 Ibid., ref. # 13, Wybory 1928 [1928 Elections], p.n.n. Among those engaged in the pro-government election campaign in the northern municipalities of Grybów County were: K. Buranych (Wawrzka), I. Kofla (head of the municipality of Wawrzka), V. Korol (Binczarowa) – he directed the BBWR campaign in Brunary Niżne and Wyżne, T. Kostelnyk (head of the municipality of Binczarowa), M. Poliansky (head of the municipality of Polany) – he also agitated in Królowa Ruska. In Bogusza the following agitated on behalf of BBWR: I. Khoroshchak (municipal head), P. Khoroshchak (municipal secretary), and H. Virkhomsky (farmer).

149 Ibid., p.n.n.

150 AP R, AKL, ref. # 72, p. 2. The Old Rusyns gave their consent to the voivodeship's proposals, fearing the loss of the position of government commissar in the People's House (*Narodnyi Dom*) institution in Lviv.

ideals of Rusyn culture."[151] Exponents of Eastern Orthodoxy such as Mykhailo Kop-chak of Tylawa, the one candidate from the Lemko region who was unsuccessful in his senate bid, starting from the sixth position on the Russian ticket,[152] took active part in the campaign.

Both parties, RNO and RAP, conducted their campaigns in three stages. The first stage consisted of assemblies organized separately by each party in late December 1927 and early January 1928, at which Election Committees and delegates for liaison with neighboring counties were chosen.[153] The second involved gatherings which brought together representatives of an entire county or several counties. They met successively in: Gładyszów (for Gorlice and Grybów Counties), in Sanok (for Sanok and Brzozów Counties) and in Rymanów (for Krosno and Jasło Counties).[154] The third stage consisted of local pre-election gatherings organized in many localities of the Lemko region.

In January and February rallies were organized with candidates to the Sejm par-ticipating. Particularly active were Dmytro Yablonsky (district 48), Orest Hnatyshak (district 44) and Teodor Voitovych (district 45), who were listed first on the ticket.[155] They traveled to many towns, making program speeches in which they discussed the possibilities for economic, cultural and educational development of the Lemko region through the help of its own deputies in the Sejm and Senate. At the mass meetings activists who were not candidates for the Sejm but were engaged in or-ganizational work also spoke. At the end of local assemblies, resolutions were passed which usually contained three points: 1 – to vote for the "Lemko ticket," no. 20; 2 – that everyone should take part in elections, "so that not a single vote is lost, the infirm and cripples must be driven there"; 3 – differences of denomination were of no importance in the elections.[156]

Despite significant involvement of Lemkos in the run-up to the election, not a single deputy from the Russian ticket was elected in the Lemko region. On the national scale the RZN obtained only one seat, which went to RZN president Pavel Korol in the Pińsk district.[157] In the area of the former Galicia the Russian ticket got the most support in the Zolochiv district (20791 votes). In the Lemko region the highest number of votes were in the counties of Gorlice and Grybów.[158]

The active participation of the Lemko population in the 1928 elections was not built on a clearly defined political position among voters. Frequently the same peo-

[151] AAN, MSW, ref. # 961, p. 225; SN 1927, nos. 5–6, p. 556 and 1928, no. 1, pp. 71–72.
[152] Holos Naroda 1928, no. 8, p. 2.
[153] Russkii Golos 1928, no. 236, p. 4.
[154] Zemlia i Volia 1928, no. 8, p. 7.
[155] Holos Naroda 1928, no. 5, p. 2 and no. 8, pp. 1–2.
[156] Zemlia i Volia 1928, no. 8, p. 7.
[157] SN 1928, no. 1, p. 72.
[158] AP K, SPG II, ref. # 14, Sprawy wyborów do ciał ustawodawczych: wybory do Sejmu i Senatu w 1928 r. – wyniki wyborów, p.n.n.

ple took part in work for the RAP and the RNO. The press organs of both parties, *Holos Naroda* and *Russkii Golos* named the same persons as members or sympathizers of their organizations. It would appear that in this rapprochement of ideologically opposed camps the still-vital common ground of "Rusyn" national identity, which Russians had not relinquished and which brought Old Rusyns and Moscophiles together, played an important role.

The RNO and RAP played a significant part in weakening the pro-government election campaign. In 1928 the BBWR did not succeed in taking Lemkos off the Russian ticket and driving them to form their own breakaway conciliatory group. Within the southeastern voivodeships the pro-government bloc took only one Ukrainian deputy to the Sejm.[159]

The RZN's union with the RNO and RAP did not, it is true, give the Lemko region a representative in parliament, but the union did energize it politically, which permitted greater elasticity in attitudes during the elections in November 1930. In mid-September in Old Rusyn circles of the Kraków province a plan was discussed for putting their own candidate in the Sejm via the pro-government ticket. BBWR agitators delegated by the district since 1928 tried to establish contact with the Old Rusyns, so on the eve of the 1930 elections the mutual relations already maintained certain traditions. During the confidential meeting in Binczarowa on 21 September it was agreed that the Old Rusyns would vote for the pro-government ticket, if Metody Trokhanovsky or another candidate whose name was not given were included on the ticket. The main candidate came from Krynica to visit the gathering for the purpose of obtaining the support of the residents of Binczarowa.[160]

On the same day there was a conference of delegates from Gorlice County in Łosie, where a plan was announced for cooperation with the government on condition that in one of the three electoral districts of which the Lemko region was comprised an Old Rusyn candidate would be included on the pro-government ticket, or, if necessary, the government would assure certain concessions for the development of dairy cooperatives, for agrarian improvements, development of cultural and educational institutions, etc. It was determined that negotiations with government circles would bring over delegates elected at the all-Lemko congress in Gorlice on 28 September.[161] At the conference in Łosie there were also activists of the Center-Left political formation present, who nonetheless did not succeed in engaging Lemkos' interest in their political program.[162]

The Gorlice congress met in the home of Yaroslav Siokalo. About 30 delegates from the counties of Gorlice, Grybów and Nowy Sącz attended. K. Bodak of

---

[159] R. Torzecki, *Kwestia ukraińska w Polsce w latach 1923–1929*, Kraków 1989, p. 251.
[160] AP K, SP G II, ref. # 5, *Sprawy ogólnoinformacyjne, sprawozdanie sytuacyjne starosty grybowskiego z 30 września 1930*, p.n.n.
[161] Ibid., ref. # 7, p. IV/2.
[162] AP K, UWKr, ref. # 51, *Tygodniowe sprawozdania informacyjne starosty powiatowego w Grybowie i Gorlicach*, p.n.n.

Rozdziele was elected chairperson of the congress. Introductory remarks were made by RSO activist Yuliian Yurchakevych, who in his long speech warned the assembly against voting for the pro-government ticket. He stated that the position of the Old Rusyns would be decided by RSO headquarters in Lviv.[163] Siokalo spoke in response to Yurchakevych. He protested against bringing the Lemkos under Lviv's control and said that Lemkos were living in a purely Polish environment, in conditions different than those in Lviv, and that they had to look after "their own interests," rather than acting according to the prescriptions of Moscophile circles in Lviv. Siokalo also spoke against imposing non-Lemko candidates for parliament on the Lemkos. His position received support from T. Yadlovsky and T. Voitovych in their speeches. The congress passed a resolution to undertake efforts for the purpose of putting a pro--government Old Rusyn candidate on the ticket, and if that proved impossible, they would expect material aid for the Lemko region. At the end of the congress an Election Committee was chosen.[164]

Conversations with BBWR representatives took place in Kraków, in which Yadlovsky and Voitovych participated. The government side rejected the proposal to get Metody Trokhanovsky on the BBWR ticket, but made a commitment to provide financial aid to the Lemko region, take into consideration the demands of Eastern Orthodox believers, staff teaching positions with Lemko teachers, grant long-term credits to Lemko institutions and create a separate electoral district for the Lemko region.[165] A report on the talks in Kraków was filed by both delegates at the meeting of the closed Election Committee in Gorlice on 12 October. The Committee heard the news of the results of negotiations and determined that contrary to Lviv Moscophiles, Lemkos would vote "for the pro-election ticket straight down the line."[166] At the same time the Committee resolved to gather again in Grybów on 19 October, and there determine its agitation tactics and agree on the text of an appeal to voters.[167]

The promised conference in Grybów took place in the apartment of Rozalia Führer and gathered the leading figures in the social and political life of the Lemko region from the Kraków province. The most prominently visible were Didovych, Dubets, Hnatyshak, Yadlovsky, Siokalo, M. Trokhanovsky, D. Trokhanovsky, I. Trokhanovsky and others. The pro-government faction was represented by I. Korzeń and W. Joniec from the Grybów branch of the BBWR. The deliberations were chaired by Hnatyshak, who stated that after the fulfillment of Lemko demands accepted by the government in Kraków, Lemkos would go to the elections "in unanimous agree-

[163] AP K, SPG II, ref. # 7, p. IV/1 and UWKr, ref. # 51, p.n.n.
[164] AP K, UWKr, ref. # 51, p.n.n. The Committee was made up of: Bodak, Yadlovsky, Kachmarchyk, Seifert, Siokalo, and Voitovych from Gorlice County; Khoiniak, Gromosiak, Hnatyshak, Fr. Pryslopsky, and M. Trokhanovsky from Nowy Sącz County; and Dubets from Grybów County.
[165] AP K, SP G II, ref. # 5, p.n.n.
[166] AP K, UWKr, ref. # 51, p.n.n.
[167] Ibid.

ment with the pro-government ticket."[168] In the discussion support was expressed for state policy in the Lemko region; only V. Dubets expressed doubts as to whether the promises made at the Kraków meeting would be kept. The Grybów conference chose an Election Committee for Grybów County, in which adherents of Eastern Orthodoxy played a key role.[169]

In the period under discussion the Orthodox population faced the necessity of solving many problems which depended on the position taken by the authorities. Among the demands made by Eastern Orthodox members of the Election Committee were: gaining permission for Orthodox priests to be given charge of register books and claims on their own church buildings and the creation of new parishes. The demands put forth by activists of Orthodox faith even caused a written intervention by the Grybów starost at the provincial level in the matter of speeding up the passage of plans for building Orthodox chasovnias in Banica, Izby, Jaszkowa, and Śnietnica.[170] Implementing their own electoral policy, the authorities unofficially supported the efforts of the Orthodox population in the direction of satisfying their religious needs, acquiring support for the government in this way.[171]

After the Grybów conference the BBWR activists from Gorlice, Grybów and Nowy Sącz began a broadly expanded campaign together with Old Rusyn activists in many Lemko municipalities. In Gorlice County the most actively engaged were K. Jamro, J. Kunigiewicz, K. Laskowski, B. Piotrowski and K. Tabor. In Jasło County political papers were delivered by Sejm candidate K. Duch.[172]

The pro-government campaign in the Lemko region met with counteraction from the opposition. The threat to the BBWR may have been the cause of the 11th ticket, a united Ukrainian ticket supported by the intelligentsia, chiefly teachers and Greek Catholic priests. The part of the intelligentsia which self-identified as Ukrainian organized visits for deputies from UNDO. In Nowy Sącz County the meetings were initiated mainly by the following priests: M. Bubniak, S. Dmytryshyn, S. Kornova, and V. Smolynsky. These visits, however, did not constitute part of a wider political campaign, but rather were a form of sporadic activity. The meetings included the visit of Deputy Biliak in Nowa Wieś on 21 July 1929 and Deputy Oleksandr Vislotsky attending a meeting in Łabowa on 28 August 1930. In these appearances they expressed criticism of the Polish authorities. They particularly spoke out against transferring Ukrainian teachers to the central areas of Poland and delegating teachers of Polish nationality to Ukrainian schools. They called Lemkos to integrate with

---

[168] AP K, SP G II, ref. # 5, p.n.n.
[169] Ibid. The Committee members were P. Khoroshchak (Bogusza), Fr. M. Khylak (Izby), V. Dubets (Florynka), M. Kuziak (Wawrzka), V. Kysilevsky (Brunary), Y. Monchak (Berest), Z. Stavysky (Śnietnica), D. Trokhanovsky (Binczarowa), and V. Vyshovsky (Królowa Ruska).
[170] AP K, SPG II, ref. # 5, p.n.n.
[171] Ibid.
[172] AP K, UWKr, ref. # 51, p.n.n; AP K, SP G II, ref. # 7, p. IV/10.

Ukrainian institutions and continuing to endure in their Greek Catholic faith. They spoke of the need to acquire at least one deputy seat in the Lemko region.[173]

The weekly reports of starosts mention the involvement of teachers in the run-up to the election. The authorities perceived pro-Ukrainian moods in Berest, Brunary Wyżne and Polany.[174] In addition to priests and teachers, some municipal officials became actively involved in the campaign, e.g. municipal secretary in Ropnica Ruska, P. Zeleny, and also farmers, e.g. V. Zlupko of Gładyszów, brother of the local rector.[175] According to the dispatch from the Nowy Targ starost to the Kraków Province Office, pro-Ukrainian agitation was also being furthered in Szlachtowa and Jaworki.[176]

Another important tendency in the pre-election agitation in the Lemko region was the campaign led by the RSO, the party which in the previous elections had gone with the Old Rusyns, and in 1930 put up a separate ticket, no. 15. The campaign was directed from RSO headquarters by Mykhailo Tsebrynsky, a journalist from Lviv. Fr. K. Chaikovsky agitated in the area. Both were candidates for the Sejm from district 48.[177] The 15th ticket was however invalidated in the district, which was justified by the lack of the amount of signatures required by electoral law.[178]

On the tickets put up in the districts of the Lemko region only the pro-government ticket, which in elections to both legislative houses received a decided majority of votes, was successful. From all of southeastern Poland, two Old Rusyns, Frs. Yosyf Yavorsky and Mykhailo Bachynsky[179] were elected to the Sejm. They also represented issues of the Lemko region in their relations with Polish authorities.

The state authorities' position toward the Old Rusyns changed in 1935. As a result of the agreement concluded between Kościałkowski and UNDO, Polish-Ukrainian relations in the RP entered a period of so-called "normalization." The Ukrainian faction supported the government in the approaching elections and received guarantees of getting 50% of the seats in electoral districts in the region of the former Eastern Galicia. The government's announcement of "normalization" in relations with Ukrainians pushed the political affairs of the theretofore preferentially treated Old Rusyns to the margins. Due to these changes they were removed from the pro-government ticket.[180] This fact led to the self-annulment of the Rusyn Electoral

---

[173] Ibid., ref. # 7, p. IV/3 and IV/4.

[174] Ibid., ref. # 5, p.n.n. In the counties of Nowy Sącz and Grybów agitation was led by among others V. Merena (head of the school in Bogusza) and A. Nishchota (Śnietnica).

[175] Ibid., p. IV/3; AP K, UWKr, ref. # 51, p.n.n.

[176] AP K, SP G II. ref. # 7, p. IV/l.

[177] *Zemlia i Volia* 1930, no. 43, p. 2.

[178] Ibid., no. 43, p. 1. Ordination required 50 signatures. *Zemlia i Volia* claimed that 102 signatures had been gathered. Additional elections were held in the Przemyśl-Sanok district on 22 November 1931, with the same results as the general election. See A. Próchnik, op.cit., p. 322.

[179] AP K, UWKr, ref. # 52, Tygodniowe sprawozdania informacyjne starosty powiatowego w Jaśle i Nowym Sączu, p.n.n.; *Smutki i radości "russkich"*, BP-U 1936, no. 38, p. 381.

[180] Only in district 62 (Zolochiv), in the fourth spot was there an Old Rusyn, I. Myskov. See *SN* 1935, no. 5, p. 467.

Committee created earlier and the Old Rusyns sitting the election out. It is true that the Old Rusyn press in its comments on the dissolution of the Committee put great emphasis on the fact that the decision did not result from oppositional leanings with regard to government actors, but simply from the fact that the Old Rusyn population deprived of its own delegates no longer had anyone to vote for, so nonetheless withdrawal from the elections meant non-acceptance of government circles.

In light of the new political reality in which Old Rusyns found themselves, the loyalty of the *Lemko Soiuz* to the state in spite of losing the support previously given by the government should be stressed. In the 1935 elections the Old Rusyn Lemkos took a different position than the Rusyn Election Committee (Bachynsky and others). In the journal *Lemko* it was stated that under the influence of disappointed hopes, tendencies to hold back from voting in elections had emerged, but the Association still held the position that the Lemko population should collectively participate in the election, to underscore that "it constitutes an organized group that can be counted on."[181] This decision was made more in terms of making a demonstration than practical considerations, but above all reflected the desire to maintain the organizational independence of the *Lemko Soiuz* from the Old Rusyn stream as a whole.

The elections of 1935, though they were held in the atmosphere of "normalization," in regard to the Lemko region revealed deviations from the terms of the Polish-Ukrainian agreement. The new electoral law eliminated the intermediation of parties in elections, initiating direct voting for candidates. The Ukrainian candidate put up in district 77 (Krosno, Lesko, Sanok) – Volodymyr Solovii, a farmer from Serednie Wielkie in Lesko County, appearing on the second ticket, which in the system of voting without deletions gave him a seat, obtained barely 13,000 votes and did not enter the Sejm.[182]

After the elections the Ukrainian press, looking for reasons for Solovii's failure, wrote about the involvement in the pre-election campaign of the Sanok starost, the Sanok school inspector, the police, and even the Sanok united organization of invalids. The local administrative authorities took steps to ensure that voters would vote for the candidate on list no. 3 – Józef Morawski, the squire in Niebieszczany.[183] According to *Dilo*, there was an official policy of putting pressure on teachers. Some District Electoral Commissions (e.g. in Bukowsko) did not allow Solovii's "private agents," and many polls were put in locations disadvantageous to the Ukrainian population. The Ukrainian press, especially those members opposed to the Polish--Ukrainian agreement, commented on these facts with suggestions that they were closely related to "the policy of isolating the Lemko region" from the rest of the

---

[181] *SN* 1935, no. 5, p. 467.
[182] Ibid., pp. 446–447.
[183] *Chomu perepav Solovii u sianitskii okruzi, Dilo* 1935, no. 244, p. 6.

Ukrainian lands.[184] Some pointed to the breaking of the terms of the agreement by the government and expressed doubts as to the future of "normalization" already on the eve of its enaction. It should here be stressed that in other electoral districts (outside the Lemko region), in accordance with the agreement, Ukrainian candidates were elected with the help of Polish votes.

As a result of the 1935 elections, Lemkos did not get their own representative in parliament. Not only Old Rusyns were deprived of the possibility of obtaining deputy seats, but UNDO as well. The idea of pushing the Ukrainian movement out of the Lemko region obscured the question of comprehensively resolving the region's issues by means of a compromise, and was one of the elements which contributed to the disastrous failure of the Polish-Ukrainian agreement. The position taken by government circles and local administration outlined above was even more in evidence in the elections of 1938, in which the UNDO candidate in the Sanok district (Hladyshovsky) did not even make it onto the ballot.[185]

---

[184] Ibid., no. 242, pp. 1–2. The exclusion of the Ukrainian candidate in the Sanok district from the Sejm formed the substance of a protest by UNDO. In response, the government promised an additional seat in the Senate, but did not keep this promise. The seat went to Y. Voloshynovsky, an advocate of conciliation from Volhynia, employed at the Province Office in the period of Henryk Józewski's term as governor. See Homo Politicus, *Pryczyny upadku Polszczi*, Kraków 1941, p. 128.

[185] V. Chesny, "Do vidoma politychnym kermanycham," *Nash Lemko* 1938, no. 21, p. 2.

Final remarks

Based on the research conducted, it should be stated that the political currents analyzed herein originated outside of the Lemko region. Beginning from the early 19th century, they first developed in Eastern Galicia. This forces us to link social and political events and phenomena occurring in the Lemko community with the transformations taking place in the Eastern part of the country and leads us to conclude that the Lemko region had close connections to the political development of East Galician centers of thought and action. This interconnectedness was sustained in the interwar period.

We face some problems when classifying the political elites. It is difficult to narrowly distinguish the elite with Lemko origins and attach to it a definite political orientation. A great many activists, it is true, lived in the Lemko region or surrounding cities, but had origins outside of its ethnographic area. This applies in particular to the intelligentsia, for whom it was easier to change places of residence. The Lemko region attracted national activists, Moscophiles and Old Rusyns; priests (Eastern Orthodox and Greek Catholic), lawyers and doctors. Migration also flowed in the reverse direction – Lemkos came to reinforce branches of institutions of varying political hues in Lviv and other cities, establishing medical practices and attorneys' offices. After getting an education it was natural for them to settle in Eastern Galicia, putting aside their Lemko origins.

It is worthy of note that the following well-known political activists of the Lemko region were not in fact Lemkos: Roman Borysevych, a representative of the Ukrainian current, Fr. Kyrylo Chaikovsky, a Moscophile, and Yaroslav Siokalo, who straddled the line between the Old Rusyn and Moscophile movements. Of course a large number of activists were of Lemko birth; the Trokhanovsky family, a group which produced both members of the Old Rusyn movement (e.g. Metody of Krynica) and the Ukrainian (e.g. Mykola of Polany) were undoubtedly Lemkos. We can observe opposing political strains in many other families, including the Bachynskys, the Barns, the Khomiaks, the Khoroshchaks, the Hnatyshaks, the Yavorskys, the Mudrys, the Polianskys, and the Pyzhes.

An analysis of the political attitudes of those Lemkos who we find both among exponents of the Ukrainian national movement as well as the Old Rusyn and pro-Russian ones, provides interesting results. We can conclude from such an analysis that Lemko origins did not have a decisive influence on a person's choice of political orientation. Of much greater importance were cultural values, including religion, language, and historical tradition. Hence the relatively easy transmission of the above political orientations onto Lemko soil, as well as the lack of native Lemko political concepts (the *Lemko Soiuz* belonged to the Old Rusyn movement which had formed outside of the Lemko region).

In the literature on the subject we find variations in the classification of the above orientations. Both the Old Rusyn movement and the pro-Russian one can be treated as separate currents, but on the other hand they can be seen as phases in the development of one process, i.e. the shaping of the modern Ukrainian national movement. The basis of its development was formed by cultural values created and cultivated by successive generations of Rusyns. The concepts of "Ukraine" and "Ukrainian," introduced by national activists in the late 19th century, were based on precisely these values, and the change of term was dictated by their desire to protect themselves from Polish and Russian influences. This occurred in this way because both Polish and Russian political thought had imported the concepts of "Rus" and "Rusyns" for their own use. Some Polish milieux considered Rusyns to be Poles, while Russians considered them Russians. The activists of the Ukrainian movement must have been keenly sensitive to this, since they decided to change their own name. The point was to arrest the process of Ukrainian culture's diminution as a result of the growing influences of neighboring cultures. This endeavor was a tactical maneuver – the concept of "Rusyn" remained in currency and for a certain time the national activists used the dyadic concept of "Rus-Ukraine." It would appear that herein lies the specific nature of the Ukrainian idea, which sometimes escapes notice from scholars accustomed to other models of development of national movements.

The Greek Catholic Church played an important role in the process of the formation of Lemko political consciousness. The political involvement of priests increased significantly during the wars in the period 1914–1920. However in the far-flung provinces the process of accepting the Ukrainian idea among the clergy took place very slowly; the delay was even more visible among the ranks of churchgoers. It seems accurate to suppose that young priests of Ukrainian orientation were too quick and forceful in their demand that Lemkos accept the Ukrainian idea, which precipitated a reaction of opposition and strengthened Old Rusyn or pro-Russian feeling. This attitude among priests pushed people away from the Ukrainian movement and fostered the growth of Orthodoxy in the years 1911–1914 and 1926–1934; it must also have influenced the desire of a group of believers to break away from the supervision of the Greek Catholic diocese in Przemyśl, which facilitated the creation of the AAL.

The Old Rusyn and Moscophile orientations were difficult to distinguish from one another in the Lemko region. This was because at the village level the rivalry between them was not conspicuously visible. Both currents used the same (though sometimes differently written) terminology, accepted among Lemkos. In looking for the reasons behind this choice of orientation, it is important to draw a boundary between ideologically-tinged feelings and self-definition on the basis of external cultural factors. It seems fit to judge that this second method of self-identification predominated among Old Rusyns. For the same reasons, a great number of peasants belonged to Moscophile organizations. So the question arises: to what extent was participation in Moscophile or Old Rusyn structures a result of political identification? In the course of seeking an answer we are led to the conclusion that for most residents of the Lemko region the deciding issue was most definitely their belonging to the eastern cultural sphere, which means that a strictly political movement among Lemkos was only beginning to take shape.

The part of Lemko society which made the choice of a particular organization on the basis of its political program should be assessed differently. This group's numbers were considerably smaller. However, we may observe a lack of consistency in organizational affiliation in this case too. A two-track attitude was typical for these persons, i.e. simultaneous membership in pro-Russian and Old Rusyn organizational structures (e.g. O. Hnatyshak, Y. Perelom, Y. Siokalo and M. Trokhanovsky).

Finally, we may observe the process of a fraction of the Old Rusyn and Moscophile intelligentsia's move over to the Ukrainian camp (e.g. Y. Kachmarchyk) – this phenomenon had earlier occurred in the region of Eastern Galicia, where in the late 19th and early 20th centuries we find the names of activists later involved with the Ukrainian movement (e.g. Lepky), which took on broader dimensions during the period of the Nazi occupation and after the Second World War.

The growth of the Ukrainian idea in the Lemko region at first was slower than that of the other currents mentioned above. This created a disadvantageous starting point for the national activists, whose political opponents defined them as agitators from the outside. It should here be underscored that the orientations discussed in this work have equal claims to being of native origin, i.e. the application of the charge of "transplantation" without the clarification that the problem relates equally to the shared heritage of each ethnic group, is unfounded. The Ukrainian national movement in the Lemko region went through a similar path of development to the one it followed in Eastern Galicia. In both cases a great many Rusyns, on their way to reaching a modern Ukrainian national consciousness, passed through the stage of Old Rusyn or Moscophile orientation, and often both, one after the other.

An assessment of the political orientations under study would be incomplete without connecting them to the nationality policy of the Second Polish Republic. The Lemko question had influence as a factor in more general Ukrainian issues. Until the mid-1930s the government conducted a policy of so-called "state adaptation" of Lemkos. In the subsequent years the Lemko region was subjected to national assimilation. Successive government cabinets made an effort to tie national minorities to the state, fostering the growth of conciliatory tendencies among Ukrainians. At the same time, conciliatory groups had a marginal role, while strong parties such as UNDO (the Ukrainian National Democratic Alliance) and the illegal OUN (Organization of Ukrainian Nationalists) were much more important. The nationalists took an uncompromising stance toward the Republic. UNDO, it is true, accepted the Polish nation-state, but this was a tactical decision. In reality it was planned to create a Ukrainian state in the future from the ethnically Ukrainian lands within Poland's borders (including the Lemko region), the USSR, Czechoslovakia and Romania. The political intentions of Ukrainian circles and the government were at variance with each other. There were objective obstacles to their convergence inherent in the national feelings of Poles and Ukrainians and their claims to the same territory. In this view the demographic plane, historical and cultural traditions, and political attitudes of both groups had not changed from Galician times and did not encourage lasting understanding. The Lemko question stood between Ukrainian politicians and the government and until the end of the RP's existence it remained a combustible problem in Polish-Ukrainian relations.

This book presents the political directions which developed in the Lemko region in the years 1918–1939, but does not exhaust the subject. Various more specific problems in the political and confessional life of Lemkos remain to be clarified by future historians, using archival sources which are often, unfortunately, incomplete.

Sources and bibliographies

Archives

Central Archives of Modern Records in Warsaw

1. Prezydium Rady Ministrów:
- Protokoły Posiedzeń RM;
- Komitet Polityczny RM;
- Gabinet Prezesa RM;
- Komisja Naukowych Badań Ziem Wschodnich.
2. Ministerstwo Spraw Wewnętrznych:
- Gabinet Ministra;
- Wydział Społeczno-Polityczny;
- Wydział Narodowościowy;
- Wydział Bezpieczeństwa.
3. Ministerstwo Spraw Zagranicznych:
- Gabinet Ministra;
- Wydział Organizacji Międzynarodowych;
- Wydział Wschodni.
4. Ministerstwo Wyznań Religijnych i Oświecenia Publicznego:
- Departament Wyznań.
5. Komenda Główna Policji Państwowej.
6. Urząd Wojewódzki w Krakowie, 1919–1939.
7. Urząd Wojewódzki we Lwowie, 1920–1939.

Archives of Polish Academy of Sciences in Warsaw

1. Materiały Ludwika Ręgorowicza.

State Archives in Kraków

1. C.k. Starostwo Powiatowe w Grybowie, 1908–1918.
2. Kuratorium Okręgu Szkolnego w Krakowie, 1922–1939.
3. Starostwo Powiatowe w Grybowie, 1919–1930.
4. Starostwo Powiatowe w Nowym Sączu, 1919–1939.
5. Towarzystwo Szkoły Ludowej, Zarząd Główny w Krakowie, 1892–1939/1940.
6. Urząd Wojewódzki Krakowski, 1921–1939.

Jagiellonian Library

1. Dział Rękopisów:
– L. Ręgorowicz, Materiały do dziejów wychowania, sygn. P. 64/64.

State Archives in Przemyśl

1. Apostolska Administracja Łemkowszczyzny, 1934–1945.
2. Archiwum biskupstwa greckokatolickiego w Przemyślu, 1921–1946.
3. Parafie greckokatolickie województwa rzeszowskiego.
4. Starostwo Powiatowe w Gorlicach, 1918–1939.
5. Starostwo Powiatowe w Jaśle, 1918–1927.
6. Starostwo Powiatowe w Sanoku, 1918–1939.

State Archives in Rzeszów

1. Archiwum ks. Juliana Łukaszkławicza.

Central State Archives in Lviv, Ukraine (Центральний Державний Історичний Архів у Львові)

1. Tsentralna Rada Rusko-Selanskoi Orhanizatsii u Lvovi.
2. Halytsyiskoie Namiestnytstvo.
3. Hreko-katolytskyi mytropolychyi ordynariat, Lviv.
4. Kraiove Silskohospodarske Tovarystvo "Silskyi Hospodar" (1899–1944).
5. Kuratoriia Lvivskoho Shkilnoho Okruhu.
6. Lvivskyi Stavropigiiskyi Instytut.
7. Naukovo-literaturne Tovarystvo "Halytsko-Ruska Matiesa" u Lvovi, 1847–1939.
8. Redaktsiia Zhurnalu *Nash Lemko*, m. Lviv, 1934–1939.
9. "Ridna Shkola" – Ukrainske Pedahohichne Tovarystvo u Lvovi, 1881–1939.
10. Ruskyi Narodnyi Instytut "Narodnyi Dim" u Lvovi, 1849–1939.
11. Tovarystvo im. Mykhaila Kachkovskoho (suspilno-kulturne i literaturne), 1876–1939.
12. Tovarystvo "Prosvita", m. Lviv, 1864–1944.
13. Ukrainske natsionalno-demokratychne obiednannia (UNDO), m. Lviv.

State Archives of Lviv Province, Ukraine (Державний Архів Львівської області)

1. Lvivske Voievodske Upravlinnia, 1921–1939:
– Podotdiel biezopasnosti i pressy;
– Prezydialnyi otdiel;
– Podotdiel po dielam tovarystv.

Ukrainian Lemko Museum, Camillus, NY, USA

1. Arkhiv Komitetu Dopomohy Lemkivshchyny, 1933–1936.
2. Arkhiv Muzeiu – korespondentsiia, 1936–1940.

Published Documents

III Narodnyi Zizd Ukrainskoho Natsionalno-Demokratychnoho Obiednannia v dniakh 24 i 25 hrudnia 1928 r. (Zvit zlozhenyi na pidstavi stenohrafichnoho protokolu), Lviv 1929.

Bachynskii M., *Promova M. Bachynskoho posla na Soim z rameny Ruskoi Agrarnoi Organizatsii vyholoshena v Soimi v sichni 1931*, Lvov 1931.

Chynnosty i rishennia provintsiialnoho Soboru v Halychyni 1891 r., Lviv 1894.

Masciukh V., *Pershe pastyrske poslaniie do Lemkiv*, Lviv 1935.

– *Pastyrske poslaniie dra Vasyliia Mastsiukha, Apostolskoho Administratora dla Lemkivshchyny z nahody Rozhdestva Khrystovoho r. 1936 do Lemkiv*, Lviv 1935.

Oświadczenie protestacyjne towarzystw i organizacyj ruskich przeciw urzędowemu wprowadzeniu terminu "ukraiński" zamiast "ruski", Lwów 1936.

Programa Russkoi Selanskoi Organizatsii (RSO), [Lvov] 1930.

Protest przeciw wprowadzeniu nazwy "ukraiński" zamiast "ruski" (rusiński), Lwów 1928.

Russkii Narodnyi Siezd, 1 noiabria 1923 g. Rezolutsii Siezda i Ustav Russkoi Narodnoi Organizatsiii s prylozheniem Rezolutsii Russkago Narodnago Sovieta ot 2 fievrala 1924 g., Lvov 1924.

Sejm Rzeczypospolitej Polskiej. Sprawozdania Stenograficzne, Warszawa 1926–1939.

Senat Rzeczypospolitej Polskiej. Sprawozdania Stenograficzne, Warszawa 1930–1939.

Siwicki M., *Dzieje konfliktów polsko-ukraińskich*, vol. 1–3, Warszawa 1992–1994.

Statut Związku Rosyjskich Organizacji Mniejszościowych w Polsce, Warszawa 1931.

Ukraińskie i ruskie ugrupowania polityczne w Polsce w dniu 1 IV 1927, Wydział Narodowościowy MSW, Warszawa 1927.

Ustav organizatsiinyii regulamyn Ruskoi Agrarnoi Organizatsii, Lvov 1931.

Periodicals

Beskid (Przemyśl) 1931–1932.

Biuletyn Polsko-Ukraiński (Warszawa) 1933–1938.

Dilo (Lviv) 1928–1939.

Droga (Warszawa) 1929.

Dzieje Najnowsze (Warszawa) 1992.

Holos Naroda (Lwów) 1928–1931.

Ilustrowany Kurier Codzienny (Kraków) 1919, 1929.

Istorychnyi Kalendar. Almanakh Chervonoi Kalyny na 1935 rik (Lviv) 1934.

Kalendar "Lemka" na zvychainyi rok (Przemyśl) 1935–1938.

Kalendar Tovarystva "Prosvita" (Lviv) 1926, 1930.

Karpatorusskii Kalendar Lemko-Soiuza (Yonkers, NY) 1954, 1959, 1960, 1963.

Karpatorusskii Kalendar Vania Hunianky (Cleveland, Ohio) 1929–1933.

Lemko (Nowy Sącz, Krynica, Lviv) 1934–1939.

Lemkivskyi Kalendarz (Toronto-Passaic, NJ) 1966, 1967, 1969.

Ludowiec (Gorlice) 1927.

Lwowski Kurier Poranny (Lwów) 1930.

Lystok (Lwów) 1939.

Magury (Warszawa) 1987, 1988.

Myśl Narodowa (Warszawa) 1934.

Nash Lemko (Lviv) 1934–1939.

Nashe Slovo (Warszawa) 1994.

Nauchno-Literaturnyi Sbornik Halytsko-Ruskoi Matitsy (Lviv) 1934.

Nauka. Ilustrovanyi misiachnyk dla naroda (Lviv) 1931, 1935.

Nova Zoria (Lviv) 1934.

Oriens (Kraków) 1935, 1937.

Rocznik Sądecki (Nowy Sącz) 1992.

Russkii Golos (Lviv) 1928, 1929.

Sprawy Narodowościowe (Warszawa) 1927–1939.

Svoboda (Jersey City, NJ) 1928–1939.

Ukrainskyi Beskid (Przemyśl) 1933.

Visti Apostolskoi Administratsii Lemkivshchyny (Sanok) 1936.

Wierchy (Kraków, Wrocław) 1935, 1993.

Zemlia i Volia (Lviv) 1928–1935.

Articles, Essays, and Memoirs

"Administrator Apostolski Łemkowszczyzny," *Oriens* 1935, no. 1.

Andrusiak M., "Zarys historii moskalofilstwa wśród Ukraińców halickich," *BP-U* 1933, nos. 34 and 35.

Baczyński M., *Kwestia mniejszościowa oraz rola i metody opozycji mniejszościowej w odrodzonej Polsce*, Lwów 1935.

Baran S., "Sianik i Yaslo," *Dilo* 1934, no. 208.

Best P.J., "Moscophilism amongst the Lemko Population," *Carpatho-Slavic Studies* (New Haven, Conn.) 1990, vol. 1.

– "Moskalofilstwo wśród ludności łemkowskiej w XX wieku," in: *Ukraińska myśl polityczna w XX wieku*, ed. M. Pulaski, Kraków 1993.

– "The Lemko-Rusnak Mountaineers and the National Question in People's Poland," *Carpatho-Slavic Studies* 1990 (New Haven, Conn.), vol. 1.

Buchatsky V., *Moskvofilstvo na Lemkivshchyni*, New York 1955.

Bukvar. Persha Knizhechka dla vseludnykh shkol, [Metody Trokhanovsky], Lvov 1933.

Chojnowski A., *Koncepcje polityki narodowościowej rządów polskich w latach 1921–1939*, Wrocław 1979.

Chołodecki J.B., *Lwów w czasie okupacji rosyjskiej (1914–1915). Z własnych przeżyć i spostrzeżeń*, Lwów 1930.

Chraplyvy E., *Silske hospodarstvo halycko-volynskykh zemel*, Lviv 1936.

Duda T., "Życie polityczne Łemków sądeckich i gorlickich w latach 1926–1939," *Rocznik Sądecki* 1992 (Nowy Sącz), vol. 20.

Dunin-Borkowski P., "Punkt wyjścia w sprawie ukraińskiej w Małopolsce Wschodniej," *Droga* 1929, no. 6.

Feldman W., *Stronnictwa i programy polityczne w Galicji 1846–1906*, vol. 2, Kraków 1907.

Franko I., *Nieco o stosunkach polsko-ruskich*, Lwów 1895.

Giertych J., *O program polityki kresowej*, Warszawa 1932.

– "Po utworzeniu biskupstwa unickiego na Łemkowszczyźnie," *Myśl Narodowa* 1934, no. 14.

Grabski S., "Kresy i narodowości," *Lwowski Kurier Poranny* 1930.

Hankevych L., "«Lemkivska Republika». Odyn zabutyi protses," *Zhyttia i Pravo* 1934, no. 2 (29).

Homo Politicus [Ivan Kedryn], *Prychyny upadku Polshchi*, Krakiv 1940.

Horoszkiewicz R., *Szlachta zaściankowa na ziemiach wschodnich*, Warszawa 1937.

Jastrzębski S., *Kim jesteśmy? O szlachcie zagrodowej w Małopolsce Wschodniej*, Przemyśl 1939.

Kedryn I., "W poszukiwaniu metryki… Kilka uwag i faktów z dziejów powojennego moskalofilstwa galicyjskiego," *BP-U* 1937, no. 15.

Kokovsky F., "Lemkivski republyky v 1918–1919 rokah," *Istorychnyi Kalendar. Almanakh Chervonoi Kalyny na 1935 rik*, 1934 (Lviv).

Kołpaczkiewicz W., "Na granicy wieków (Jeden etap ewolucji i myśli politycznej Starorusinów)," *BP-U* 1938, nos 5 and 6.

– "Na granicy wieków. Staroruski Guliwer na falach polityki wszechświatowej," *BP-U* 1938, no. 9.

Konstantynovych Y., "Muzei Lemkivshchyna v Sianotsi," *Nova Zoria* 1934, no. 52, Scholarly supplement.

Kozik J., *Między reakcją a rewolucją: studia z dziejów ukraińskiego ruchu narodowego w latach 1948–1949*, Kraków 1975.

– *Moskalofilstwo w Galicji w latach 1849–1866, na tle odrodzenia narodowego Rusinów*, MA thesis (typescript), Jagiellonian University, Kraków 1958.

Kruhelsky A., *Tylavska skhizma na Lemkivshchyni, ii istoriia i teperishnyi stan*, Lviv 1933.

Kuryllo T., "Nashi bursy," *Kalendar "Lemka"* 1936 (Lviv).

Lemkivska problema. Napysav Lemko, Lviv 1933.

Łemkowszczyzna, n.d.p. and n.p.p.

Lewandowski J., "Konflikt polsko-ukraiński na tle konfliktów narodowych w Europie środkowo-wschodniej w XIX i XX w.," *Warszawskie Zeszyty Ukrainoznawcze* 1994 (Warszawa), vol. 2.

Markov D.A., *Russkaia i ukrainskaia ideia v Avstrii*, Moskva 1915.

Moklak J., "Kształtowanie się struktury Kościoła prawosławnego na Łemkowszczyźnie w Drugiej Rzeczypospolitej," in: *Przez dwa stulecia, XIX i XX w.*, ed. S. Pijaj, Kraków 1993.

– "Mychajło Kaczkowśkyj i czytelnie jego imienia na Łemkowszczyźnie," *Magury '87* (Warszawa) 1987.

– "Political Orientations among the Lemkos in the Inter-War Period: 1918–1939," *Carpatho-Slavic Studies* (New Haven, Conn.) 1990, vol. 1.

– *Relacje między ukraińskim ruchem narodowym a moskalofilstwem w Galicji Wschodniej w latach 1866–1890*, MA thesis (typescript), Jagiellonian University, Kraków 1985.

– "Republiki łemkowskie 1918–1919," *Wierchy* (Kraków) 1994, vol. 59.

– "Życie polityczne i religijne ludności łemkowskiej powiatu krośnieńskiego w latach 1918––1939 (na tle całego regionu)," in: *Krosno. Studia z dziejów miasta i regionu*, vol. 3, ed. S. Cynarski, Rzeszów 1995.

Naumenko J., "Ukraińskie formacje wojskowe w czasie wojny światowej (1914–1918 r.)," *BP-U* 1934, no. 2.

Papierzyńska-Turek M., *Sprawa ukraińska w Drugiej Rzeczypospolitej 1922–1926*, Kraków 1979.

Pełczyński E., *Prawosławie w Galicji w świetle prasy ruskiej we Lwowie podczas inwazji 1914–1915 roku*, Lwów 1918.

Pełeński Poray Z., *Polityka UNDO w świetle autonomicznej deklaracji Centralnego Komitetu UNDO z dnia 7 maja 1938 r.*, Lwów 1938.

Petrovych Y., *Halychyna pidchas rosiiskoi okupatsii 1914–1915*, Viden 1915.

Podleski E, *Rusofilizm a ukrainizm*, Lwów 1931.

Polianskii I., "Perebih sporu o slovo «pravoslavnyi» v Tylavi, ta jeho vyslid: vybukh relihiinoho rozdoru na Lemkivshchyni," *Visti Apostolskoi Administratsii Lemkivshchyny* (Lviv) 1936.

Potocki R., *Polityka państwa polskiego wobec zagadnienia ukraińskiego w latach 1930–1939*, Lublin 2003.

Prach B., "Apostolska Administracja Łemkowszczyzny," in: *Łemkowie w historii i kulturze Karpat*, vol. 1, ed. J. Czajkowski, Rzeszów 1992.

Prus-Faszczewski T., *Małopolska Wschodnia a zagadnienie obronności państwa*, Warszawa 1939.

Przysiecki F., *Rządy rosyjskie w Galicji Wschodniej*, Piotrków 1915.

Pulnarowicz W., *Rycerstwo polskie Podkarpacia (Dawne dzieje i obecne obowiązki szlachty zagrodowej na Podkarpaciu)*, Przemyśl 1937.

Radziejowski J., *Komunistyczna Partia Zachodniej Ukrainy, 1919–1929. Węzłowe problemy ideologiczne*, Kraków 1976.

"Ruska Bursa w Horlytsiakh," *Holos Naroda* 1928, nos. 36, 43, 44, 45.

"Ruska Ludowa Republika Łemków," *Magury '88* (Warszawa) 1988.

Shakh S., *Mizh Sianom i Dunaitsem*, Munchen 1960.

Shpylka P., "Vyzvolni zmahannia skhidnoi Lemkivshchyny v 1918 rotsi," *Lemkivskyi Kalendar 1967* (Toronto–Passaic, NJ) 1966.

Śliwa T., "Kościół greckokatolicki w Polsce w latach 1918–1939," in: *Kościół w II Rzeczypospolitej*, ed. Z. Zieliński, Lublin 1980.

Smerekanych P., "Do 60-littia «Nashoho Lemka»," *Nashe Slovo* 1994, nos. 33 and 34.

Smoleński J., "Łemkowie i Łemkowszczyzna," *Wierchy* (Kraków 1935), vol. 13.

Stawecki P., *Następcy Komendanta. Wojsko a polityka wewnętrzna II Rzeczypospolitej w latach 1935–1939*, Warszawa 1969.

Tarnovych O., "Lemkivshchyna v chasi vyzvolnykh zmahan," *Svoboda* 1933, no. 271.

Tarnovych Y., *20 rokiv nevoli. Lemkivshchyna pid polskym iarmom*, Krakiv 1940.

– *Ilustrovana istoriia Lemkivshchyny*, Lviv 1936.

– *Verhamy Lemkivshoho Beskydu. Mandrivnyi providnyk po Lemkivshchyni*, Lviv 1938.

Teodorovich I., "Lemkovskaia Rus," *Nauchno-Literaturnyi Sbornik Halytsko-Ruskoi Matitsy* (Lvov) 1934, vol. 8.

Tomaszewski J., *Rzeczpospolita wielu narodów*, Warszawa 1985.

Tomczyk R., *Ukraińskie Zjednoczenie Narodowo-Demokratyczne 1925–1939*, Szczecin 2006.

Torzecki R., *Kwestia ukraińska w polityce III Rzeszy (1933–1945)*, Warszawa 1972.

– *Kwestia ukraińska w Polsce w latach 1923–1929*, Kraków 1989.

Vanchytsky S., "Lemkivshchyna – Samotsvit Ukrainy. Ohlad ukrainskoho suspilnoho zhyttia na Lemkivshchyni 1918–1944," *Lemkivskyi Kalendar na Bozhyi 1969 rik* (Toronto–Passaic, NJ) 1968.

Winiarski I., *Rusini w Radzie Państwa 1907–1908*, Lwów 1909.

Index for proper names

TECHNICAL EDITOR
Jadwiga Makowiec

PROOFREADER
Małgorzata Szul

TYPESETTER
Katarzyna Mróz-Jaskuła

Jagiellonian University Press
Editorial Offices: Michałowskiego St. 9/2, 31-126 Krakow
Phone: +48 12 631 18 81, +48 12 631 18 82, Fax: +48 12 631 18 83

GPSR Authorized Representative: Easy Access System Europe, Mustamäe tee
50, 10621 Tallinn, Estonia, gpsr.requests@easproject.com

www.ingramcontent.com/pod-product-compliance
Lightning Source LLC
Chambersburg PA
CBHW081658120626
46550CB00010B/2944